Józef Lubomirski

Safar-Hadgi

Or, Russ and Turcoman

Józef Lubomirski

Safar-Hadgi
Or, Russ and Turcoman

ISBN/EAN: 9783337168322

Printed in Europe, USA, Canada, Australia, Japan

Cover: Foto ©ninafisch / pixelio.de

More available books at **www.hansebooks.com**

SAFAR-HADGI

OR

RUSS AND TURCOMAN.

FROM THE FRENCH OF
PRINCE LUBOMIRSKI

NEW YORK
D. APPLETON AND COMPANY
549 BROADWAY 551
1878

CONTENTS.

		PAGE
INTRODUCTION	. . . . . .	3
I.—EMINEH	. . . . . .	5
II.—CAPTAIN RELIEFF.	. . . .	18
III.—THE WOLVES.	. . . .	33
IV.—THE REVOLT	. . . . .	42
V.—THE SCANDAL	. . . . .	52
VI.—THE EMPEROR'S LIEUTENANT	. . .	62
VII.—THE EMIR OF BOKHARA	. . .	83
VIII.—SAFAR-HADGI	. . . .	97
IX.—THE EXPEDITION	. . . .	112
X.—THE CAMP	. . . . .	123
IX.—OOROOMDAY'S STORY	. . . .	133
XII.—THE BATTLE	. . . . .	145
XIII.—THE PRISONER	. . . .	155
XIV.—LISE	. . . . .	165
XV.—THE NEWS	. . . . .	174
XVI.—THE SLAVE-MARKET	. . .	181
XVII.—MOHAMMED	. . . .	198
XVIII.—SAFAR'S DWELLING	. . .	206
XIX.—THE TURCOMAN PRINCESS	. .	216
XX.—THE ACCUSATION	. . . .	226
XXI.—THE WEDDING	. . . .	235
XXII.—THE SPY	. . . . .	245
XXIII.—THE ARREST	. . . .	260
XXIV.—THE TRIAL	. . . . .	272
XXV.—DELIVERANCE	. . . .	282

SAFAR-HADGI.

INTRODUCTION.

GEOGRAPHERS designate under the common name of Turkistan the vast region lying between the sea of Aral and the Caspian Sea, the Celestial Mountains, the "Roof of the World," the Hindoo-Koosh Mountains, and the mountains of Khorassan. Yet those who have made a closer study of the country observe among its inhabitants a marked diversity of types, races, and general characters. The Turkomans of the south belong to the Caucasian race; the Turkomans of the north, the Kirghiz, the Uzbecks, and the Kipchaks, are Mongols; and the Tadjiks—called Sarts at Khiva—are hybrids. The first four are courageous, indomitable, barbarous, and, for the most part, nomadic; while the last are sedentary, pusillanimous, given to mercantile pursuits, and readily accessible to the influence of civilization.

Although Turkistan has from time immemorial been the hot-bed of Moslem fanaticism, the Kirghiz are Buddhists, and there are Hindoos of the religion of Brahma, and Parsee fire-worshipers. Christians alone have ever been the object of inexorable persecution. It is only within the last ten years that, thanks to the efforts of the Russians, readier means of communication have been introduced, and European commerce and science have now begun to penetrate more freely into these mysterious regions. The arid and uninhabitable sand-plains are at present crossed by numerous caravans; and these, protected by the Russian eagle, can thread their way, almost free of danger, through the entire Turkistan territory, to the post marking the limit of the czar.

From month to month and day to day that post is placed farther and farther off; and even now, as we trace these lines, the antique khanate of Khokan, with no inconsiderable portion of the possessions of the Emir of Bokhara, acknowledges allegiance to the Emperor of all the Russias.

Tashkend, a city of some sixty thousand inhabitants, and formerly the capital of a beylic dependent upon the khanate of Khokan, is the administrative and military centre of the Russian possessions in this part of Asia. The Governor-General of Tashkend is the supreme ruler of the country; he is invested with power of life and death; soldiers and officers, natives and colonists, are alike submissive to his will, and he holds in his hands all authority, civil, military, and religious.

Too far distant from St. Petersburg, and not yet sufficiently securely annexed to the empire, Turkistan is not regarded by the czar's government as Russian territory. The governor-general rules the province according to his own ideas or to local requirements, without heed to the laws of the empire, and is alike irresponsible in an administrative as in a financial point of view. He sends embassadors to the neighboring emirs, to the Khan of Khiva, and to the Afghan princes, and treats on equal terms with the Son of Heaven, whose dominions are contiguous to the new Russian possessions.

The country thus governed is twice as great in extent as Germany and France together; hence the necessity for the governor-general to appoint other functionaries, who, with the title of governor, and invested with powers nowise inferior to his own, administer the public affairs of provinces too remote from the chief town to be conveniently placed under his immediate authority.

No sooner has a new conquest been achieved by Russian arms in the Bokharan territory, than an order, transmitted from Tashkend, converts it into a Russian province, transforming the most populous town into a seat of government, and usually appointing the commander of the triumphant troops as sovereign chief of the recently-acquired possession.

Thus it was that Samarcand became, not long ago, the capital of a Russian province.

I.

EMINEH.

THE antique palace of Timour, comprising a number of edifices scattered amid vast gardens and defended by a fortified inclosure, has been made the residence of the general commanding the troops of the district.

The general's house is a roomy structure, whitewashed without, and surrounded by a wall likewise whitewashed. The several palaces of the inclosure, set apart in other days by the Emirs of Bokhara for their seraglios, harems, or tribunals, now afford shelter to the governor's family; studding the grounds at intervals, they strike with their whiteness in sharp contrast upon the sombre verdure of the groves, and, bathed in the sun's rays, ever most effulgent in these climes, they present a brilliant and cheerful aspect to the eye.

In the main building of Timour's palace is a spacious hall, which has recently been furnished in the European style. Ample velvet hangings of deep blue drape and screen the loop-holed windows and the ogee doors; thick Persian carpets are spread here and there upon the floor; and a few pieces of furniture from one of the principal establishments of St. Petersburg are symmetrically arranged throughout the apartment. Between two windows stands a piano-forte; elsewhere are graceful shelves laden with French and Russian books in elegant bindings; and upon two Boule cabinets are photographs of the czar and the czarina, resting on golden tripods, between a pair of Chinese porcelain vases.

The most shaded corner of the hall is occupied by a sort of lounge, close to which stands an oval table covered with a fabric of dazzling hues. Reclining on the lounge is a woman, wrapped in a pearl-gray dressing-gown with violet facings; a scarlet bashlick sits negligently upon her head, and a rose-and-lily foot is toying with a violet slipper, which it dangles up and down measuredly in space. Fair tresses of flaxen hair escape in disorder from beneath the bashlick, and mingle their golden tinge with the chatoyant blue velvet of the lounge.

The deep expression of her black eye, now indolently haughty, when completely overshadowed by the long lashes, now piercing and cruel, when illumined by sombre scintillations, is nevertheless always pure, limpid, domineering, and imperious; the nose straight, with quivering nostrils; the mouth small; lips vermilion, humid, though perhaps too thin; teeth white, keen-edged, and closely set.

The woman as she lay was thrillingly beautiful; nor could the severest critic have discovered, in that charming, delicate, and transparent being, one single, the slightest, imperfection. The first sight of this adorable creature elicited unbounded admiration; yet a more attentive examination of her features showed their very regularity to be too rigid; her eye was observed to lack that power which penetrates and charms, and which embellishes the otherwise most insignificant female countenance—and the feeling of admiration gave place to one of fear.

Just now her face was distorted with rage, and the white, ring-adorned hand, upon which her cheek rested, quivered slightly with nervous agitation.

Kneeling on the carpet, not remote from the lounge, was another woman, also beautiful, but of an order of beauty quite unlike the first: a tall, shapely creature, of pure Caucasian type. Her countenance was of Biblical symmetry, and her long, black hair descended in two tastefully-braided tresses much below her waist. She was attired in a garment of scarlet silk, unconfined save by a yellow girdle, and reaching to the feet, upon which were morocco boots, also yellow, with brazen heels and pointed toes, curved upward after the Oriental fashion.

"I ask of you neither excuses nor pretexts," said the lady, with a voice tremulous with impatience. "I wish you to answer me why, contrary to my command, you dared beyond the precincts of the palace?"

The maid smiled, but made no reply.

"Hearken, Emineh!" she continued, in a tone of growing agitation. "You know me. You have by this time observed that all here must bow to my will, and that I cannot brook delay. This morning I arose and had myself to put on my slippers. You were not at hand. Yet, you are aware that this is your duty, and how much pleasure I take in seeing you perform it. To-day I have been deprived of that pleasure. But, never mind. Answer me, and I will pardon you for this time. Come! Speak, fear not, I say!"

The Turkoman girl's smile assumed an expression of disdain, but she spoke not a word.

"Emineh!" exclaimed the lady, in a low murmur, "until now I have had pity on you. You are the daughter of one of the emirs of your country, and never yet have your shoulders felt the lash. But, take care not to try my patience too far! Take care!"

Emineh shrugged her shoulders, and, now for the first time opening her lips, uttered a half-suppressed laugh of scorn.

The lady's face for a moment grew pale with anger. She hastily stretched out her arm and convulsively pressed the spring of a small bell within her reach upon the table.

A shudder passed over the maid, but her mocking smile became more and more bitter.

When the last vibration of the bell had died away upon the air, a lugubrious silence pervaded for a few moments the vast hall, and the lady and her maid stared at each other with brooding brow, and visage livid with rage and hatred.

"Let the non-commissioned officer in charge of the Cossack escort be sent to me immediately," said the lady to a servant in livery who had just appeared at the threshold. When the servant had withdrawn, she said to Emineh: "It is not yet too late! Speak! Ask to be pardoned!"

The maid seemed not to have heard; the menacing expression of her eye had subsided into a vacant, wandering gaze, as it were in a world visible only to herself.

"Speak! I counsel you—though it be but a single word! This silence exasperates me! Hear me, I beseech you! Oh, do speak!" gasped the lady, suddenly springing up and placing herself before the girl.

Emineh, still kneeling, rapidly turned her eyes upon those of her mistress, as vivid fire flashed from her sombre pupils.

"Down with those eyes, slave!" shrieked the lady, "or I'll have them plucked out by the executioner!"

A prolonged peal of mocking laughter from the damsel reverberated through the hall.

Like a lioness infuriate, the lady crouched as if she would spring forward; but, suddenly changing her intention, she turned about, ran to the table, and struck upon the bell three or four blows so violent as to set the very spring a-grating with a strident jar. The summons was answered by the same servant, now not a little bewildered.

"That non-commissioned officer is long in coming."

"He has been sent on duty by his excellency. As soon as he returns he will come and receive your orders, madame."

"I presume there are others in waiting in the antechamber. Let any one of them be sent."

"The aide-de-camp of the day is the only—"

"Then bring the aide-de-camp of the day!" And as the domestic appeared to hesitate—"Go!" she exclaimed, in an irrepressible outburst of rage. "You all seem to set me at defiance to-day!"

Slowly and majestically Emineh stood up, raising her tall figure to its utmost height; and the lady, cowed, moved nearer to the bell.

"Since your slaves can compel me to do so," said the Turkoman girl, in a muffled, guttural tone, "I maintain before them and you the humiliating posture to which your vanity condemns me; but one of your equals and mine is now about to enter, and it were not becoming that I should remain voluntarily on my knees."

"Go on! You may defy me now as you please:

your punishment can be none the more nor none the less severe for it."

The heavy drapery of a side-door was lifted, and an officer of some thirty years entered, whose commanding stature and bronzed visage revealed much energy and determination of character. A long black beard descended upon the front of his tunic of dazzling whiteness; and a pair of golden epaulets, sparkling in the subdued light, showed his rank to be that of captain.

The lady, on perceiving him, was unable to disguise a passing sensation of uneasiness; her brow contracted into a frown, and she seemed undecided, though only for a moment; then, steeling herself against perhaps a generous impulse:

"Captain Relieff," said she, pointing with her finger toward Eminch, "that girl has incurred my displeasure, and I charge you to see that she receives fifty lashes!"

A shudder swept through the whole frame of the man. Advancing a step, he muttered:

"Perhaps I did not hear aright?"

"Have I to repeat my orders?" she asked, angrily.

"That is not my province," he replied; "such offices should belong to the executioner!"

Then, approaching the lady:

"Martha," he said, in French, "you are acting wrong, and your caprices, which at times carry you too far, may be the cause of your losing the esteem of honorable people, and (who knows?) even the devotion of those who, like myself—"

Casting upon him a haughty glance, she interrupted him, and asked in the same language:

"What do you say?"

"That I might cease to love you."

"Are you going to execute my orders?"

"No!"

"Well, then, for having taken the liberty of finding fault with my conduct, you shall this very instant kneel and kiss the hem of my robe, and ask my pardon." As she spoke, a snowy finger pointed to the carpet, while an imperious glance from her half-closed eyes, magnetized the officer. After a moment's silent contemplation of the lady, slowly, very slowly, he bowed his knee and raised to his lips the hem of her pearl-gray dressing-gown.

"I will tell you, Serge, that you are a very great fool!" said she in a scarcely audible murmur, her eyes at the same time shedding beams of fondest expression upon the captain.

"What now? What is this I see here?" broke in abruptly from behind a voice half merry, half threatening. "Relieff on his knees before my wife! What does all this mean?" The Governor of Samarcand stepped forward with a mien of inquiry not completely exempt from wrath. The general was a man of fifty, of athletic frame, somewhat overladen with flesh, and debonair but altogether unimpressive countenance.

The aide-de-camp, more than a little abashed, hurried to his feet, and shuffled to the background to conceal his embarrassment.

"My dear," said the lady, with entire self-possession, "the captain was begging my pardon, and very luckily too, for him, for I had just made up my mind to call you. I sent for him to come and have this girl chastised for her disrespect toward me; but my request proved to be distasteful to the gentleman, for he refused to obey, and that very cavalierly too. So I had just decided to make appeal to you, when the captain returned to a sense of his duty, and acknowledged his fault."

As soon as the general caught sight of Eminch, whose presence he had not noticed at first, his countenance underwent a sudden change, and assumed the impassioned air of a bear in love. Seizing his wife's hand and kissing it, he exclaimed: "The slightest want of respect toward you I shall punish with the greatest severity. That is a crime I shall not be very apt to pardon!" Then turning to face the officer, his brow still gathered, he said:

"My wife's orders must be obeyed in Samarcand as if they were my own, without hesitation or murmuring! I had given commands to that effect before! You shall remain under arrest in your room for a fortnight."

"My dear," interposed the lady, "I do not ask so much of you this time; the captain has acknowledged his fault."

"I do not agree with you, madame," interrupted Relieff; "and, since his excellency is of opinion that I deserve punishment, I desire to be punished."

"Then you will be good enough," she rejoined, dryly, "to submit to the punishment which I prescribe for you, and which will simply consist in the execution of my order concerning that girl."

Eminch, still smiling ironically, suddenly turned her eyes toward the officer, with what he deemed a suppliant look. He had hitherto paid but little attention to the girl; but, examining her now, he was struck with the comeliness of her appearance, and yielding to that sentiment which so readily and forcibly appeals to our sympathy in behalf of a pretty woman, he said:

"I have refused to obey, general, because I believed corporal punishment to be abolished in Russia. I fear such a measure would produce an unfavorable impression among the people whom you govern, and—"

The general, red with impatience, stopped him short, exclaiming:

"In Russia they may do as they see fit; I am sole master here, and I will act as it pleases me! My will is the law. I have said already that my wife's orders are supreme. Do not compel me to repeat it. To disobey her is a crime in Samarcand. A crime, sir! Do you hear?"

So saying, the general riveted his gray eyes upon his aide-de-camp, endeavoring at the same time to look as stern as possible. Relieff, not the least intimidated by the frown of his superior, advanced a few paces, and bowing in obeisance before Martha, "Madame," said he, "but a moment ago, upon my knees, I asked your pardon for myself: will you now grant me permission to kneel a second time, and sue for pardon for her?"

"No, no; that you shall not!" exclaimed Eminch. "I will not consent to that. Who asked you to intercede for me, Ooroos?"[1]

[1] The name given by the Turkomans to the Russians.

Filled with amazement, Relieff remained silent; the general shrugged his shoulders; and Martha stood up, and, leaning languidly upon her husband's arm, murmured:

"All these discussions have so wearied me that I do not know whether I shall have the courage to walk to my chamber. Indeed, Alexander, you ought to have the gallantry to carry me," she added, smiling.

The general lifted the fragile creature in his herculean arms, and pressed her fondly to his bosom; and neighing boisterously with very joy, hurried off in the direction of a door.

"Oh, dear me, not so quick!" she said, merrily. "You will make me still more tired." Just as the general's shoulder touched the hangings of the door, Martha, one hand entwined around her husband's neck, pointed with the other toward Emineh, and said to Relieff, "Fifty lashes, you know!"

The captain, followed by the Turkoman damsel, retraced his steps to the waiting-room. On beholding him, a native, who occupied one of the benches which alone formed the scanty furniture of the apartment, arose, and saluted him with a gesture of deferential friendship. Safar-Hadgi[1] was a Turkoman from the countries beyond the Daria, and very influential among the Tadjiks. A zealous Mussulman by conviction, he had five times performed the pilgrimage to Mecca, and had seen Constantinople, Smyrna, and Damascus; nor was European civilization wholly unknown to him. Still later he had been sent by the Khan of Khiva as

---

[1] Hadgi, pilgrim, bestowed as an honorary title upon such of the Mussulmans as have performed the pilgrimage to Mecca.

embassador to the Russians at Orenburg; after which Safar-Hadgi, all at once and without any apparent reason, retired from active life, and fixed his residence at Samarcand, at that time belonging to the Emir of Bokhara. Although still young (Safar had not yet completed his fortieth year), he soon enjoyed high consideration among his new countrymen; and his erudition (he knew the Koran by heart), wealth, and benevolence, secured for him the rank of *ascacal*.[1] At the time of the Russian conquest he was still at his post. He was one of the first to subscribe to the new order of things, and the czar's government found in him a faithful and devoted ally. Upon all occasions he used his incontestable influence with the inhabitants of Samarcand to induce them to accept with resignation the administrative reforms established by the conquerors, and bear without repining the yoke—tolerably easy on the whole—imposed upon them by the Christians.

Safar-Hadgi was magnificently attired in a silken robe of scarlet, with sable border, and fastened at the waist with a scarf of blue cashmere, ornamented with golden tassels; his turban, likewise blue, was made of a woolen fabric of delicate texture; and silver buckles, mounted with costly gems, embellished his yellow-morocco boots, with pointed toes, curved upward, according to the invariable custom of the country. Although of the purest Mongol type, his features were regular and beautiful; and a white hand was wont to stroke his silken and well-cultured beard. Relieff approached him with outstretched hand, and greeted him cordially:

[1] White-head.

"Good-morning, hadgi. You desire, I presume, to see the general?"

"Yes," replied Safar. "I have come to inform his excellency that the measures he requested me to propose to my countrymen yesterday have their entire approbation."

"Good news, hadgi," said Relieff—"good news for us and for all Russia! . . . Ah! did all your countrymen but resemble you!"

Meantime Eminch, who, on perceiving Safar, had buried her face in her hands, quivered involuntarily at the sound of his voice; then, advancing a few paces and placing herself in the full glare of the sunlight, she uttered three words in an unknown dialect. Safar-Hadgi shrank backward, awe-stricken.

"The emir's daughter here, with face uncovered to the gaze of an unbeliever! Oh, pray, captain, what does this mean?"

"The daughter of an emir?" inquired Relieff, astonished.

"Yes, of the greatest, the mightiest of all. . . . How comes she here?"

"How can I tell? For the time being she is the slave of the governor's wife, and her gracious excellency has directed me to see that she receives fifty lashes for having disobeyed her."

"Lashes! Allah Akhbar! You speak in jest?"

"By no means. Tell me," said Relioff, in a tone of irony, "you, who are so fond of the Russians, will you take upon you to see the order executed? Here it is in writing: I will sign it. You are known to all our soldiers. Conduct your emir's daughter to the guard-house yourself; it will afford you a pastime while you are awaiting the audience which the general will, I fear, not be able to grant you before an hour or so. Do you say yes?"

The Turkoman drew up to the captain, and, his brow contracted in a scowl, inquired, "Is it to me that you speak?"

"Most assuredly," replied the officer. "Whom else can I address here, since we are alone?"

Already Safar's hand was in the act of seizing his poniard, when some words uttered by the maid in the same dialect as before promptly soothed his ire.

"Be it so, then," he said. "I will obey you, tyrant; but the curse of Allah be upon you and yours to the sixth generation!"

Relieff smiled, but his smile was one impossible to depict. "Ungrateful wretch that you are!" said he. "There is no manner of question that I cannot execute orders of that sort myself." And, shrugging his shoulders, he disappeared within the governor's apartments.

II.

CAPTAIN RELIEFF.

THE white houses of Timour's ancient city had assumed a purplish tinge in the fading glimmer of the setting sun. Each Mussulman town then bursts into life. The monotonous cries of the muezzins calling the believers to prayer fall in shrill notes from the minarets, and cross each other in the air; and the people, one and all, issuing from their mysterious dwellings, hasten to the mosques in eager throngs along the narrow streets.

At that hour of the day Samarcand is peopled with types and costumes of most varied casts and forms: Tadjiks in long robes and quadrangular *toques*, which give them a sort of resemblance to Russian priests; Uzbecks with martial strut and peaked bonnets; Tartars of the desert in their rags; and Indians in violet caftans—all forming a striking contrast with the Russian officer, with his fine white shirt and gold-lace shoulder-straps.

Relieff trudged musingly along toward the ramparts, by the side of those streams which invariably take the place of sidewalks in Samarcand; and with the switch which he held in his hand he clipped off heedlessly as he went the blue and yellow flowers that grow in bunches on the banks of the canals. On two or three occasions the measured hissing of the switch caused Tadjiks crouching in the water at their ablutions to shrink with fear or anger. Relieff, however, neither heard nor saw anything, but mechanically followed a path he had often trodden before, so completely was he absorbed in thought.

At last he reached the ramparts. Before him was a sort of temporary wooden barrack, of recent construction, but so rude and uncouth in form beside the high and graceful wall against which it was built, that it resembled a hideous parasite clinging to the neck of beauty. On the long platform which extended into the street was an officer, still young and beardless, pacing up and down, and abstractedly twirling a mustache as yet to come; and some soldiers, in coarse gray shirts, huddled around the door, gazed curiously along the street. On perceiving Relieff, the officer uttered an exclamation of joy and hailed him by name.

The captain approached the platform, and said:

"Oh! It is you, Bassalsky. You are on guard, eh?"

"You cannot think I am here for pleasure? You are a nice fellow! You are quartered quite near, and yet you never trouble yourself to find out who is on duty, or whether it may chance to be a friend! It is not kind, old boy. You should come and help a fellow to pass the time."

"This is one of my dull days; or, as you would say, I am undergoing a metamorphosis, and turning into a bear."

"Pshaw! Are you not just on your way from the palace?"

"Not exactly. I have been knocking about the town for the last two hours."

"Then, you do not know the news?"

"No."

"The governor-general is to be here next week. Klotz has just brought an order to double the posts outside, and put on patrols beyond the ramparts. It appears the general is decided upon having the ditches and bastions well guarded, and all parts of the fortifications most open to an attack."

"Ho, ho! So General Kaufmann[1] is coming?"

"We shall have plenty to do. What a lucky fel-

[1] General Kaufmann, the Governor-General of Russian Turkistan.

low you are, not to have any of this stupid garrison-duty, as we have! You are always stuck in the palace!"

"Yes," rejoined Relieff, with a laugh; "and in the palace I see the governor's lady, with whom Captain Bassalsky is over head and ears in love."

The young officer blushed, and stammered out: "How insupportable you are! You know that it is not true."

"Indeed?"

"On my honor!"

"Do not pledge your honor, for you would be telling a lie. . . . After all, why should you make a secret of it? What do you see wrong about it? She is handsome, you are young, and pastimes are not numerous in this country. Love one another, good people, and much good may it do you!"

"What an air of sincerity! I assure you you are in the wrong; for, while it is true that I envy your good fortune, it never came into my head to follow your footsteps."

"My footsteps?—did you say my footsteps, captain? Are you aware of the meaning of the word you have just uttered?"

The youth replied timidly: "It is really impossible to chat with you; at the slightest word you are off like a match."

"You are right, and I am wrong. But, then, were you only to know how many disappointments I have had through life, how many dreams of happiness destroyed! . . . Nor do I say this with the slightest reference to Martha Nicolaïewna. What can she ever be to me? Mino is not the stuff of which your amorous swains are made. You, Bassalsky, are altogether different; when she gives you her hand to kiss, you are happy for a fortnight after it. The other young officers are in the same case as you. And she knows it too; and accordingly there are several officers to whom she extends that privilege every fortnight, in order to keep them all in breath. She is pretty, and they are unoccupied: it is a diversion for her, and a pastime for them. You are right; she is right; they are all right. What is that to me? I am not her husband."

"Relieff!" exclaimed Bassalsky, in a tone of reproof.

"What! You would have me believe it to be untrue? . . . As for yourself, Bassalsky, you who have a true heart and a warm soul, let me give you a word of advice: flirt as much as you please with the countess; but when once you leave here, forget that woman, and let not the remembrance of her linger a moment in your breast beyond the last poplar of Samarcand."

"Seriously, you are going mad!"

"Alas! I am mad no longer; I was once mad. If you only knew—"

Relieff was interrupted by a non-commissioned officer who came forward with four men, and, saluting Bassalsky, said, "Captain, the patrol you ordered out is now ready."

"What a bore!" cried the young officer. Then turning to Relieff, he asked, "Will you accompany me?"

"Gladly," replied the captain; and then he added

in a low murmur to himself, "Just as well to have it all out at once."

The night was cool, calm, and cloudless; a few stars already twinkled in the sky; the leaves of the poplars rustled in the desert-breeze, and the balmy country air was peculiarly refreshing and invigorating to breathe after the overwhelming heat of the day.

The two captains, followed by the patrol, passed out through the city-gates. On their left was Samarcand with its golden cupolas and multitude of minarets; around them, gardens and white houses imbedded in the verdure of trees of a century's growth, and surrounded by immense poplar-groves; and in the background, the snow-covered crest of Mount Kohak.

The officers walked a long time in silence. Bassalsky, observing his companion to be plunged in deep thought, was loath to interrupt him; and as for Relieff, he seemed oblivious of the presence of his friend, when suddenly he seized Bassalsky's arm, and, holding it in tight clasp, he began: "Have you the slightest idea of what that woman is? She is soulless, heartless, and unfeeling! Are you aware that long ago, in our own country, over there"—and he pointed with outstretched hand toward the west—"in the government of Moscow, where she lived with her father, she was beloved, as never woman was loved before, by a man from the same neighborhood? Do you know that they had loved each other from childhood, and that their families, equals in all respects, had been united in the bonds of friendship for centuries? Do you know that their betrothal had been celebrated and their marriage appointed to take place two months later, and that her betrothed had set out for St. Petersburg and Paris to order the bridal presents?"

"Indeed, I do not perceive your meaning."

"Then it happened that the colonel in command of the regiment stationed in an adjacent town had been guilty of some misdemeanor, and the emperor dispatched Count Molotoff, one of the generals of his suite, to institute an investigation. And when the absent one returned from Paris, he was apprised that Martha's marriage with Count Molotoff was fixed for the following Sunday. He went to her, trembling and confounded, a death-chill in his soul, menaces upon his lips, and entreaties in his heart. Can you imagine her reply?—'I am of a domineering disposition, and with the general I shall have what you could never give me: the absolute rule over countries as extensive as our whole government; with a nation of slaves to hearken to my will on their knees, with their faces bowed in the dust. What can you offer me in exchange for that? The humdrum and dependent life of a rich country-woman.'

"'But you pretended to love me?'

"'Assuredly, I do love you, more than I love the general, and you are infinitely more to my liking than he. But what does that amount to? One's lot for a whole lifetime must not be dependent upon a mere caprice.' He cast himself at her feet, prayed, besought her, drenched the carpet with his tears; and when, spite of all that, the accursed marriage took place, instead of plucking the fatal passion from his breast, the idiot gave up his former manner of life, joined the service, and from town to town, and place to place, went begging a glance from her whom he had learned to regard as his own. Yet, do not suppose that all this importunity was irksome to her, or that, wounded in her woman's pride and sense of propriety, she either repelled the man or made the least complaint to her husband. No! Too glad to exercise such an influence over a man of his stamp—for, aside from his ill-starred passion, the luckless fellow was not devoid of worth— she sometimes encouraged, though she often rebuked, him, but nevertheless retained him constantly in her immediate surroundings. How much disdain, humiliation, and shamefacedness, has not that man voluntarily submitted to; while she remains ever frigid, ever smiling, ever implacable!"

"Yes, you must have suffered fearfully."

"I!" exclaimed Relieff; and he fixed his eyes fiercely upon his friend's. "Who has mentioned a word about me in all this story, captain?"

"But I thought .... I supposed .... Indeed, my dear fellow," said Bassalsky, out of patience, "where, then, have you had an opportunity of learning all the details you have been referring to?"

"At St. Petersburg. You know it is a *large* little city. After their marriage the count brought his wife to court. I was at St. Petersburg at the time. There, just as it does here, as it does everywhere, Martha's beauty attracted attention, and for several weeks the countess was the theme of all conver.ations; her name was on every tongue."

"Then pardon me, Relieff; but what you now do is not right; you are not acting in conformity to your principles and your usual upright character, which all of us do well know. You, perhaps, calumniate this woman."

"Have I not been living these three years with her and her husband? Have I not been an eye-witness of her caprices—always selfish, sometimes cruel? Has she not this very day attempted to get me to apply the lash to a slave, guilty, in all probability, of nothing more than having made an awkward bow on her shoe-strings?"

"Indeed!"

"Yes; at first I refused, but I afterward went upon my knees and begged her pardon!"

"And yet you pretend not to be in love with her?"

"I! in love? Ah, no! I am no longer in love with any one! And, after all, she looked irresistible when, with half-closed eyes, she said to me, 'You shall kneel down and beg my pardon.' I obeyed. Do you know why? Because, in bending my knee before a creature so perfect, so adorable, I experienced an ineffable pleasure that thrilled my whole being. It is all past now. Never again can she look so beauteous as at that moment, never! To me she is no longer even pleasing. I do not love her. I love no one; do you understand?" And he clinched Bassalsky's arm as if he would crush it in his grasp.

"Come, now, my dear fellow, keep calm!"

"Have I not made a point of disobeying her this very day? I commissioned Safar-Hadgi to attend to the flogging of her Turkoman damsel. He is not like those thick-headed Tadjiks, and I suspect he saw my intention was, that she should have an opportunity to escape."

"You did? And what will the general say to that?"

"If the man is weak enough to allow such orders to be given to an officer, I can only pity him. But do you think he supposed for an instant that I was going to lead his wife's serving-woman to the whipping-post? It was quite enough—too much—to be obliged to sign the order. There was not a single soldier in the antechamber, and, as the Turkoman is noted for his devotion to the czar, no one will be astonished that I handed over the order to him. If he has not executed it properly, what is that to me? Can you imagine that, in his cool moments, the general will follow the matter up? Nonsense! But, even if he should, what of it?"

"It is sometimes hard to make you out, Relieff."

"Nonsense! Why so? Because I rebel against infamy? I thought it would be an act of friendship to open your eyes as well as I could, that is all. You think, perhaps, it is jealousy. If so, you are mistaken, I assure you. Let you profit or not by my words, that is your own lookout, and . . . . Now let us change the subject."

The two officers had by this time reached the avenue of poplars that leads up to the north gate, and the soldiers of the patrol, seeing their superiors engaged in close converse, had entered the city some minutes before. Just then a man and a woman issued from a side avenue, and exactly at the spot where Bassalsky and Relieff were standing, a score of yards or so from the ditch; so that both parties met full face to face. The man's dress was that usually worn by the Turkomans on a journey or at war; and the woman's, a long garment of blue linen, that covered her from head to foot.

"Safar-Hadgi!" exclaimed Relieff.

"I was not looking for you," replied Safar; "but, since I have met you, I will tell you what I have to say."

"What have you to tell me, hadgi?" inquired Relieff.

"Your orders have been obeyed."

"What! you have had the lash given to your emir's daughter?"

"More than that; I asked the executioner to allow me to take his place. Such was the hamoun's request."

"Why so? You must be gone mad!"

"Hear me a few moments. When first you Russians came here you were already known to me; I had seen your cities, your civilization, and the well-being of your people; I had read your books, and found them instructive; and I had studied your laws, and found them to be wise. I then thought Allah had sent you here for the good of my poor, distressed country, and from that very day, Safar-Hadgi, as all of you know, was your truest friend and most devoted ally."

"That is true, indeed, hadgi!"

"But now, Ooroos, when I see that you are no less wicked than our own emirs, that your tyranny is no less odious than that of our former rulers, and that our destiny is to suffer still and bow to the caprices of a barbarous master, I have changed my mind. It is better to live under the law of the servants of the true God than under that of unbelievers, since the tyranny of the one is by no means milder than that of the other. This woman, whom I respect and revere, has received the lash at my hand; first of all, to save her from the contaminating touch of the executioner, and then to shut out from my breast every sentiment of forgiveness for you and yours! So now, unbelieving dogs, I have declared war against you, and you shall learn to your cost how I take vengeance!"

While Safar was speaking thus defiantly to the officers, Emineh seemed to peer, with anxious gaze, down through the palm-fringed avenue. For some moments two black spots had been visible near the end of the walk, and were evidently in rapid motion; and, as the last syllable of the Turkoman's harangue vibrated in the air, two camels, whose feet sank noiselessly into the black, deep sand, halted beside the maid. A Tartar djigweet was mounted on one of the animals, and led the other by a hair halter passed through its nostrils. Immediately upon coming to a stop, the camel knelt. Emineh touched Safar with her finger, and he, with the rapidity of lightning, seized her in his brawny arms, sprang upon the camel's back, and uttered a long, shrill whistle. The camel arose and was off like an arrow.

"A curse upon you all, Oorooses! tyrants, unbelievers, thieves!" shouted Safar.

"What! brigand!" exclaimed Bassalsky. And he took aim with his revolver at the fugitive. "There is a parting salute for you!"

He fired, but the ball whizzed inoffensively through the air, and was spent among the dense foliage of the poplars. Relieff had, with a quick movement, raised the muzzle of the weapon as it went off. The Turkoman pushed his camel to the top of its speed, and soon was out of range.

"What did you do that for?" shrieked Bassalsky. "The devil take you!"

Relieff pointed to the two camels, now only to be descried in the distance as a cloud of brownish dust.

"Look," said he; "they are so small, and Russia is so large! What can they do?"

"No matter for that; they deserve to be chastised for their insolence. You now have yourself a dangerous enemy in Safar."

Relieff was pensive for an instant. "No," said he, "it is better as it is. I unquestionably offended him this morning, and to kill him would have been an act of cowardice. Besides, I can take care of myself when necessary."

The detonation had attracted some soldiers to the spot, and they gathered in an anxious group around the officers.

"It was only the captain's pistol that went off," said Relieff. Then, taking his friend's arm, he said: "Come, it is time to go in. I will come and keep you company. We can send for some of your comrades and play a game of lansquenet, if you feel so disposed."

It is five o'clock in the morning. Four candles flicker in the sockets of brazen candlesticks, and their fluctuating glare, falling upon the creviced cross-beams of the guard-house, forms fantastic and lugubrious shadows. On the table near the candlesticks are cards, greasy and worn at the corners ; and pieces of chalk bestrew the green cloth, almost disguising its natural hue beneath their whitish dust.

Two men are seated at the table, Relieff and Bassalsky. The former is engaged in counting gray, red, and violet bank-notes, and doing them up in packages ; while the other, holding his head between his hands, follows his companion's every motion with anxious gaze.

"What luck !" said Relieff, as he pinned up the last bundle. "That makes forty thousand rubles that I have won !"

"Besides six thousand that I owe you," rejoined Bassalsky, with a husky voice.

"You have lost a great deal, have you not ?"

"Thirty-seven thousand rubles !"

"Perhaps you will not be able to pay all to-morrow morning?"

"I shall find money."

"If you *can ;* if you cannot, you are dishonored, for you are aware that in campaign there is no trifling with gaming-debts."

"Oh, at all hazards—"

"But if you have not two-thirds of the sum at your quarters, where can you expect to get money in a newly-conquered country?"

Bassalsky hung his head.

Relieff pushed the bank-notes over to him, and said, "There, take—" and observing the hesitation of the young officer, who could not believe his eyes, he added, "Go on, take it!"

"Oh! thank you!—my eternal gratitude—"

"Will be too much altogether. You have thanked me, that is sufficient."

"Never mind, my dear fellow—you may believe me—all my life—"

"That will do, I say."

"The gratitude I owe you—"

"Nonsense! you do not owe me so much gratitude as you think. One day or another I will let you know the motive that impelled me to render you that slight service."

Bassalsky was completely at ease in his mind, and he burst into laughter.

"Come, come, Relieff!" said he; "do not spoil my good impression of you by your customary skepticism, which, by-the-way, is merely feigned."

"There, enough about the matter! And, besides, you can do me a favor, if you wish, just now. I feel rather heavy, and I do not want to go to bed. It will soon be daybreak, and the gates will shortly be open. Just have them opened for me immediately, and lend me a horse and a gun; I have a desire to take a ride through the country."

Bassalsky went hastily to the door, and gave orders to a soldier; and then turning to Relieff, he observed: "It seems as if you never slept?"

"Rarely," replied Relieff, heaving a sigh. The two friends continued chatting a few minutes longer, and then the soldier came to announce that all was in readiness. Bassalsky went to the door and called to the sentinel, who was pacing up and down at his post on the platform, "Allow his excellency's aide-de-camp to pass out." And the men on guard repeated one to another, "Allow his excellency's aide-de-camp to pass out."

III.

THE WOLVES.

Five wolves issue with stealthy step from the wood that borders the road leading from Samarcand to Bokhara. Hurriedly they cross the narrow space between the forest and the highway, disappear a few moments in a ravine, and rise again into view on the opposite side, ascending a steep acclivity which overlooks the road. On reaching the top they lie down, and their gray bodies are confounded with the sand of the hummock, so that it is impossible to distinguish them at a distance. A convulsive shiver agitates their hair and ears; their jaws are clinched with rage and hunger, and their phosphorescent pupils strained in persistent and eager gaze along the gently-winding highway. Two dark points, moving with great rapidity, are visible afar.

The spot here referred to lies near the border of the desert. Mount Chabonata, the sanctuary of Samarcand, is still within sight to the north; on the right all is jungle as far as the eye can reach; the reed-cane waves in the breeze, faintly sparkling in the uncertain light of the stars; and the Zerefchan glides unseen through the gigantic grass, revealing its presence by a mild and plaintive murmur. To the left lies the vast, interminable forest, whose sombre mass forms a striking contrast with the yellow tinge of the landscape. To the south the blue sky, where it seems to touch the earth, darkens to a brownish-gray; the yellow of the reed-cane also grows darker, and appears to form at the horizon a dividing line between the blue sky overhead and the brownish sky in the distance. This sombre background and the reed-cane, resemblig palisades planted by the hand of man, mark the commencement of the desert.

The black points grow larger: two camels are flying in the direction of the desert. One of the wolves arises, stealthily crosses the road, and lies down on the sand on the opposite side.

The camels are nearing rapidly. On one of them is Safar-Hadgi, holding Eminch in his arms; and his camel is led by the Tartar djigweet mounted on the other. Suddenly the camels tremble as if terror-stricken, and redouble their speed. The wolf on the right springs to his feet and descends, followed by his four companions; and all five set out silently and swiftly in pursuit of the fugitives.

Close by the road, and behind the mound, stands a mud-hut, deeply imbedded in the sand. It is occupied by an aged Tadjik, who sells tea and cakes to the caravans that pass. This night the Tadjik was standing at the door of his hut. He saw the sinister beasts of prey running like dogs around the silent travelers; he saw the sleeping djigweet's pointed bonnet dangling in the air; and he saw the linen sack in which Eminch was wrapped, like a corpse in a shroud, flapping against the camel's side with a muffled, dull, and hollow thud. And the whole scene bore an aspect so weird and fantastic in his eyes that he retreated within his hut, spitting upon the ground.

"Scheitan!" he exclaimed in a loud voice; "Allah's curse upon him!"

The Tadjik's imprecation awoke the djigweet, who cast an inquiring glance all around. The wolves were following close by, and in the thick dust raised by the camels' feet their eyes shone like sparks in the midst of a column of smoke.

"Hey!" cried he, shaking Safar with his hand, and pointing to the wolves.

"Let them run!" replied the hadgi. "They will not dare to attack us."

The sound of the human voice produces strange echoes in those wilds where it is so seldom heard; and each syllable, reverberated with a lugubrious intonation, strikes upon the ear as the cry of some unknown wild beast.

The five wolves stopped short, pricked up their ears and snuffed the air, then cast a peering glance in every direction, and started off again in their noiseless, wild pursuit of the camels, whose speed had not been slackened an instant.

The black line which abruptly crossed the yellow line of the reed-canes gradually disappeared, and both lines were confounded in one uniform sombre shade; the murmuring of the Zerefchan, which here makes a sudden bend, could be distinctly heard; and a bamboo bridge across the stream, and linking the desert to the habitable world, seemed to repose upon gigantic piles. The fugitives saw the bridge, their only chance of escape; but the wolves, too, perceived it, and, rending the air with their lamentable howlings, quickened their pace to reach it before the camels.

"Hey! hey!" cried the Tartar, with a disdainful chuckle; "they will not dare to venture into the desert! Do you hear how they howl with fury?"

Just then the reed-canes were bent as if borne down by a violent gust of wind; the camels, terror-stricken, trembled and crouched as if about to kneel; and the wolves slunk off with flattened ears, crawling along the road on which but a few moments before they had been bounding full of courage.

"Allah! a tiger!" shrieked the djigweet.

Two luminous balls were seen hovering in space; a terrific roar burst upon the travelers' ears; then a short silence ensued, which was broken by a human yell of agony and a noise as of bones cracking. Safar felt a violent shock. His camel uttered a rending groan of suffering, and, turning about, set off with the rapidity of the wind. In obedience to a sudden impulse of humanity, the hadgi attempted to stay the animal in its flight; but he discovered the strap which had been attached to the bridle held by the djigweet hanging unconfined on the camel's neck. The Tartar, as he was dragged to the ground, had snapped the bridle and lacerated the nostrils of the animal, which, frenzied with pain and affright, had become entirely ungovernable.

The subdued growls of the tiger, still audible for a while, grew gradually less distinct, and finally ceased to be heard. On looking behind, Safar saw the wolves spring up, as it were from under the ground, and resume their chase with unremitting obstinacy. His eyes met the ardent pupils of one of the five, and the famished animal uttered a howl, which was promptly answered by the rest in terrific chorus. The tiger was at his repast; the wolf had seen fear depicted in the eyes of the man, and informed his fellows of his discovery, and their howling was one of rejoicing in anticipation of their approaching feast.

Safar felt his blood run cold. Eminch, till now a silent spectator of the awful scene, raised her eyes.

"Hanoum," said her companion, "this accursed animal is seized with vertigo; I have lost all control of him, and I fear we are lost."

"Allah is all-powerful!" replied the Turkoman maiden.

The jungles were fast disappearing in the distance; two lonely poplars stood in bold relief upon the horizon; far beyond them were other trees, and, still farther, the white walls of Samarcand might be descried in the gray mist of the morning.

"The accursed beast is carrying us back to Samarcand!" cried the hadgi, "and we shall fall into the hands of the unbelievers."

"Oh, no!" rejoined Eminch, in a tone of meek supplication. "Yesterday morning, you, the servant of my father, laid the lash upon his daughter, and your eyes were filled with tears. Rather than to let me fall again into their hands, you will strike me to the heart, will you not?"

"You shall be obeyed, hanoum!" replied Safar,

and drawing a poniard from his girdle he seized it with his teeth. A smile of sadness played on the maiden's lips as she beheld the weapon gleaming in the twilight. "Your hand will not tremble, Safar?" she said.

"No!"

Meanwhile Samarcand was growing plainer to their view, and Safar could already distinguish the four dome-like monuments and the confused mass of structures constituting the citadel. A narrow line of fire fringed the eastern horizon, and bathed the city in its rose-tinted rays.

Suddenly the foremost wolf made a prodigious bound and sprang upon the camel's croup, plunging its sharp claws deep into the animal's flesh; but, unable to retain its hold, it fell, and the camel with a furious kick dashed it far upon the sand, never to rise again. Goaded by the pain of the new wound, the camel seemed literally to fly through space. The city was now but a hundred paces distant, and the deep moats were in full view. Safar drew himself up, and after a moment of wild meditation—death in front of him—death at his feet—he snatched the poniard from his teeth. A gunshot was heard. The four surviving wolves fled in terror toward the desert. A second gunshot followed close upon the first: the camel, with one leg broken, fell heavily to the ground, and its riders, suddenly separated, were precipitated to a considerable distance on either side of the animal.

Between the poplars, a Russian officer, mounted on a black horse, was hastily reloading his carbine. Safar-Hadgi arose, and, poniard in hand, advanced toward the spot where Eminch was still lying. The officer took aim at the man. "Stop!" cried he, "or you are a dead man!"

The hadgi recognized Relieff. "Ha! you again!" he exclaimed. "Well, then, finish your work and kill me!"

Relieff, slinging his carbine upon his shoulder, replied: "You mistake: I have no intention of killing you. You wrongly suspect me of having willfully insulted you. Last night I saved your life and gave you your liberty. I have just now saved your life a second time—and I again give you your liberty. Fly!"

A smile of disdain curled the hadgi's lip. "Knavish and cruel, like all your kind!" said he. "Fly! do you say? It were madness to venture in the desert on foot with this woman; and you know that to reënter the city-gates would be to expose myself to immediate arrest. Spare us, then, your hypocritical protestations."

"Hadgi—"

"I am ready to die; but you shall not have this woman with life!"

With poniard in act to strike, Safar rushed upon Eminch; but Relieff, with the quickness of thought, put spurs to his horse, and the animal bounding forward dashed the Turkoman to the ground. The steel had been almost up to the girl's breast, which she in part laid bare to insure the blow.

Foaming with rage, Safar sprang to his feet, while Relieff alighted from his horse.

"You are right!" said the latter, flinging his carbine far from him; and waiting until the hadgi, who did not cease to brandish his poniard, had come up to him, he reached the bridle to him, and said, "Here, take my horse and be free!"

The weapon dropped and was buried in the sand. So much noble-heartedness could not fail to make impression upon the Turkoman's savage nature. He stood for some moments motionless with astonishment. But his emotion was of short duration. "I may have been deceived," said he, in a low murmur; "however, it is too late. The insult was too cruel to be repaid by your present generosity. I cannot forget it."

"Be that as you please!"

"In sparing me you spare an enemy to your country, for I am and shall be its enemy forever! No! Ooroos, kill me! take my life! Believe me, it will be better for us both. But, since pity has entered your breast, save the emir's daughter, and I will forgive you for my death!"

"Idiot! how can I save her, unless I have your aid? Do you think it is for your sake that I compound thus with my duty? Hate me you may, if that can afford you any pleasure: for my country, what has it to fear from such a pygmy as you are? So, then, up and away! No further discussion: I might be unwilling to hear you."

The tone in which the captain spoke stung Safar to the quick, and he hesitated still; seeing which, Emineh approached the officer, and, laying her hand upon his shoulder, asked him with her melodious voice, "What is your name?"

Relieff looked at her amazed. "Serge," said he, laughing.

"Serge," rejoined the maiden, "I understand your intentions toward us, and I thank you." And taking from beneath her veil a carnelian medallion, on which was engraved a verse from the Koran in Arabic characters — "Keep this in remembrance of me," she added. "It belonged to my father, Emir-Al-Oumra.[1] Heaven knows what fate has in store for you; and this talisman may one day be the means of saving you as you save me to-day!" Then, placing her hand in his, "I accept my liberty from you, and thank you for it, brother!"

Relieff bowed his head respectfully as he held her hand. "Your *souvenir* shall never quit me! But, pray hasten your departure, for the gates will shortly be opened."

At an imperious sign from Emineh, Safar, still silent and sombre, got into the saddle, and Relieff aided the girl to mount behind her companion. When he saw her comfortably seated, he raised his right hand to his *képi* in a gesture of supreme courtesy, and struck the horse gently with the rod in the other. The steed bounded galloping off.

Safar, too, had involuntarily raised his hand to his forehead and breast—his usual mode of saluting the emir.

"All these natives—Tadjiks, Uzbecks, Kipchaks, and Turkomans—are as stupid as their boots," soliloquized Relieff, shrugging his shoulders.

[1] Elder brother of the Khan of Khiva.

IV.

THE REVOLT.

The drums beat the reveille, and the portcullis of the drawbridge was raised, and the gates of Samarcand were boisterously thrown open by the soldiers on guard.

As Relieff passed under the archway, his attention was arrested by a long line of heavily-laden camels literally obstructing the street, and, lazily reclining beside them at full length on the ground, a number of Tadjiks listlessly smoking their short black pipes. They belonged to a caravan from Bokhara, awaiting the opening of the gates in order to pursue their journey to Khokan.

Elbowing his way through the crowd of animals and men, Relieff reached his quarters before seven o'clock, and, after a refreshing wash and a change of linen, seated himself at his desk with the intention of writing to Russia. Two hours elapsed, and the sheet of paper lying before him was yet untouched by pen. There he sat, with his head supported by both hands, until aroused by the sudden opening of the door. On turning to see who entered, he felt two tears trickling down his cheeks, and furtively dashed them off with the back of his hand.

"Captain Bassalsky!" announced an orderly. And Bassalsky's laughing eyes were peering over the man's shoulder.

"I have come to return you your money, old boy,"

cried he. "Just imagine what I found awaiting me when I got home! A registered letter! Couldn't have come at a better time! Of course my first race was to you. This, you know, does not change in the least my deep, my sincere gratitude to you. I need not tell you, Relieff, that you will always have a friend in me, for life or for death!"

"Whew! my dear fellow! not quite so fast, if you please!" replied Relieff, whose countenance had by this time resumed its mask of haughty indifference. "I risked nothing by the loan. You never would have attempted to keep the money altogether in any case; and as it is, were *I* to ask *you* for some, you would not think of refusing me! So, you see, it was a lucky hit that I made—that's all!"

A hearty laughing-fit prevented Bassalsky from answering at once. By-and-by, his hilarity subsided in a measure, and he said: "Agreed, then! You are the most skeptical of men, and there is no getting you to like anything or anybody."

"There may be more truth in what you say than you suspect. At all events, of the services rendered by each of us to the other this day, mine to you was certainly not the more important."

"I rendered you a service?"

"Yes, by lending me your horse, which, I may as well tell you, I have disposed of. I have given it to some one desirous to escape from this place."

"How? Who was it?"

"I took your horse without so much as asking your permission! So, you observe, I was not dilatory in repaying myself for the slight obligation I had placed you under. How much am I indebted to you?"

"You are by no means indebted to me, my dear fellow; only too happy—"

"I don't understand it so at all," interrupted Relieff in a determined tone.

"Well, well! I'll take one of yours in the place of it."

"Agreed! take your choice."

"Now, then, for an explanation."

"Some other time—when the storm has burst."

"What storm?"

Just then the same soldier as before pushed the door ajar and said: "One of the general's orderlies has come to say that your highness's presence is required at the palace."

"All right; I shall be there immediately." And, shaking Bassalsky by the hand, "There is the lightning already," he said, laughing.

At a late hour in the morning two women stole softly on tiptoe into Countess Martha Nicolaïewna Molotoff's chamber, and gently shook the rose-colored muslin curtains by which the sleeper's couch was surrounded on every side as a safeguard against the incursions of myriads of bloodthirsty mosquitoes. The countess raised her eyelids for an instant, and, heaving a deep sigh, drowsily inquired, "What is it?"

"It is nine o'clock, countess," answered one of the maids.

"Very well. I will rise."

The first maid poured into a large porcelain basin some perfumed toilet-water, whose delicate fragrance pervaded the whole apartment. Martha now opened her eyes completely. One of the maids took from a wardrobe a white *peignoir* bordered with point d'Alençon, and held it unfolded in her hands, while the other knelt to search for her lady's slippers, and, having found them, remained upon her knees at the bed-foot in readiness to put them on her mistress.

The countess observed each movement of her maids. By-and-by, with a drawling voice, she called, "Eminch!"

The first maid answered, "We have not seen Eminch this morning."

"How! not seen her this morning again?" exclaimed the dame. "This is downright rebellion! Let her be brought here this very instant."

"She has not made her appearance since your excellency sent for her yesterday morning."

"She has not been in the palace all night?"

"No, madame," stammered the maid, overawed by the shrill, overbearing tones of her mistress. "We supposed your ladyship had given orders—"

"By whose authority do you *suppose?* Ha! she is not here!" And she pressed her lips together in a ferocious smile. "Mary can dress me all alone," said she to the servant who was still kneeling.—"You, Katharine, go tell the non-commissioned officer-of-the-day that I wish to see him in my boudoir."

She dressed herself hastily, without bestowing as much attention as usual upon her toilet, and in a few minutes she was in her boudoir, where she found the non-commissioned officer already in waiting.

The soldier had seen nothing, heard nothing. Inquiry was made at the guard-house, and an answer promptly came, to the effect that, according to her ladyship's orders, Eminch had been flogged, and had then been handed over to the person accompanying her, no instructions having been received to retain her in custody.

"The person accompanying her!" exclaimed Martha. "I wish to see Captain Relieff immediately."

The captain was sent for at once. In the mean time, the palace was turned upside down, for the countess ordered diligent search to be made for her Turkoman captive. As fast as her maids could go and come, she dispatched them in every direction in quest of tidings, and as they came back without any, she gave way to violent outbursts of passion, paced wildly up and down the room, and railed at the messengers most unmercifully.

After half an hour of useless search, the countess was informed that Eminch was nowhere to be found, on hearing which her fury knew no bounds, and the terrified maids would not dare to enter her boudoir; so the orderly who came to announce the captain's arrival had no choice but to brave the danger in person, and face the terrible dame. No sooner had he uttered the first word than Martha flew to the drapery which separated the boudoir from the *salon* and dashed it aside with a violent gesture. Relieff seemed to be engaged in attentive examination of the czar's portrait; his countenance was rather pale, and a frigid smile played about his lips.

Warned of the countess's presence by the noise she made on entering, he turned his head, and immediately saluted her with a profound inclination of the body. Without the slightest motion of the head in return, or even a word of welcome, Martha asked, imperiously, "Have my orders been executed?"

"What orders?" inquired the officer.

Raising her voice to the shrillest pitch she could attain, she said, "Did my slave receive the fifty lashes?"

"I am under the impression that the infamy has been accomplished."

"What am I to understand?"

"I suppose the poor creature has been flogged."

"You suppose!" cried Martha, indignant. "You are under the impression! Have you gone mad? Will you tell me that?"

A calm gaze of irony accompanied Relieff's reply. "I know that I signed the order! You do not imagine, do you, that I ever, for a single instant, intended to lead the girl to the whipping-post?"

"Or that you could tell where she is at this moment—eh?" rejoined the countess, in a threatening tone.

"Pardon me, I can tell you exactly." The aggressive tone of this reply was distinctly perceived by Martha. She felt conscious of an approaching struggle, and resolved to let it come.

"Ha!" said she. "Then I trust you will be good enough to do so."

"In all probability she is galloping across the desert, in the direction of Bokhara."

Martha knit her brows. "Your jesting is unseasonable, sir," she said.

"I am not jesting."

"You would have me believe that a woman, unprotected, and without money or food, would pass beyond the gates of Samarcand, and venture alone in the desert?"

"But she was not alone."

"She had a companion, then! And some one to aid her to escape, too?"

"Most assuredly."

"And you know who it was that aided her, doubtless?"

"I do."

"And you will tell me his name, I hope?" cried Martha, as she drew nearer to the captain in a menacing attitude.

"Whenever it may please you."

"Speak, then! Speak now! It was—"

"I!"

"You?" shrieked the countess, falling back again to the spot where she stood before.

"I, myself!" repeated Relieff, looking her full in the face.

"Ah! This is going too far!" she exclaimed, quivering with rage at the aide-de-camp's provoking replies. "This time it is too much, and you shall be punished for your insolence." She attempted to run to the bell, which was on a table in the opposite angle of the room; but to reach it she must pass the spot where Relieff was standing, and observing the expression of fixed determination in his eye, she stopped short, undecided what course to adopt.

"Do not act rashly, Martha!" remonstrated the captain.

"Allow me to pass!" cried she, recovering from her indecision; "or you shall pay for this hour of revolt with your life."

"I have a few words to say to you," replied he, without any change in his calm and collected demeanor. "Wait till I have said them. You are about to summon your husband. Do you know what will follow? He will either refuse to punish me, and you will have had your pains for naught; or else he will be weak enough to yield . . . . to what I shall indulgently call your whims—"

"Relieff!" she interrupted in a paroxysm of rage, "for your own sake, be silent, and stand aside. The end of all this will be serious for you!"

"Not until I have finished! . . . . You shall hear me out, and then you may act as you see fit . . . . Then," he went on coolly and firmly, as before, "any penalty inflicted for having favored the escape of a woman whom no law of the empire recognizes as a slave, cannot be very severe. But be it what it may, it would constitute an injustice."

"Your language at this moment constitutes a rebellion against your superiors!"

A short, nervous laugh of defiance preceded the officer's rejoinder: "I was not aware that I was addressing a superior. I am speaking neither to a general nor a colonel."

The countess stamped her foot, and sprang forward in the hope of forcing the aide-de-camp aside; but perceiving him still smiling and motionless, she once more stopped short, breathless, and relinquishing all further effort to overcome the passive resistance of the officer, she muttered, her lips contracted by the violence of her fury: "Go on! continue to the end!—My turn will come by-and-by!"

"The result, then, will be," he pursued, "that inasmuch as there is no reason why I should silently submit to an injustice, I shall report the case as soon as I have suffered my punishment. I am one of those persons whose reports are read, as you are aware, madame. An inquiry will be instituted. And do you think that your actions and your husband's pusillanimity will meet with approval in St. Petersburg? Do you presume that, in these days of reform and progress, the fact alone of having caused a woman to be flogged, in an empire where slavery has recently been abolished, will not prove sufficient to call forth the well-grounded dissatisfaction of your husband's superiors? You would fain strike me lifeless with your glances," continued Relieff, laughing and raising his finger to the level of Martha's brow; "but I do not fear them. I am not one of those men who may be put out of the way or assassinated with impunity! What I wished to say to you, madame, is briefly this: If you should call your husband, and the reproachful story of this morning find an echo outside the walls of this apartment, the mysteries of Tamerlane's palace shall be unfolded by me to my comrades, and, after having, as a matter of course, tendered my resignation, I shall forward my report to St. Petersburg. Now," added the captain, stepping aside and bending in a profound bow, "ring, madame; the passage is clear for you."

Anger, and the consciousness of her own powerless condition, had for a moment distorted her delicate features. She sank into an easy-chair, completely overcome by the vehemence of her passion.

"Begone!" she gasped; "and never enter this place again."

"I ought to have done so two years ago," replied he; "but, were I now to desist from coming here, how, pray, should I attend to my duty with his excellency, your husband?"

Exasperated by the irony that lurked in this remonstrance, the countess drew herself up in a threatening attitude, and shrieked, "Quit this place, I say—begone!"

Three or four servants, alarmed by their mistress's cries, rushed into the apartment and found her sitting in the easy-chair in a state of exhaustion, pale, and with her hair in the utmost disorder; while Relieff, with bowed head, seemed to be in the act of taking leave.

"Her excellency has a nervous attack," observed the captain. And, as if to confirm the assertion, Martha was seized with a sudden laughing-fit, which was almost instantly followed by a flood of tears, and she fell heavily to the ground writhing in a violent convulsion.

V.

THE SCANDAL.

Eight days had elapsed since the events narrated in the preceding chapter, and Relieff still continued in the discharge of his functions as first aide-de-camp to Molotoff. Regularly each morning he repaired to the governor's quarters, carefully avoiding, however, to pass through the countess's apartments. And Martha seemed also to shun the captain; nor did they meet once during the entire week.

Molotoff, in all probability, was unaware of the outbreak between his wife and Relieff, there being in his manner of receiving the latter no noticeable departure from that cordial frankness usual between Russian generals and their aides-de-camp.

The countess had for some time past been in the habit of giving a reception to the more distinguished officers of the garrison three times a week, and had had a list of their names drawn up for the purpose of insuring scrupulous regularity in the order of the invitations. Every officer whose name was thus enrolled was certain to be invited to tea at the palace once a fortnight at least. The aides-de-camp were alone excepted from the general rule, they having by right of their position the privilege to attend the countess's routs without the formality of a special bidding. Previous to his quarrel with Martha, Relieff had never been absent from a single one of these entertainments;

but from that time his visits ceased altogether. His evenings were thenceforth usually spent in play in the rooms of one or another of his fellow-officers; and, as for Bassalsky, he saw him every day. This young gentleman made no effort to conceal his ever-growing admiration for Martha, who had for some time back made him the object of a flattering exception, by sending him special and gracious invitations to every one of her parties.

A degree of coolness and constraint had become observable in the manner of the two friends, though, perhaps, no one could with precision have assigned a reason for the change; yet they themselves were cognizant of it, and each of them did all in his power to disguise it under a show of the most sincere friendship.

It happened, however, one day, as Bassalsky was unusually extravagant in his praises of the countess, that Relieff grew impatient, shrugged his shoulders, and changed the subject of conversation. Bassalsky, presuming he knew the cause of his friend's irritation, could not suppress a smile of irony, which he did not seek to conceal. That day the two friends separated without so much as a shake of the hand.

Meanwhile, Relieff, who for several days had been successively the guest of his comrades, resolved to assemble them at his quarters for an evening at cards. Although the dwelling of the governor's aide-de-camp was one of the handsomest in the city, and had in earlier days belonged to a wealthy dignitary of the khanate, the chief room of the house was furnished in a most unpretending style — sofas all around the whitewashed walls, a table of white-wood in the centre, a brazen lamp suspended from the ceiling above the table, and a simple matting on the floor.

At one o'clock in the morning the games were interrupted by the announcement of supper. The guests were all in high spirits, for the playing had been remarkably even; and, plate in hand, they fell to devouring with evident relish the caviar and slices of ham and cheese that were served on capacious dishes. In one corner of the room an army of champagne-bottles, and other bottles containing native wine, were symmetrically arranged around an immense glass bowl, brimful of ice.

Klotz, the governor's second aide-de-camp, who had joined the party just as the collation had begun, was chatting with the master of the house. This officer was held in little esteem in the regiment, owing to his incorrigible habit of flattering everybody on every occasion, and often without occasion; though his weakness was so well known that no one paid any attention to it. In former times, however, it had been the means of bringing him into rather disagreeable scrapes: indeed, his almost forced stay at Samarcand was due to the discovery of his unfortunate mania by the general whom he had served as aide-de-camp before he came to Molotoff. Though that general was by no means an imbecile, Klotz had, by his high-sounding praise and open admiration of his commandant's wit, and even of his person, which was the reverse of prepossessing, soon insinuated himself into his good graces. The general was delighted with his aide-de-camp until, one morning at breakfast, having mentioned the czar's expected arrival at Moscow: "What good fortune!" exclaimed Klotz.

"How? what good fortune!" inquired the general, looking up in amazement.

"Why, are we not nearer to Moscow than to St. Petersburg?"

"Well, and what of it? We shall not see the emperor in any case."

"Oh! no matter for that: we shall still be closer to his majesty."

The general could only express his surprise and disgust by a look of pity mingled with contempt. He had seen what the praises lavished on his own person by his aide-de-camp were worth; and so completely was his predilection changed to dislike that from that day forward he harassed the poor wretch unremittingly, not even stopping at injustice, until the latter was heartily glad to petition to be transferred.

Notwithstanding that severe lesson, Klotz persisted in his systematic and indiscriminate flattery, the news of which having preceded him to Samarcand, he was there treated by every one, from the governor to the lowest officer, with a sort of indulgent indifference, which, however, he by no means resented.

"But, how the deuce could you, old boy," said he to Relieff—"you, the soul of Martha's parties, choose one of her days for your *fête?*"

"The merest chance!"

"Say rather a lover's pout."

"A lover's *what*, did you say?" asked Relieff, whose countenance had suddenly assumed an expression of extreme severity.

"Well, well! There, now! hst! hst!—the brave, the handsome, the dashing Relieff—is out of sorts—"

The captain shrugged his shoulders. Just at that moment the door was opened, and in strutted Bassalsky, in full uniform and highly pomaded. Relieff advanced to meet him with outstretched hand. "How late you have come, my dear fellow!" said he, in a tone of friendly reproach.

"Martha Nicolaïewna detained me: first of all she chose me as her partner at whist; then we chatted and laughed a great deal—you understand, old chum—"

"I understand."

"No, you don't—you don't understand sufficiently. What a charming creature she is! so easy in her manners, so handsome, such a distinguished air—then her way of treating us just like friends of hers."

"Yes, yes!"

"Come, now, Relieff, you must grant that she is the most adorable creature in existence."

"My dear Bassalsky, your brain has been turned by looking at her so long—you had better come and have a bite of something!"

"No, no! I will neither break bread nor eat salt with you, nor be seated within your tent, until you have joined your voice with mine in the praises of our countess!"

"You have soon forgotten my advice to you, my dear fellow," said Relieff, with a movement of impatience.

"What! still on the same boasting strain as before? I would advise you to find something better to do."

"Come, now, that is enough. Here, take this slice of ham."

"Oh!" exclaimed Bassalsky, laughing, as he approached the table, "have you really the assurance to refer to the nonsensical stories you told me on that evening?"

Relieff now lost patience altogether. "I never jest, sir," said he, dryly, and in a low tone.

"So you dare to ask me to believe all that you said?"

"My dear Bassalsky, do let me entreat of you to let the subject drop."

"Ah! I see! In that case, of course, let us think no more of it; but the fact is, it was a capital joke, and once I was on the point of believing the whole story."

"Look you here!" interrupted Relieff, glancing fiercely at Bassalsky, whose persistent arrogance had by this time almost deprived him of his self-command; "what silly crotchets are passing through your brain? What I told you was true. I had hoped this subject should not again be broached between us; but since it has, I will repeat that it was the precise truth, on my honor! Do you believe me now?"

"I do not!"

Relieff shuddered. He seized Bassalsky's arm, and clasping it fiercely—"It is lucky for you that you are in my house, sir," said he.

"Consider yourself entirely relieved of your obligations as the master of the house," replied the officer, "for, even under your roof, I cannot give ear to your calumnies."

Relieff had regained his self-control. He stepped forward and whispered in Bassalsky's ear: "Poor fool! do you not see that you are compromising a woman's reputation and your own honor?"

"No! no! It is you who are afraid lest your calumnies be made known.—Gentlemen, hearken, all of you!" he cried.

The officers approached him inquiringly. Relieff, propping himself against the table, had grown somewhat pale, while Bassalsky soon found himself in the centre of an anxious group of comrades.

"What is all this about?" asked several officers.

"Oh, Bassalsky has been drinking a little too freely, you know," said Klotz, with a honeyed smile, "and as the charming northern gentleman is unaccustomed to our sun, the wine has gone to his head."

This remark exasperated the young officer. "Ah! I have been drinking, have I? We shall see about that!—Relieff claims to be Martha Nicolaïewna's lover."

"Silence!" broke in Relieff, in a voice of thunder. In an instant every mouth was sealed. Then, resuming his usual tone, he went on, calmly, yet mockingly: "My dear Monsieur Bassalsky, you are an imbecile and a coward. What you state is untrue!—it is a base falsehood!"

"Wretch!" shrieked Bassalsky, as he sprang forward.

The officers made a move to get between them.

"Allow me, gentlemen, to chastise this insolent fellow!" cried the young man, struggling to release himself from their hold.

"Gentlemen, I have a few words to offer in my own justification. Pray, hear me first," said Relieff, "and meantime secure that desperado."

The officers drew up in a circle around Bassalsky, who was stamping with rage.

"By-and-by," continued Relieff, addressing him, "when I have finished. A deadly outrage, a duel, proves nothing ; the accusation still remains ! I am ready to give you satisfaction, but I must first justify myself, and repair, in as far as it is in my power, the injury done by your inconceivable folly.—Hear me, then, gentlemen ; you shall be my judges ! I will abide by your decision."

"Go on, Relieff," said the officers.

"This, my 'friend for life and for death,' now standing before you," pursued Relieff, smiling, while Bassalsky became flushed, and his passion abated in a measure, "declares he heard me boast of being the countess's lover. This is entirely false, for I never said any such thing. One day, however, having noticed that the gentleman had set his eye upon her, and was so lost in admiration as to be unable either to eat or to sleep, giving vent, besides, to his feelings in terms more enthusiastic than respectful — such conduct seemed to me ridiculous in my friend, and injurious to the lady ; so, then, with the best intentions in the world, I related to him the story of—"

"You told me of your intimacy with her," interrupted Bassalsky.

"I did not. I even protested energetically against your repeated efforts to bring me personally upon the scene."

"Yes, granted! Yet it was not hard to perceive that—"

"Be it so! I was talking of myself, if you will! What did I say? That I had been engaged to the countess? So I had. That the countess had consented to marry another during my absence at Paris, regardless of her plighted faith to me? That, nevertheless, I had persisted in adoring her, craving a smile, and begging not to be deprived of the pleasure of beholding her? Yes, I said all that! Did I say anything else?"

"No! But that was sufficient."

"Ah! That was sufficient! Where, then, do you find the statement that I was the countess's lover? Is it at all probable that a man in my position, having become the lover of a woman he had intended to marry, would remain faithful throughout two whole years? Is it usual for an accepted lover to complain, or beg for smiles? What more did I tell you? That the countess was a heartless, soulless creature? Since you force me to repeat it in public, I will do so, and vouch for the truth of the assertion! But did I ever say to you that she was not a woman of virtue?—Gentlemen, I swear to you that my lips have never touched the tip of Martha Nicolaïewna's fingers!—Am I believed?"

"You are believed, Relieff!" cried the officers with one voice.

"I love—pardon me—I did love the countess with all the powers of my soul! She has chosen another for her husband, and I did say to this gentleman that the motives for that choice appeared to me lacking in dignity—more than this, my opinion still remains unchanged. I told him, besides, and repeat now to you, that it was cowardly and unmanly in me to have followed that woman, then married to another, to submit to the humiliations that were offered to me and accept the position I have held in this place. I consider this last act reproachful in the extreme!"

"Enough, enough, Relieff!" urged the officers. "We need to hear no more."

"No, my friends, I feel bound to refute the accusation of calumny cast in my face by this young madcap. My dear comrades, I shall be obliged to leave you, for, if my intimacy with the countess was merely humiliating to my dignity while it remained a secret, when once made known to the world it renders my position here insupportable. I shall, therefore, seize the earliest opportunity to quit Samarcand, being unwilling further to compromise one whom I no longer love, or to leave her reputation at the mercy of the whims and thoughtlessness of youths who have as yet no knowledge of the world! Now, gentlemen," he added, gently touching the shoulder of the two officers standing nearest to him, "pray allow me to pass." And making his way to the centre of the circle, he stood facing Bassalsky : "You wished to chastise me," said he ; "here I am."

The young man, fairly driven to distraction, seized his cap and hastened out of the room.

VI.

THE EMPEROR'S LIEUTENANT.

On the 18th day of May, 187–, General Kaufmann, aide-de-camp general to the emperor in Russia, and Governor-General of Turkistan, made his entry into Tamerlane's ancient capital.

The houses were gayly decked with Russian flags, the thoroughfares newly swept, and troops were drawn up in line along the streets through which his supreme excellency was to pass. By daybreak the Tadjiks, eager to catch a glimpse of their new master, had begun to assemble along the line of march and form in groups upon the house-tops.

The sun shone full upon the white walls of the houses, which reflected the dazzling light on the four-cornered bonnets of the Tadjiks as they swayed to and fro in regular cadence; and the effulgence was rendered still more intense by the sheen of the polished bayonets bristling on the top of the conical piles of muskets symmetrically stacked in the middle of the streets.

Though it was yet an hour before noon, the heat was already oppressive; and the soldiers were glad to stoop and wash the perspiration from their brows in the cool water of the stream. The hum of voices proceeding from the groups of Tadjiks on the terraced roofs, and from the military below, interrupted at intervals by a stray horseman hurrying past in the direction of the palace, would again swell into a soft, musical, and airy murmur.

Toward half-past eleven, a battalion of artillery passed through the town. The gray shirts of the men and white tunics of the officers were blackened with the dust of a protracted march; and dust mingled with sweat coursed down their weary faces in streams of mud.

The battalion was closely followed by a troop of mounted artillery; and the clanking of harness and accoutrements, the rumbling noise of the wheels and the neighing of the horses, constituted a sort of martial din which for a quarter of an hour or so disturbed the comparative silence of the expectant multitude.

At length an aide-de-camp came galloping up, announcing "The general!" Then there was a rush of soldiers hastening to their guns, while the groups of Tadjiks advanced as near as possible to the edges of the roofs.

A colonel issued from a house close by, still in the act of buttoning his uniform, and gave the word of command, "Fall in!" The noise and bustle shortly subsided, and a profound, respectful, solemn silence ensued. A dark cloud now became visible at one end of the street, and for a moment intercepted the view of the city walls. An irregular detachment of Cossacks, from the Ural Mountains, with their blue tunics and fur bonnets, mounted on their diminutive horses, and carrying their long lances in their hands, advanced in disorder, taking up the entire width of the street. In the centre of the detachment a vast, ungainly carriage was drawn heavily along by four horses abreast.

The dense volumes of dust rendered it impossible to distinguish the features of the occupants of the vehicle. But the flags were lowered, the drums beat a salute, and the troops presented arms, the barrels of their guns glistening in the sunbeams, as the aide-de-camp general passed. The Tadjiks, notwithstanding they had not so much as caught a glimpse of the crown of his cap, whispered one to another, " He is grand ! "

General Kaufmann was in excellent spirits ; the recently-conquered people seemed to accept his rule without a murmur. As the carriage moved onward, he was engaged in converse with Molotoff, who had gone to meet him beyond the ramparts. " Yes, general," said he, " matters would be perfectly at rights in the country were it not for these Kipchaks. The savages begin to grow too daring, and I think we shall have to make an end of them. It appears to me that an expedition is indispensable."

" Immediately after your supreme excellency's departure, I will set out at the head of the campaign myself."

The viceroy, casting a glance of rebuke at him, said: " You? What folly ! A general of his imperial majesty's suite, and Governor of Samarcand, expose himself to the mercy of such outlawed plunderers ! The slightest reverse might prove hurtful to the authority and prestige of the Russian name ! No, no ! a major will do very well, and more than do, for the purpose ! Is there not, general, among your higher officers a major in whom you can have confidence, and whom you would like to distinguish ?

" I do not think of one at the present moment,

general; but I shall look, and I know I shall find one."

"Find one, then! Any officer who brings those bandits under subjection will receive a reward befitting a brilliant action. I can leave you some of my artillery. Those high-handed scoundrels must have their courage cooled!"

Here the conversation ended, the procession having halted, owing to a deputation of Tadjiks intercepting the passage.

At a signal of dismissal the escort pursued its way down a side-street, and fifty other Cossacks, forming the rear-guard, took up their position behind the carriage. Another small escort, still farther behind, was obliged to halt during the delivery of the Tadjiks' address. It was composed of half a dozen persons on horseback—Bagnovo and Klotz, aides-de-camp to Molotoff, and two of General Kaufmann's aides-de-camp—riding by the side of an old man and a lady. The old man, who was not of the military profession, wore a white costume and a large straw hat, and appeared to be ill at ease on his horse, exclaiming incessantly against his present mode of locomotion. The lady, on the contrary, managed her steed with consummate ease and address. Her features were fine, regular, and of a pleasing expression, and the heat of the march had given a rosy hue to her naturally pale complexion. With her delicate and tastefully-gloved hand she held her horse securely, though it pranced and reared with impatience; and kept up a lively conversation with the officers by her side, apparently heedless of the animal's restive movements. "This is a delightful ride!"

she exclaimed; "fresh scenes greet the eye at every step, revealing an unknown world!—liberty, sunlight, and space! Just the life of my dreams!"

"Don't torment your horse so!" cried the old man, petulantly; "he might throw you off!"

"I defy him to do that, papa!" rejoined Lise, in a decided tone, as she patted the animal's neck. "Besides, there is no danger of him making the attempt; Sbogar obeys me as if he were—"

"A man," interposed Klotz. "Everybody in the town will obey you still better than he, for none will dare to make the slightest movement of impatience."

"Indeed?" was the girl's mock-earnest rejoinder.

"We shall do all in our power to render your sojourn agreeable. Samarcand will be privileged above all the cities in Turkistan in possessing two stars, one of which, alas! is a shooting-star."

"If it is for me that you intend that rather too flattering distinction, pray lose all anxiety," she replied; "I shall perhaps stay sufficiently long to be burdensome."

"What good fortune for the inhabitants!"

"Really! The Uzbecks and Tadjiks would appreciate my presence among them?"

"I do not allude to these savages; I am speaking of ourselves, the Russian officers."

"But I have not the least desire to live among you Russian officers; I see too many for that everywhere I go. I have come here to observe, run about, and gather information, and that will certainly be a more pleasing occupation than listening forever to the same story over and over again."

One of the governor-general's aides-de-camp burst into loud laughter. "Elizabeth Yegorovna has long accustomed us to her witty sallies: you, too, gentlemen, must get used to them, and learn to bear them with smiles."

"Oh! who would not willingly submit to a thousand deaths in exchange for a single smile from such an adorable person as Mademoiselle Lise!" declaimed Klotz.

Lise knit her brow, and, leaning over, said in an undertone and with visible impatience to the same aide-de-camp who had spoken immediately before Klotz: "That is a declaration."

"Phew! Pay no attention to him," replied the officer; "this is Klotz, you remember—you know what I mean?—the emperor in Moscow."

"Ah! indeed?—Ha! ha! ha!"

The Tadjik deputation had now finished their address, and the Cossacks moved on, followed by the small escort at a gallop; and in a few minutes the procession was out of sight at the turning of the street, leaving nothing behind but a long cloud of brown dust.

Meantime Relieff, in his capacity of first aide-de-camp to the governor, had remained at the palace, for the purpose of superintending the preparations for the reception and dinner to be given by Molotoff to the emperor's lieutenant. After inspecting the apartments allotted to the illustrious guest, he repaired to the dining-room, where the table was already laid, and the butler was busied in a final review of the wines and hors-d'œuvre. What was the captain's astonishment on observing the glasses and decanters so arranged as to form General Kaufmann's name!

"What is the meaning of this?" he inquired of the butler.

"Monsieur Klotz so ordered it."

"But in this way no one will have a glass within reach; and how the devil are the guests to drink?"

"Precisely the remark I made; but I was told that it was no matter, and that, provided the generals and the countess had glasses beside them, the others could do without them."

Relieff laughed heartily. "Change all that forthwith," he said — "or, no," he added, consulting his watch, "the general will be here in a quarter of an hour; I will attend to it myself while you go and dress." And, still laughing, Relieff began to set the decanters and glasses in the proper order, and was so absorbed in the operation as not to notice that the door had been opened.

Martha, in a costume of blue cloth, well fitted to set off to full advantage the graceful elegance of her figure and gait, entered the dining-room buttoning her gloves. Upon her head she wore a small square hat also of blue cloth, surrounded by a white veil which floated in the air. Thus attired, the countess was adorable.

On perceiving Relieff, her mouth formed into a sort of mysterious smile, neither spiteful nor hostile, nor yet altogether kindly.

With slow and measured tread she approached the captain, who continued arranging the table service, and with her perfumed glove touched him gently on the shoulder. Relieff turned quickly, and, seeing the countess, bowed:

"Serge," she began, in her mildest tone, and a look expressive of tenderness, "have we then become enemies?"

"O madame! that term is too harsh; let us say *indifferent*, at most."

"Why even indifferent? Is it on account of the scene of the other day? Oh! I forgive you with all my heart. I forgive you for your bad opinion of me too, and of which you make no mystery! I know all, sir!"

"Ah! have you heard—?"

"All!—You judge me wrongly, Serge, and you are unjust."

"You must have heard also that I was not your enemy, of which I gave proof by my determination to quit Samarcand?"

"Why go away? What folly!"

"It appears to me more desirable for both you and me that I should. Besides, there is no longer any reason why I should prolong my stay."

"Are you, then, quite indifferent to *me* now?"

The insinuating tone of this inquiry was anything but composing to Relieff. He did not answer, but bowed in silence in a manner which he intended should convey assent.

"Really? Well, let me tell you, my dear Serge, I do not believe one word of it."

"Nevertheless, it is so," replied he. "I love you no longer; and I bitterly regret that I ever did love you." As he spoke his voice was choked with emotion, but his tone was sharp and decided. He bit his lips with anger.

"What course do you intend pursuing, then?"

"To ask to take part in the first expedition that is sent out. As I hope to gain distinction, I shall petition for the command of some one of the posts situated nearest to the enemy's territory."

Relieff was calm, yet beneath that outward calmness there was perceptible a certain bitterness which touched Martha's heart to all appearance, for she reached her hand to him, and, with her most sympathetic look—

"Serge," said she, "do not be foolish! I am headstrong and capricious; but I am not dangerous, on the whole, provided," she added laughing, "my will is obeyed. There, let it be a peace!"

He withdrew a step, and, without taking the proffered hand, "What are your terms?" he inquired. This time the countess fell back a step, evidently wounded. "I do not understand you," stammered she.

"You must need my services, for this kindliness is not natural in you. So I frankly ask you on what terms you are prepared to conclude the peace. I hope I am clearly understood?—Believe me, Martha, you have no need to resort to subterfuges and mystifications in order to obtain from me anything compatible with my honor and dignity. So, let us remain, as we are, enemies, and speak out boldly. I await your pleasure!"

She could not bring herself to believe in such a downright revolt on the part of one who, until within a few days, had been her submissive slave; so she smiled, though not without considerable effort. "Do not say any more of these things to me, but give me your hand," urged the countess. "I may have been unjust to you; but suppose I should—" She seemed to hesitate.

"Suppose you should—?" inquired he, as if to urge her to complete her sentence.

She tore one of her gloves, and her eyes flashed fire. "Were I to tell you that your very rebellion renders you nobler in my eyes; that I have begun to feel that ambition cannot alone constitute happiness; and, finally, that I look upon you as the greatest of great men, and the strongest of the strong—"

"The general! the general!" cried a soldier, rushing breathless into the dining-room. She glanced at a mirror, adjusted a minute lock of hair which had escaped from beneath her hat, saying to Relieff as she passed him, "Are you going to remain here?"

The captain shook his head, drew his hand over his brow, and followed her, stifling a deep sigh.

The Talari-Timour[1] is a long, narrow yard, surrounded by a species of cloister or covered foot-path. The celebrated Koctach—green-stone—which Tamerlane had used as a stepping-stone to his throne, is outside the chief entrance of the governor's palace. If tradition is to be believed, this colossal stone was transferred from Brusa to the spot where it now stands. Upon the wall behind the stone are two firmans, bearing the signatures of the Sultans Mahmoud and Abdul-Medjid, granting the emirs permission to say prayers on Friday. An Arabic inscription, written

[1] Timour's audience-hall.

in Cufic characters upon a brass plate, carried off, it is said, from the treasury of the Sultan Bajazet-Ilderim, testifies to the ancient splendor of the Tartar conqueror.[1]

On the other side of the yard is an arched doorway, leading to the ancient Aynckham, or emir's abode, now set apart as the governor-general's residence.

It was in the Talari-Timour that Martha was to receive the emperor's lieutenant. The yard was full of people: officers, civil functionaries, leading Tadjiks, and Uzbecks, were already assembled there. Just as Martha entered, and the crowd pressed forward to meet her, the door on the opposite side was thrown wide open, and both generals appeared on the threshold. The officers saluted after the military fashion; the Uzbecks first placed their hands on their foreheads, then raised them up toward heaven; the Tadjiks prostrated themselves on the ground, and his supreme excellency, General Kaufmann, passed along between a double row of bowed heads, until he reached Tamerlane's stone, where the beautiful Martha, with mien of haughty unconcern, awaited him. The old man and the pretty horsewoman—who have already been introduced to our readers—followed in the footsteps of the general. After the usual forms of welcome had been exchanged, Kaufmann took the old man by the hand. "Madame," said he to Martha, bowing courteously, "I have the honor to present to you Yegor Alexandrovitch Goreff, one of our most distinguished scholars. Yegor Alexandrovitch wishes to spend a few months

[1] Vámbéry, "Travels of a Pretended Dervish."

in Samarcand, for the purpose of devoting himself to scientific research. He is recommended to me by his imperial highness the grand-duke, heir-apparent, and his daughter the grand-duchess. Your husband knows them well, and on presenting them to you, madame, I would seize the opportunity of begging you to grant my request that hospitality be offered them, and their sojourn in the city be rendered agreeable."

Although, at the sight of Lise, Martha's brow became slightly contracted, she bowed graciously to the emperor's lieutenant and her new guests, and said, "Your wishes, general, shall be commands for me."

"No one has the right to give orders where you are, madame," replied Kaufmann. Then turning to the old man: "I have already informed you, Yegor Alexandrovitch, that in our provinces the governors are all-powerful; I can vouch for the kind protection which General Molotoff will grant you at my request; but you behold before you the real sovereign of these parts," continued the viceroy, somewhat archly, however, "and my power must of necessity yield to hers. Endeavor to secure her good graces as early as possible."

"I shall use every effort to merit the distinction of being numbered among the lady's most respectful and submissive subjects," replied the *savant*.

"I should be charmed to have so distinguished a scholar for a subject," rejoined Martha, laughing. "But will your supreme excellency do me the honor of accepting my arm, that I may show you to your apartments?—Monsieur Klotz, you will be good enough to see this gentleman to his; as for the young lady, my own chamber is at her disposal for to-day; to-morrow we shall endeavor to provide her with more commodious quarters."

"A thousand thanks, madame!" said the young girl.

"That voice!—and that face! where have I seen it?" thought Relieff, still mingling in the general crowd of officers.

"Have the goodness to await me here an instant," went on Martha; "I shall be back in five minutes.—Come, general!—we have barely time to make our toilet for dinner."

"I am, madame, the humblest of your subjects," replied the emperor's lieutenant, as he bowed and offered her his arm.

When Klotz withdrew in company with the old man, Lise, left quite alone, looked all around her and soon fixed her eyes on the handsome countenance of Relieff, precisely at the same moment as he was intently examining hers. Uttering an exclamation of joy, she flew to where he was standing. "Cousin Serge!" said she.

"Lise!" cried Relieff, who had now fully recognized her.

"What! you, Serge—whom we all supposed to be in Italy or Switzerland—here, a soldier, in this out-of-the-way country? Now, do you know, Master Serge, I feel perfectly happy?"

"Dear cousin!"

"Will you not embrace me, sir? There!—What splendid walks we shall have together! You will initiate me into this savage life. Ah! how glad, indeed, I am!"

The young girl clapped her hands with delight, never observing the cloud which passed over the officer's brow.

"Yes, my dear Lise, I will remain in Samarcand all the time you are here."

"It will be a long time, then, for I have resolved to force papa to make his visit as extended as possible."

"Silly girl! Then you don't know—?" Relieff stopped short. "Yes, of course, I will stay—I was about to leave; but now I—no! no! I'll stay!"

"So you had intended to quit Samarcand?"

"Yes!"

"What tragic air is this that I observe with you? Are you in any trouble? You must hide nothing from me! But first of all, before you do anything else, tell me, how are you situated here?"

"And how are you situated?"

"Oh! as for me, since my mother's death I have been traveling over hill and dale. Father has become member of several scientific societies, and is constantly on the move."

Relieff interrupted her, for he had just perceived Martha coming toward them.

"I have been appointed to seat the guests at table," said he; "I shall place you by my side, and we can chat at our ease during dinner."

The countess came up to them, and, addressing Lise, "Are you acquainted with Monsieur Relieff?" she inquired.

"We are cousins, madame."

"Ah!—But will you accompany me to my chamber? You must be in need of repose before dinner."

The young lady was struck with amazement at the frigid, almost aggressive tone in which Martha addressed her, and at the harsh, sardonic expression of Countess Molotoff's features at that moment.

"I am prepared to follow you, madame," she said; then turning—"I shall see you by-and-by, Serge."

Relieff followed both ladies with his eyes until they had disappeared beneath the archway leading to Martha's apartments.

"Oh, no! I will not go away! It is now my duty to remain here and defend this girl," soliloquized the captain.

The dinner was drawing to a close. Martha presided at the feast, and had seated the governor-general on her right, and Yegor Alexandrovitch on her left. The guests were numerous; a few ladies, wives of the higher officers of the garrison, all either ugly or insignificant, in gaudy, ridiculous, and extravagant toilets, had been invited merely to fill up the table. Beside them, Martha, who had put on a magnificent low-necked dress, sparkling with diamonds, had the appearance of a brilliant star. The ladies' eyes were all turned toward the centre of the table, passing alternately from his supreme excellency to the countess, and from the countess to his supreme excellency, which latter addressed them from time to time with much urbanity of manner, while Martha scarcely favored them with some curt phrase, delivered in a tone at once patronizing and ironical.

The dinner had passed over in comparative silence, for those who were not absorbed in the contemplation of their excellencies did not, out of respect, dare to raise their voices above the limits of an almost inaudible whisper.

Among these last were Lise and Relieff; yet their conversation, though held in a low tone, appeared to be quite animated. Lise had already related to her cousin how her father, deeply affected by her mother's death, had given himself up heart and soul to science; how he had solicited and obtained a government mission abroad, that mission consisting of a journey to Turkistan, and particularly to Samarcand, for the purpose of inquiring into the origin of the Iranian and Turanian races; and how she herself, having been advised by her physicians to seek a more genial climate than that of St. Petersburg, had, instead of repairing to Nice, as suggested by them, induced her father to take her along with him. When she had finished the narration of these things, and of many others besides, it remained for Relieff to begin the recital of his adventures.

Accordingly, he explained how, after having first served in the Guards, and reached the rank of lieutenant in that corps, he had, in the exercise of his right, been enabled to enter the line with the rank of captain. But, spite of the reiterated questions of the young girl, he would not reveal to her the real motive which had led him at first to join the army. He hinted at an inordinate passion for travel and adventure, losses at play, his friendly relations with General Molotoff—gave as a reason everything he could think of, in fact, save the truth.

"This very morning I was about to ask to take part in an expedition which we thought would be organized before long; but your arrival, my dear cousin, has brought about a change in my plans. The friend of your infancy must surely be of some service to you, were it only in doing the honors of this out-of-the-way country in your behalf. Hence I will stay, and I am entirely yours to command."

"That is really very kind of you, cousin."

"Allow me to look at you and admire you. How pretty and charming you are! Who would have recognized in such an adorable young miss the little madcap who used to run about in torn dresses, and manage to have her hands scratched by all the cats in the neighborhood?"

"Now do stop, Serge," remonstrated Lise, laughing. "I warn you beforehand that I detest compliments; so, if you wish to please me, you must abstain from them. Sound, sincere friendship, as in old times, uncontaminated by falsehood or flattery!" she added, with her usual air of decision.

"Oh! I am quite agreed; but yet you *are* charming, you know!"

"There you are again!" she rejoined, chidingly.

"You will have no lack of admirers. What means can you take to prevent them from telling you—"

"Oh, I know how to keep them at their distance."

"Your heart has never begun to speak yet?"

"Alas! no," replied Lise, with a comic smile;

"nor does it expect to find any one to speak to in Samarcand, unless, indeed, it address you, the least tiresome of all the men I see here."

"Ho! ho! you prohibit compliments, and yet you use them yourself!"

"Impertinent fellow! to turn my own weapon against me! Seriously, though, I have never had anybody to think of or sigh after; my existence has hitherto been passed in the society of my father and a few old *savants*."

"As for me, I—" He was interrupted by a prolonged "Hush!"

General Molotoff was standing, glass in hand. "Gentlemen," he began, "I propose the health of our illustrious guest and venerated chief, his supreme excellency General Kaufmann! May the country at large, the country in the enjoyment of peace, happiness, and wealth, unite with me in wishing long life, honor, and prosperity, to his imperial majesty's lieutenant, Governor-General of Turkistan! Hurrah!"

"Hurrah!" responded the guests, with one voice.

A flourish was executed by the military band, the banqueters in regular succession touched glasses respectfully with the general, and then all became silent, for his supreme excellency had made a sign that he was about to speak. The stillness was such that a fly might have been heard crossing the room; and all present were busied in making ready beforehand to express their profound admiration of the coming speech. Glass in hand, the governor-general arose, and, bowing to Martha, commenced: "Madame, in omitting to drink your health, I trust you will pardon my infringement of the rules of good-breeding, when you have heard the other toast which I intend proposing." On a sign of acquiescence from Martha, he went on: "Gentlemen, the Kipchaks and Turkomans, accustomed to brigandage and plunder for many centuries, have exhausted our patience by their depredations and rapine in the territory now under the protection of the Russian eagle. His excellency General Molotoff and myself, satisfied of the urgency of putting a stop to these grievances, have resolved upon sending out a battalion of our brave soldiers to bring those indomitable savage hordes under subjection. The expedition will be one of risk and hardship, and may not prove successful, inasmuch as those taking part in it will have to cross vast, unexplored deserts, and face courageous and cruel enemies. If I am unable to promise those brave hearts victory—that being in the hands of God alone—I can promise them speedy and signal revenge in case of their defeat! Gentlemen, I drink to the success of this expedition and the officer who will command it!"

"Long life to his excellency!" shouted the officers.

Then, addressing Molotoff—"General," said the emperor's lieutenant, "I should desire to be able to associate a name with my toast. Could you not point out an officer to command the expedition?"

Molotoff was going to reply, but he was forestalled by his wife. "Will your supreme excellency," she began, "grant me the privilege of saying a few words in relation to this matter?"

"Madame," replied Kaufmann, somewhat astonished, "you are in your own house, and it is ours to demand that permission of you."

Martha smiled archly, and went on: "I would beg, then, to name an officer whose fervent desire is to follow the expedition, according to his own avowal to me this morning. He is one of my husband's aides-de-camp, and I believe I do him pleasure by soliciting in his behalf a favor which he himself would perhaps never have had the boldness to ask for. The officer is Captain Relieff!"

Had a thunderbolt fallen in the midst of the assembly, it would not have caused the captain such an impression of surprise as did Martha's words. He sprang to his feet and stood bolt upright in act to speak, but Molotoff, stupefied, was already stammering: "Relieff! my first aide-de-camp! Impossible! you must be in err—"

An imperious glance from the countess forced the words back down the love-sick governor's throat.

"Am I not right, captain?" she inquired across the table. "Did you not say you wished for an opportunity to distiuguish yourself fighting the enemies of our czar and our holy faith? Explain that I am not in error, and that I meet your desire by demanding this favor for you of his supreme excellency!"

Relieff plainly perceived that the question thus presented would admit of but one answer. So he replied: "It is true! I thank you, madam!"

"Bravo!" cried the emperor's lieutenant; "I know you, captain, and I know that, thanks to your position and your fortune, you have an enviable career open before you. You give proof of your patriotism by demanding to participate in such an expedition and under such circumstances. You are, however, only a captain, and I said this morning to General Molotoff that I desired to have a whole battalion, under the command of a major, sent against the Kipchaks. I will not, then, go back of my word! By virtue of the powers conferred upon me by his imperial majesty, I promote you, Captain Relieff, to the rank of major, and drink to your health, cordially, and with all my soul!—Gentlemen, to the health of Major Relieff, commander-in-chief of the expedition! Hurrah!"

"Hurrah!" rang out every voice.

The clinking of glasses and the hum of voices, now grown quite boisterous, still resounded for a long time in the room. Relieff, after touching glasses with the emperor's lieutenant, thanked Martha with a smile that forced her to lower her eyes, and then returned to his place at the table, deaf, insensible, and speechless, amid the congratulations which showered upon him from every direction.

"That woman has quite a friendship for you, has she not?" whispered Lise.

"How should I know?" murmured Relieff.

The feet of the chairs, pushed by their occupants as they rose from the table, produced a grating noise upon the floor; and the guests repaired, two by two, to the *salon* for coffee.

Relieff alone had not yet left his seat. Sombre and pensive he sat, with his head resting between his hands.

"What the deuce put that idea into your head, old fellow?" said Molotoff as he passed him.

VII.

THE EMIR OF BOKHARA.

Seid-Mozzafar-Dinn-Khan, Emir of Bokhara, was seated on an ottoman of scarlet cloth, and surrounded by a number of books and manuscripts; and opposite to him, on square carpets, four Bokharian ulemas,[1] stroking their beards and counting over the ebony beads of their chaplets. In front of the carpets and close to the ottoman, the chief ulema, who also discharged the functions of *reis*, or guardian of the religion, was busied in turning over the leaves of an Arabic folio. This functionary was a puissant personage in the khanate. Supreme chief of the religion, his influence often counterbalanced the despotic power of the emir, and his person was held sacred and inviolable. In one corner of the hall, an aged man, clothed in a rich furred robe, and wearing a green turban on his head, was engaged in converse in a low voice with an individual of some forty years, whose black, silken beard strongly contrasted with the pallor of his visage. The eyes of this last personage were painted with kohl, and a bonnet of astrakhan, with high, pointed crown, formed the covering of his head.

The old man was Chakrullah-Djelal-El-Dinn, the first vizier; and the person with whom he was conversing, Mirza-Mohammed, who held the important office of chief of police. He had been sold as a

---

[1] Ulema, mollah, imam—names of Mohammedan priests.

slave to Nasroullah-Bahadour-Khan, father of the present emir; and, by dint of knavery, sly cunning, and the duplicity inherent in his race, had managed to insinuate himself into the favor of Mozzafar. First slave, then confidant, he had gradually risen to the post he occupied at the time when the events of our history render it necessary for our readers to accompany us to the "noble Bokhara."

Seid-Mozzafar-Dinn is a man of fifty, of middle stature and with an apparent tendency to corpulence. His teeth are beautiful, beard thin, and complexion olive, and his features on the whole might have been agreeable, were it not for the cold, inflexible expression of cruelty of his small gray eyes, deeply sunken in their orbits. When he fixed his eyes upon any of his subjects, his icy, searching gaze intimidated the boldest, especially when the latter reflected on the absolute power exercised by the tyrant. He was the youngest son of Nasroullah-Bahadour, who hated him, and in order to get him out of the way had sent him to the obscure village of Kermene. On the emir's death, his situation underwent a sudden change; finding himself in possession of the supreme power, he set about imitating his predecessor's example in every particular, and soon made himself known for a profligate and bloodthirsty despot, capable of all kinds of excesses.

At the commencement of his reign, he had to put down the revolts of some members of his family who disputed his right to the throne; and he was next obliged to make war against the Kipchaks, Turcomans, and Khokans; but his arms were victorious in all encounters. The glory of his name soon spread throughout Central Asia; but his success only puffed up his pride, and made him still more cruel and despotic than at first. He had in the beginning paid little heed to the Russian advances in Khokan and at the northern extremities of his territory; indeed, with characteristic Mussulman apathy, he never gave the matter a thought. What was it to him if his vassals and Mussulman brethren were conquered, provided their misfortunes did not touch himself directly? From time to time he would give orders to have the Giaours exterminated, and would give himself up anew to his indolent carelessness.

The taking of Samarcand, which he had for several years chosen as his summer residence, was an unexpected and cruel blow for him. That city was but one hundred and fifty miles distant from Bokhara, hence the Russians were almost at the gates of his capital. Wild, ungovernable anger took possession of him; he beheaded two of his ministers, and projected an immediate expedition against the unbelievers, and nothing short of the advice of his most influential favorites (which advice cost some of them their lives) could deter him from attacking Samarcand with his handful of undisciplined soldiers. Finally he made up his mind to await reënforcements, which he solicited throughout all Turkistan, in the name of the religion threatened with destruction and of the country already exposed to the inroads of the invaders. The preparations for the expedition absorbed all his energies, and the hatred and desire for vengeance which now filled his breast were only equaled by the indifference with which he had hitherto regarded the Russian name.

For the present, however, he had given truce to his political considerations, and was discoursing on the subject of religion with the reis and ulema.

"I do not agree with you, venerable reis," said he; "I believe that not more than two seconds passed between the moment when our holy prophet (may the blessing of Allah be upon him!) was taken up by the angel and his return, after having beheld paradise. Just reflect, the prophet found two hundred and forty-seven drops of liquid still in the vessel, did he not?"

"Granted!" replied the reis.

"Now, the vessel was not large, for it was upon the prophet's table. Let us suppose, as I said the other day, that it held twenty-five hundred drops: an admissible supposition, inasmuch as twenty-five hundred drops constitute a certain volume."

The reis, after a moment's reflection, expressed his conviction that "it must not have contained a larger number."

"Yesterday I caused a vessel containing that quantity of water to be upset in my presence, in the same manner as the prophet must have upset his—that is to say, suddenly, with the elbow or the sleeve, just as a person would do who was surprised or frightened by an unexpected apparition. Well, then, in no instance, even when the glass was not altogether tipped over, but only inclined to one side, did the operation last longer than two seconds!"

"All that may be true, sire; but then Ichac-Hadji has it that the prophet (may Allah's blessing be upon him!) was neither surprised nor frightened at the sight of the angel. He arose hastily, but only through courtesy; his sleeve grazed the top of the table, and the result was an accident of very frequent occurrence, and one which all of us have observed, namely, a revolving motion in the vessel. Now, such motion may last a minute without the minutest drop of water falling over the edge, and only then happens one of two things: the vessel either regains its upright position, or falls to one side. If it falls, the water, as your majesty very justly remarks, is poured out in two seconds. But sixty seconds and two seconds make in all sixty-two seconds; hence the prophet (may Allah's blessing be upon him!) had sixty-two seconds to travel through heaven."

"It was you that discovered that, Ichac-Hadji?' inquired Mozzafar of one of the ulemas.

"I myself, your majesty."

"Go tell my *haguadar* to count over one hundred *tenghes* to you, as a reward for your knowledge." Mozzafar then addressed another of the ulemas who had been listening to the discussion with calmness and meditation: "Rahmet-Hadji, I believe I told you to give the Koran another reading; have you done so?"

"I have, sire."

"Very well, what is your opinion regarding the precepts of Islam?"

"*Farz* points out the line of conduct, as prescribed by God and transmitted by the prophet. *Sunnet* is the tradition emanating from the prophet himself, without the divine inspiration."

"True; but what say you of *Vadjib* and *Mustahab?*"

"These are only religious advices given by more recent interpreters of the Koran.

"Therefore, you do not hold the *Vadjib* and *Mustahab* to be obligatory?"

"No, sire."

Mozzafar smiled. "So then, I, who practise the precepts in question, might just as well dispense with their observance, and the reis is not obliged to punish such as neglect them?"

"That is my opinion, sire."

Mozzafar's brow became suddenly contracted. "Hearken, Rahmet; the theory you now advance constitutes rebellion and indifference in matters of religion. I called you here to a free discussion, and will therefore not order your death; but my religion enjoins upon me to punish you." So saying, he struck his hands together twice, and the chief of police came forward and prostrated himself before the throne. The ulema changed to a livid color, trembled in every limb, and turned his eyes imploringly toward the reis.

"Mohammed," said the emir, "you will take this man and have him bound, naked, upon a camel, his face turned in the direction of the animal's tail, and his head bare, that the sun may give him sounder ideas than he now possesses; and cause him thus to be marched through the whole city three consecutive days, and for four hours each day."

"To hear is to obey," replied Mohammed.

"Pity!" stammered Rahmet.

"The executioner will lead the camel and cry out, 'Behold how the emir punishes lukewarm Mussulmans who deny the obligation to observe the holy precepts of the *Vadjib* and *Mustahab.*'"

The ulema, a tall old man, with a long white beard, dropped from his carpet to his knees and held up his clasped hands to the reis with supplicating mien, well knowing that a single word from the chief of the mollahs would suffice to prevent his sufferings. The reis, however, only shrugged his shoulders, probably regarding the affair to be of too little consequence for his intervention. With wailings and lamentations the old man dragged himself to the emir's feet, and, striking his forehead against the flags—"Pardon!" cried he, "I acknowledge my error!"

A still deeper scowl covered Mozzafar's countenance. "So, it was to contradict your master that you gave utterance to your heretical opinion. Your crime is all the more enormous! Let his tongue be cut out, Mohammed, to prevent his blasphemy in future!"

The ulema was pitiful to behold, as he wept and howled and rolled himself on the floor, abjuring his doctrine and his science. For a few seconds the emir gloated upon the old man's contortions; at last he made a sign to Mohammed, who went out and returned immediately, followed by two soldiers of the prince's own guard. The ulema continued his supplications. The emir opened his mouth in a prolonged yawn. "Away with that brawler!" said he, bitterly; "he tries my patience!"

The soldiers dragged away the mollah, who, with his eyes bathed in tears, did not cease to implore the emir's mercy, in a tremulous voice, until he had passed the threshold of the door.

"You will attend to that imbecile by-and-by," said Mozzafar to the chief of police. "What news about the city?"

"Your subjects are happy, and bless Allah for having given them such a master as you! Nothing new in Bokhara, sire!"

"Ah! so my subjects are so fond of me as all that?"

"There is not one of them that does not, when he mentions your name, add the prayer, 'May he live one hundred and twenty years!'"

"Well and good! But what about those accursed Oorooses?"

The functionary here put on a countenance suited to the occasion.

"Have you anything to report?" went on the emir.

"Only this morning my agents arrested a Turcoman, in company with a woman. They stated themselves to be fugitives from Samarcand, and desirous to obtain an audience of your sublime majesty. I had them put into prison."

"Why not have brought them here?"

"I wished to be assured they were not Ooroos emissaries, to assassinate your majesty. It was my intention to question them first, and search them, and then usher them into your presence; but just then I received the order to come and contemplate your sacred beauty, and I have had no time to attend to them since."

The emir smiled benignly. "You are wrong, faithful Mohammed; I fear no assassins, and it is my will that my subjects shall be enabled to enjoy the light of my countenance at all hours of the day, and so be convinced of my justice and my unchanging bounty toward them." Then, with a cordial wave of the hand, he added, " Go fetch me those prisoners forthwith."

Mohammed was about to obey, but the emir stopped him. "After all," he pursued, "as prudence is, unfortunately, a virtue in kings, have them searched and escorted hither by four soldiers; and let fifty other soldiers be in readiness at the door to come to my aid should I require them. Go."

When Mohammed had gone, Mozzafar feasted complacently on the outbursts of admiration which his courage elicited from the ulemas and the vizier; and, his vanity completely satisfied, he asked of Chakrullah, " What have you to say to us this morning, vizier?"

"May it please your majesty, the Kipchaks are massing on the Amu, and a message from Merv informs me that the Turcomans will probably agree to furnish us a contingent of ten thousand horse."

" Excellent tidings!"

"Before deciding finally, they are awaiting the return of an envoy dispatched to Samarcand for the purpose of consulting one of their old leaders, who enjoys a high reputation among them for his knowledge and bravery."

"And what of the Khan of Khiva?"

" The taking of Samarcand has made a deep impression upon him. He has, nevertheless, remained indifferent, so far, to the advances of the Russians. He informs me that a friend of his, living in Samarcand, talks of the strength of the new conquerors, and of how dangerous it would be to make an attack on them.

Besides, he is aware that they do not persecute Mohammedans."

"Seid-Mohammed has always been a friend of mine."

"The emir of emirs, his eldest brother, with whom I am in correspondence, has, however, promised me to use all his influence with the khan to get him to come to your aid. I think, your majesty, we may rely upon ten thousand Uzbecks."

The emir arose, and, casting a haughty glance upon those present, stretched out his hand toward the west, and said: "We shall have an army of a hundred thousand men! What will the handful of Giaours who profane the sacred soil of Tamerlane be able to do against us?"

"Nothing, indeed, sire," replied the vizier, with a low reverence.

"We shall soon take the field, vizier."

"Your majesty would do well to reflect. Your life is too necessary to the happiness of the kingdom to risk it in battle. The Russians have bullets that kill afar, and their machinations are terrible, for they are protected by *Scheitan*."[1]

"We shall reflect, vizier."

All at once a tumult was heard in the adjoining hall. Mozzafar grew pale, and cried out lustily for help; for assassinations are of so frequent occurrence in these countries that the slightest uproar is regarded with considerable apprehension. The door was dashed open, and Safar-Hadgi rushed into the apartment, followed by Mohammed and four soldiers en-

[1] Satan.

deavoring to seize him. The affrighted emir fled back to the extreme end of the hall, and in the precipitation of his flight ran over the prostrate ulemas.

Safar-Hadgi was no longer the dashing Turcoman to whom the reader has been introduced heretofore; he now cut a sorry figure, with his clothes hanging in rags about him, his turban soiled with mud, and his visage blackened with dust, streaming with perspiration, and livid with rage.

Behind him were two soldiers escorting Emineh, wrapped in the same long linen garment as when we last saw her, and with the same silent and haughty mien.

Mozzafar still kept up his clamor for help; the ulemas, in consternation, would not dare raise their heads, which seemed as if riveted to the floor; and the soldiers gesticulated with fury, though prudently keeping out of reach of a poniard that Safar-Hadgi brandished right and left. The reis alone, with an air of scornful placidity, secure in the respect which his presence inspired in every Mussulman breast, looked on the scene around him with an ironical smile of unconcern.

Meantime a number of other soldiers, attracted by the emir's vociferations, hurried into the room, and, having by a rapid glance satisfied themselves of their numerical strength, were about to spring forward; but Safar turned round, and with an authoritative gesture shouted: "Back! touch me not! I am now in the presence of the emir, and, that being all I desired, you have nothing more to fear from me!" He replaced the poniard in his breast and folded his arms.

"Sire," said he, addressing Mozzafar, "I mean you no hurt. Pray be reassured, and allow—"

In obedience to a secret sign from the emir, who had by this time recovered his self-possession, seeing that no violence was intended to his person, ten *sarbares*[1] surrounded Safar.

"Unnecessary," said he. "I have already told you I intended you no hurt."

Mirza-Mohammed stepped forward. The pallor caused by the recent emotion had not yet disappeared from his countenance, though fear had given place to a species of brooding rage.

"This is a very dangerous man, your majesty," said he. "After having caused him to be brought to the palace, I gave orders to have him searched, and on his person were found pistols, a poniard, a large sum of money in gold coin, and diamonds of incalculable value, three or four millions of tenghes—all hidden beneath his rags."

"Diamonds!" ejaculated the emir, his eyes glistening with cupidity.

"At first he allowed himself to be searched unresistingly; and he made no move until his companion's turn came, when he gave a few nervous twitches: he then became quiet again. Nothing of a suspicious character was found on the woman, your majesty. She is very handsome, and is certainly neither a Turcoman nor a Tadjik."

Mozzafar looked fiercely at him. "Did you raise her veil?"

Mohammed felt he had taken a step in the wrong

---

[1] Regular soldiers of the emir's body-guard.

direction, for the emir made no light matter of a transgression of the Islam precepts, and it might go hard with the functionary for his rashness.

"Oh! sire, never!" he replied, affecting holy indignation.

"How, then, do you know she is handsome?"

"I was so informed by the person I directed to search her."

"How did this rebel make his way here?" inquired Mozzafar, softened by Mohammed's answer.

"When his pockets had been emptied and his turban unrolled, I ordered him to be stripped, lest he should have some weapon concealed under his clothes. No sooner had he heard my instructions, than all at once he became quite ungovernable, and, making a desperate effort, he burst his bonds, drew a poniard, with which he mortally wounded two of my best men, and then hastened directly to this hall, with the intention—"

Thus far Safar listened passively, but on hearing these last words he stopped Mohammed short. "Silence, slave!" he shouted; "I will now address your master myself."

Mozzafar's pride, rendered doubly sensitive by the humiliating exhibition he had just given of his own cowardice, was deeply wounded by the Turcoman's arrogant tone. So, feeling secure behind his ten soldiers, he rejoined: "Silence, yourself! The emir is only addressed in answer to his questions!"

"You shall be obeyed, sire!" said Safar, bowing.

"Because you cannot help obeying me!" retorted Mozzafar, with a diabolic smile. "Be brief in answering my inquiries. Where have you come from now?"

"From Samarcand."

"What brought you to this place?"

"I had a communication to make to you."

"Ah! Who is that woman?"

"I am not at liberty to answer, your majesty. All I can say is, that she is a Mussulman lady, saved by me from the hands of the unbelievers."

"Enough!—Mardja,"[1] he went on, addressing Emineh, "raise your veil!"

Emineh shook her head negatively. At a sign from Mozzafar a soldier snatched away her veil, and all present were dazzled by the Turcoman maid's incomparable beauty. Even the emir himself was seized with admiration, and his small gray eyes sparkled with fire.

"You will repent that action, emir," said Emineh, in her usual grave and melodious voice. "You have transgressed the law of the prophet!"

A slight contraction was visible in the reis's brow.

Safar raised his hand to his breast, and his eyes flashed with the fire of indignation.

"Enough!" said the emir; "let her veil be restored to her! This woman I shall retain for my harem. As for the man, let him be beheaded!"

"You are too expeditious, emir!" exclaimed Safar. Then, drawing his poinard, he knocked down the two soldiers nearest to him and sprang forward. Mozzafar, frightened, took refuge behind the mollah.

"Seize him! kill him!" he shrieked.

[1] Woman.

But Safar had had time to reach the spot where the reis was seated. Breaking a silken thread which he wore around his neck, he drew out a red medallion and held it before the eyes of the chief of the ulemas. "Do you recognize that sign?" he asked.

"The seal of the Shereef of Mecca!" exclaimed the stupefied reis, with a reverential inclination of the body. Then, placing his hand upon the hadgi's head, and casting an imperious glance on all around him, he said, in a tone of marked solemnity: "Let no one touch this man; he is under the protection of Islam!"

VIII.

SAFAR-HADGI.

The ulemas, entirely recovered from their fright, had raised their heads and looked inquiringly at their superior, and Mozzafar, fairly overcome by the recent shock to his nerves, had dropped once more upon his ottoman.

"What does all this signify, reis?" he inquired.

"It signifies that this man is the bearer of a firman from the Shereef of Mecca, enjoining upon every Mussulman to help him in case of need. The firman is graven on stone, in sacred characters, and sealed with the seal of the prophet. The shereef's maledictions would fall upon the head of any believer who should do hurt to the saintly personage bearing the talisman. There are barely ten Mussulmans in all Islam thus recommended."

Mozzafar, who, so far as his own kingdom was concerned, had elevated the faith to the level of fanaticism, clearly saw he was vanquished. He uttered a sort of wild roar; and, turning to the soldiers: "That man is free," said he.—"You may withdraw."

The order was superfluous. At the voice of the reis the sarbares, led by Mohammed, had gathered in a group, like frightened sheep, in the darkest corner of the room. They went out slowly, one by one.

"Reis," said Safar, "touch the reverse of the medallion, and there you will find something which will inform you still more amply concerning me."

The reis pressed with his finger, and the medallion opened; a small golden plate fell to the floor, and one of the ulemas picked it up and presented it to his superior. While the reis was engaged in deciphering the characters engraved upon the plate, his countenance alternately assumed an expression of stupefaction, respect, and fear. When he had completed the examination he replaced the plate within the medallion, and handed the latter back to the hadgi.

"Brother," said he, "is there anything that I can do for you?"

"Riches which do not belong to me have been taken away from me. One part is the property of the association, the other that of the Turcomans whose interests were intrusted to me in Samarcand. Pray have the riches restored to me, and the woman that accompanied me, and is retained here against her will, delivered to me."

The reis nodded his head in sign of acquiescence. "This man," said he to Mozzafar, "is the supreme chief of the association of Nakichbend dervishes. His request, sire, must be granted."

"Most certainly," replied Mozzafar, chuckling. "Your riches shall be returned to you. As for the woman, that is another thing. Inasmuch as you belong to the order of Baha-El-Dinn-Nakichbend, you have taken the vow of poverty and contempt of the things of this world. None, not even the supreme chief himself, is exempt from the laws by which it is governed."

The reis turned his eyes toward Safar with a look which meant that the emir was in the right. The hadgi was nonplussed for a moment.

"The gems and the gold found with you are not yours, say you?" pursued Mozzafar. "It is well: take them back. But the woman in your company does not belong to the association of holy dervishes. She pleases me: I am the lord of the soil, and I keep her. She will be my slave. Thereby I do you no injustice, do I?"

"This woman cannot be your slave," rejoined Safar, who had by this time quite recovered his self-possession. "Her birth is equal to yours; she is the daughter of the Emir-Al-Oumra (emir of emirs), brother to the Khan of Khiva.

Glancing at him with serpent's eyes, Mozzafar exclaimed: "Silence, old man! Who will vouch for the truth of what you say?"

"I swear it by the beard of the prophet!"

This oath is one of great solemnity in every Mussulman's mouth; and the saintly character of the person who had now uttered it admitted of no doubt as to his veracity; yet Mozzafar was determined to carry on the struggle.

"How did she come into your charge?"

"Shah-Mourad, Khan of Khokan, had asked and obtained her hand in marriage; the caravan escorting her was surprised and pillaged by a band of Turcomans, and these in turn fell into the hands of a Russian regiment. I found the hamoun a prisoner by the order of the wife of the Russian Governor of Samarcand, and I aided her in making her escape, with the intention of delivering her up to her father, once my master, and still my friend."

"Your friend!" interrupted Mozzafar, scornfully. "But it matters little!—Vizier," added he, "send a messenger to Choorakhan to demand officially of Emir-Al-Oumra his daughter's hand in marriage for me."

Safar felt that all hope was lost for him, the reis having resumed the perusal of his manuscript, as if thereby to signify that he would take no further concern in the debate. Fierce anger brooded in the Turcoman's breast, but he restrained himself, being aware how dangerous it might prove to give way to his passion just then. He bit his lips savagely until drops of blood rolled down upon his beard; observing which, the emir smiled, and his smile exasperated Safar all the more. "In the name of the association of which I am the head, I demand the protection of Islam for the emir's daughter.—Reis, I call upon you to keep that woman in your house until the messenger returns."

Mozzafar writhed under the insult as if he had been bitten by a serpent. Yet, being much given to ostentation in matters concerning religion, and feeling, besides, that an overt act of opposition to popular fanaticism might be attended with peril, he swallowed the affront and awaited, with a semblance of composure, the reis's reply.

The chief of the mollahs looked up from his book and nodded assent, preparatory to reciting the formula of acquiescence. For this, however, the emir did not give him time. "Enough!" broke in Mozzafar. "I consent. Let the woman be taken to the reis's house!" And Eminch was escorted away by the soldiers.

Mozzafar stroked his beard, and, summoning his Asiatic duplicity to the rescue, he stifled the pique of the man and the mortification of the despot. "Now that all our dissensions have come to an end," said he, "it only remains for me to tender to you the hospitality due to so venerable a dervish."

The chilling expression of Safar's eyes as he fixed them upon Mozzafar, in a stern, persistent gaze, so disconcerted the latter that he was forced to look in another direction.

"I am on my way to Bokhara," said the Turcoman, "and my only motive in coming here was to see you. The impertinence of your slaves has hitherto prevented me from apprising you of important news, the chief object of my journey. Emir, the Russians are preparing an expedition against you, and before a month has elapsed the attack will have begun!"

Mozzafar stood up, and, turning pale with fury, shrieked: "The Russians? It's false, I say! They will never dare to attack me!"

"The Russians will dare anything," rejoined Safar,

with a shrug of the shoulders; "and, unless you act promptly and with energy, they will crush you like a worm!"

"Insolent slave!" howled the emir, trembling in every limb and foaming at the mouth.

"Emir," replied Safar, eying him composedly from head to foot, "I am not your slave, and your insults to me are an outrage upon our religion! Beware! It were easy for me to have abandoned you to your blindness and folly; but I am not your enemy, and I have been mortally offended by the Russians. Hear me, then, for you will shortly behold me in the proper light, and will assuredly repent of your words and deeds of this day."

The reis had arisen from his seat; and the ulemas, already awe-stricken by the cruelty inflicted upon one of their number, huddled together close by his side. As for Mozzafar, perceiving that all present would side with the hadgi, he suppressed his resentment. "Speak!" he exclaimed, addressing Safar.

The latter, turning toward Chakrullah, said, "You must have received a communication from Merv—"

"But—" stammered the vizier.

"Answer! By whom was it sent?"

"I am not sure that I ought to tell," began Chakrullah hesitatingly.

"You certainly ought not," interposed Mozzafar. "Do you not see that this fellow, instead of giving news, is seeking for information? What, vizier! Intrust my secrets thus to an unknown man!"

"Your correspondent's name is Kandjan-Bek," said Safar, in a tone contempt. "He writes that the Turcomans await the decision of a certain Safar-Hadgi before uniting their forces with yours."

"Allah!" exclaimed the vizier.

"Emir-Al-Oumra informs you that he can promise nothing before hearing from Samarcand, from the same Safar-Hadgi."

Mozzafar interrupted him to say: "It is indeed unnecessary to question my vizier, if that is all you have to tell us. Safar-Hadgi, formerly minister of Mohammed-Seid, is celebrated throughout all Turkistan for his learning, his bravery, and his piety!"

"I am that Safar-Hadgi!" said our hero. And he made a low reverence.

A glance of inquiry from the emir was met by a nod of assent from the reis.

"Why, then, did you not apprise me of your name at once?" asked the embarrassed Seid-Mozzafar-Dinn-Khan.

"Did you allow me an opportunity to do so? At all events, I may frankly say my capacity of chief of the Nakichbends will offer a surer guarantee for my personal safety than the fleeting renown of my name."

"So, then," murmured Mozzafar, with half-clinched teeth, "you hold my crown and my life in your hands!"

"Even so!" was Safar's calm reply; "but, as I bear you no hatred, I will help your cause with all my might." Advancing nearer to the prince, he added, "Will you but place your hands in mine?" After a brief hesitation, Mozzafar yielded; and Safar, clasping the emir's hands in his own, said: "Thus we seal our alliance! Bear it well in mind!"

"Thus we seal our alliance!" repeated Mozzafar in a low murmur.

"I swear by the beard of the prophet that before a month has rolled over, I shall have twenty thousand horse, Turcomans and Uzbecks, assembled, and will march them to meet you on the Amu, where an equal number of Kipchaks await you this very moment. Order a horse for me, with provisions and clothing. I set out to-night.

Mozzafar called to Mohammed to approach. "You have heard what has been said. You will obey Safar-Hadgi's orders, and you will furnish him, besides, an escort of a hundred mounted sarbares to accompany him to the frontiers of my territory."

"I require no escort on Mussulman soil; but I thank you nevertheless," replied Safar.

"So, then, you are all-powerful for *me;* but I can do nothing for *you!*"

"We shall settle our accounts another day."

"Yes, another day!" murmured the emir. And, rising, he bade him farewell.

"May Allah pour down his blessing on your head!" returned the latter.

Mohammed accompanied him to the palace-gate. When they had entered the court-yard, Safar turned abruptly and said to the Persian: "Are you aware that I have it in my power to have you beheaded?"

Mohammed bounded backward, gasping, "How so?"

"By just apprising the emir of what my fellow-traveller did not deign to disclose to him: that you *did* raise up her veil, and that you secreted the diamonds found in her apparel. You will not have long to wait: your time will come shortly."

"It is false! I have no diamonds."

Safar seized him by the skirt.

"You have them with you now! see there!—in that pocket!—shall I call?"

Mohammed clasped his hands together, crying, "Mercy! I will surrender everything!"

"You are still in my power, dog! and, if you wish for mercy, you must first merit it!"

"I am your slave, my lord!" exclaimed the functionary.

"I leave all these diamonds in your charge; you will give me an acknowledgment for them. By-and-by, if I am satisfied with your services, it may be that I will allow you to keep the lot you attempted to rob the emir and myself of. Have you your tablets here?"

"No, my lord."

"Again the lie! I saw you take them out of your pocket when I was being searched."

Mohammed, overwhelmed, gathered himself into a half-crouching attitude, that he might lift his eyes upward to Safar in a look of supplication mingled with hate.

"Write!" commanded Safar, "and no more treachery, or this very instant I will deliver you into the hands of your master."

The Persian drew out the tablets, wrote a receipt, and handed it in trembling to the terrible hadgi, who scanned it over and placed it in his turban.

"This receipt I shall leave for safe keeping with

the reis, with whom, as you know, Shiite dog, you are not in very good odor. Should any evil befall me, or I not be back here from Bokhara in one month from now, he will hand it over to the emir. So, I warn you, be prudent! In case of need, you shall receive my orders, and the least hesitation on your part to obey will be the signal to bring your acknowledgment to Mozzafar's eyes. If I am pleased with you, you shall be rewarded bountifully. You may go! I need you no further."

As he was about to withdraw, Safar added: "You will order two horses, saddled and appointed, to be brought to me this evening at the Rhigistan caravansary; and let the djigweet in charge of them bring me some clothing and the gold I had with me. Go!"

Mohammed went back into the palace, and Safar disappeared in the direction of the Rhigistan.

Meantime, the emir, having dismissed the reis and ulemas, and being entirely alone, began to give vent to the long-pent-up rage with which the late humiliation had filled his breast. Mozzafar rolled to and fro on the carpet, biting the cushions, and uttering wild cries, interrupted now and then by a flood of tears or a torrent of imprecations, or such exclamations as—"Braved and taunted by a begging dervish!"

His yells attracted the servants of the palace, who, with fear and trembling, gathered in groups behind the doors, in readiness to hasten to his first signal. They had not long to wait. The emir clapped his hands, and a slave sprang forward. "Mohammed! Quickly!" cried the prince. "If he is not here before I have finished pulling off the beads of this chaplet, I will have your feet cut off." In an instant the slave was out of sight.

Undoing the string of the chaplet, Mozzafar began pulling the beads off and throwing them on the ground with ferocious precipitation. Five minutes had expired, and the only noise to be heard was that of the beads falling on the flags, and the heavy breathing of the emir. At length the last bead dropped, and went rolling over to the window. Mozzafar heaved a sigh of relief: Mohammed was not yet there; and consequently the slave was soon to pay the penalty of his tardiness. The last bead was still faintly oscillating when Mohammed entered, followed by the slave. The latter cast an anxious glance at the prince, who pointed with his finger to the empty chaplet-string. The slave became pale, and swooned away on the flags. Mohammed prostrated himself at a respectful distance from the ottoman.

"Did you hear what outrage that dervish heaped upon me?" inquired Mozzafar.

Mohammed crawled close up to the ottoman, as if hoping by that act of humility to soothe the rankling wound left in his master's breast by Safar's insolence.

"Hearken to me," went on the emir. "The boys are my subjects, yet I am at times constrained to resort to dissimulation with them; and the reis is under the protection of our holy religion; while you are but a slave, and all you have and are you owe to me!"

"Sire!" replied Mohammed, kissing the fringe of the ottoman, "I know I am your property."

"In order to retain my favor and good-will, you must obey me blindly. To-morrow, before sunrise, this

Safar must be in my power; I must have him under my heel, and make him expiate his insolence by new and unheard-of tortures, which you and I shall meditate together."

"I will make effort, sire," said Mohammed, now rising to his knees, "to obey your orders, though if I should attempt to have him arrested I may be forced to release him. You yourself know his person is inviolable."

"For that reason I command you to act secretly. He has to perform a journey across the desert, and he had the madness to refuse the escort I offered him. In traveling alone over our sandy plains one has many risks to run. His disappearance would astonish nobody. Bear all this in mind, for I must have that man. The continuance of my favor rests upon that condition."

"You shall be obeyed!" exclaimed Mohammed, rising to his feet.

"As for this worthless worm here," said Mozzafar, standing up too, and pushing with his foot the still prostrate and inert body of the slave, "have him carried out and both his feet cut off, that he does not know how to make use of." And the emir withdrew to the inner apartments of the palace, while Mohammed remained standing before the ottoman, with his eyes fixed upon the ground, and his mind on the rack, as he reviewed the horrors of his present situation. To disobey the emir would be dangerous, on the one hand; and, on the other, his life was in Safar's hands— for he felt certain that the offense of concealing the diamonds would not be pardoned by Mozzafar, whose favor he enjoyed only in return for his supposed fidelity. After having thus mused a few minutes, he stepped backward, and, pushing the still motionless slave roughly with his foot, he cried: "Up, dog! and hear what I have to say to you."

The slave uttered a low groan, and, rising to a sitting posture, turned his eyes upward to the functionary, revealing a countenance wild with terror and dismay.

"You heard the order given by the emir while you were playing dead, did you not?"

The slave only answered with a sob.

Mohammed looked down at him with an air of affected compassion, and added: "Now, suppose I were not to execute that order, but to let you off, could I be sure of your gratitude?"

The slave on hearing this arose to his knees, and, hugging Mohammed's feet, fell to kissing them with a sort of convulsive ardor, as he exclaimed, in broken accents: "Oh! sure, sure! only tell me what you wish; I will do anything, everything!"

"If I say 'Steal,' you will steal? If I say 'Kill,' you will kill—'Die,' you will die?"

"Yes! yes! But not that! Oh, not that!"

Gently raising him to his feet, Mohammed, with his mildest voice, asked him his name.

"Hahib, my lord."

"Up, then, Hahib! and off to my palace. By-and-by I will tell you what I have for you to do." And as the slave continued kissing his feet, and uttering half-stifled, inarticulate sounds expressive of joy and gratitude, Mohammed repeated the order, adding: "Come! haste! and you must change your costume and your face, so that none, not even your father, would recognize you." Then hastening to the courtyard, he gave some orders to two of his men who were awaiting him there; and, gathering up the long folds of his flowing robe, he started off with a run in the direction of the Rhigbistan, the inhabitants of Bokhara looking after him with amazement, and asking one another, "Has Scheitan carried off our emir, that his damned spirit runs thus wildly through the streets?"

A happy thought had germinated in the Persian's fertile brain, namely, that, if he could manage to assassinate Safar before the latter had conferred with the reis, he should then have no reason to fear being denounced, and he might keep the diamonds and chop off Hahib's feet. The very idea of so much good fortune rejoiced Mohammed's heart, for he had a special passion for gold and blood.

It is six o'clock in the evening. The white houses of Bokhara are tinged in red by the ruddy rays of the descending sun, and the muezzins are calling the believers to prayer. The mysterious dwelling of the reis is plunged in silence; but the square lying between his house and the grand mosque presents a scene of animation quite unusual for the hour. Vagrant mendicants wander through the adjacent streets, and strange, suspicious faces flit up and down, casting anxious looks toward the high wall that surrounds the abode of the spiritual chief of the khanate.

"An Ooroos emissary attempted to assassinate the emir," said a Tadjik to a Turcoman standing near him in the square; "he killed several soldiers, and effected his escape after having spit upon the Koran. He is now hiding in the city, awaiting a favorable opportunity to penetrate into the reis's house."

"Had he only attempted to kill the emir," rejoined the Turcoman, "that would not have been so much of a crime; but spitting upon the Koran—!"

"Yes!" chimed in a mendicant; "Mehemet the ulema saw him spit on it!"

"Death to the unbeliever!"

Some Tadjiks passing on their way to the mosque were stopped by the Tadjik who had spoken to the Turcoman. "Brethren," said he to them, "come and help us to defend our reis's dwelling."

"What is the danger?" inquired the others, anxiously.

"An unbeliever has spit upon the Koran!"

"Death to him!"

The square before the grand mosque was soon filled with a dense crowd. Mohammed, concealed behind a sort of inclosure, was talking with some of his men who had come to report to him, and rubbing his hands with contentment, as he gazed complacently on the assembled multitude.

The door of the reis's house was opened wide, and the chief of the ulemas, accompanied by a number of priests, and leaning upon Safar-Hadgi's shoulder, appeared on the threshold and took the direction of the mosque.

"Too late!" murmured Mohammed. And he slowly regained his palace, where Hahib was in attendance to receive his orders.

IX.

THE EXPEDITION.

Countess Molotoff was reclining listlessly upon her lounge. "I am quite serious, Monsieur Bassalsky," said she; "and I sent for you to-day, to give you a sound rating."

As she spoke in a tone of no great severity, Bassalsky, who was seated at a considerable distance, drew his chair closer to the lounge. "Scold me, beat me; I will kiss the rod that chastises me; take my life, and my final breath shall be drawn uttering your name!"

"Well, well! let me tell you," continued Martha, assuming a more frigid tone, "that you are very unreasonable, and that your extravagant manners will compromise me in the end. Your expressions of adoration tendered to the woman might perhaps be excusable, but allow me to say they are out of all character when addressed to the wife, and, above all, to the wife of your general. It is positively disrespectful to me!"

"Oh!" exclaimed he, bending in a low reverence, as if he would fling himself prostrate at her feet. "I respect you as a divinity of a nature superior to my own! I kneel before the spot where you stood, and have never dared to kneel before you!"

"You give no proof of respect for me. My name is ever in your mouth, and you are continually defending me and taking my part, as if I required a defender; and you go into ecstasies when praising my beauty and grace, and what not, before your fellow-officers! My beauty and my grace, sir, are like the sun, and shine for all; but you would have people believe that you are a favored mortal, and monopolize the whole of the rays yourself! All this," she added, changing from a burlesque tone to one of gravity and determination, " is displeasing to me!"

Bassalsky felt that, this time at least, the reproof was in earnest, and he was deeply mortified.

"What have I done to merit?—"

"You speak of my person with too much freedom," replied Martha, dryly. "You were heard to say somewhere yesterday—no longer ago—that at a word from my mouth you would throw yourself into the fire. Such things, sir, may perhaps be *done*, but they should certainly never be *said!* "

"It may have been wrong to *say* it, but I am ready to *do* it," rejoined the young man, in a scarcely audible murmur.

She turned round to conceal a smile of contempt and a look of triumph, muttering, half articulately, "Indeed?"

Bassalsky, notwithstanding, felt as if he would burst with joy. "Just try me!" said he.

Martha turned rapidly, and, looking him full in the face, said, in a resolute tone: "I will try you, then. Do you promise to do anything I ask of you?"

"Oh!" ejaculated Bassalsky.

This exclamation, the only sound his exultation had left him power to produce just then with his voice, was so clearly affirmative that the countess was compelled to suppress a second smile of scorn.

"Well, then, make love to Mademoiselle Goreff!"

This unexpected request so stunned him, that for a moment he was in danger of falling backward off his seat, while Martha gathered her shoulders in an almost imperceptible shrug.

"Make love to—!" gasped the officer. "Oh! taunt me as you please, forbid me your presence, but do not ask me to do that!"

"It is as much for your own interest as mine that I give you that advice. I suppose you must be persuaded that you have nothing to expect from me. Why lose your time and your youth? Lise is handsome, rich, and of good family, and she will make an excellent match for you. If I mistake not, she has no great dislike for you as it is, for the reason, as she tells me, that you never talk nonsense to her. But, see how your fine zeal has abated the very first time you have an opportunity to please me! Do you refuse?"

Bassalsky was completely annihilated. He stood rolling his cap between his hands, and looked so abashed and so sheepish that the countess lost all patience.

"The task would seem to me to be neither difficult nor irksome. Lise is pretty, witty, and elegant in manner.

"I scarcely know how she is. I have hardly had an opportunity of looking at her yet," said he. And he drew a sigh as he spoke.

"Well, you must look at her, and do all you can to please her."

"Why torment me thus? Why this cruelty?"

Giving way for a moment to a nervous movement, Martha rumpled her pocket-handkerchief between her hands; but she immediately recovered her composure. Yet her countenance wore an expression of marked serenity, for the young man's obstinacy, however flattering to her feminine vanity, was decidedly displeasing to her. She perceived, notwithstanding, that without a little dissimulation she could scarcely gain her end. "Do you not observe," she remonstrated, "that you have almost compromised me as it is? You are anxious to become aide-de-camp, and yet you seem not to notice that the general, who was at first disposed to gratify you, now puts you off from day to day and week to week. Now do you understand?"

Suddenly, as if, through the clouds which had hitherto darkened the sky of his imagination, he had perceived a small spot of blue, Bassalsky struck his forehead with his clinched hand, exclaiming: "Ah! imbecile that I was! Yes, I understand! I am ready to do whatever you desire!"

Once more the countess turned away, but this time it was to wipe off some large drops of perspiration which had gathered on her brow. Her countenance at that moment wore an expression at once of extreme lassitude and irrepressible disgust; however, she had still sufficient self-command to master her feelings, and even to assume an air of frank good-nature. "Now I am satisfied!" said she, holding her hand to the young officer, who raised it to his lips with an impassioned gesture.

"You must begin this very day," she pursued. "I will appoint you as Mademoiselle Lise's cavalier for the excursion to-morrow. You will accompany us in the carriage."

"You can do whatever you see fit with me," said he, ardently.

A servant announced his excellency. A moment afterward Molotoff and Relieff entered the countess's chamber arm-in-arm.

"Here is Relieff," said the general; "he has just barely time to take a friendly leave.—Quick! my dear friend—kiss my wife's hand : the troops have been awaiting us for some time."

At sight of the aide-de-camp, whom she had not seen since the departure of the governor-general (which took place the next day after his arrival), she experienced a momentary embarrassment. As for Relieff, he approached with becoming dignity and ease of manner; true, his manly, open countenance betokened a certain degree of apprehension ; but no trace of anger or of rancor lurked in the expression of his eye.

It is a Russian custom for the lady to kiss the forehead of the gentleman who kisses her hand ; and in the present instance the countess adhered to that usage. It seemed to the aide-de-camp that her fingers clasped his in a rapid, convulsive pressure, and that her lips were burning when they touched his brow. By a spontaneous movement, his lips united in a second and more prolonged contact with her hand than at first.

When he raised his head, a death-like pallor was on his visage. Martha's eyelids drooped to hide (who knows?), perhaps a tear, and, for the first time in her life, a genial glow pervaded her whole being. The major's pallid features appeared to her fancy as the indication of a still-surviving and ardent passion; and she was moved to pity, and her breast was filled with poignant regret for the past. For a moment she felt her senses lulled in a sort of misty dream, in which other scenes than those around her opened to her view: Relieff—the Relieff of her virgin days—the handsome, the brave, the devoted Relieff, lay stretched a bloody corpse upon the red sand of the desert! Then the red of the sand and the red of the gore seemed to mingle together, and, as it were from a fountain, gushed forth upon her guilty brow, and a sting of remorse awakened her to reality again. The dream of a moment was dispelled, but the remorse persisted. Had the successive emotions of the past few minutes brought about a passing change in the countess? Who can say? Certain it is, however, that all at once her stern nature relaxed into genuine amiability, and she seemed bent, for the time being at least, upon showing kindness to all around her. "Monsieur Bassalsky," said she, in a gracious tone, "pray go and ask Mademoiselle Goreff to come here. She will doubtless be pleased to embrace her cousin once again before his departure."

Before Bassalsky could reach the door, Molotoff detained him, and said hurriedly to his wife: "Impossible, my dear; we have no time to spare."

"I thank you, madam," added Relieff—"I thank you sincerely; but I have already taken leave of my cousin, in whose company I spent the whole morning. I left her making ready to come and rejoin us beyond the ramparts."

Martha was deeply wounded by this speech. How was she to believe that the man who had once adored her beyond any one on earth had been unable, in the course of two whole weeks, to find time for more than the few minutes of almost official leave-taking which he now devoted to *her*, and yet have spent the entire morning of the day of his departure with *Lise?* This thought filled the countess's haughty heart with indignation.

"Ah!" said she, "I was not aware." Then rising from her seat, she went on: "Well, then, gentlemen, I will not say adieu! inasmuch as we shall meet again. It is time for me too to go and make ready. Monsieur Bassalsky, you will wait here till I return: you must not forget that you are our cavalier." And she left the room without bowing to any one present.

"Come, come along, loiterer!" cried Molotoff, twisting the handle of the door in a sudden fit of impatience. But at that moment Bassalsky approached his old friend. "Major," said he, "accept my wishes for the success of your glorious expedition." Then, with outstretched hand and lowering his voice, "and my sincere apology, too, my dear Relieff."

The major replied with a bow of exquisite politeness, but he did not take the proffered hand. "Many thanks, captain; I accept both your well-wish and your apology."

Bassalsky either could not or would not understand the major's reserve.

"We are friends again, are we not?" he ventured to ask.

"Oh! sir. . . . Friends? No! What should we

gain by being friends ? This is probably the last time we shall meet." And with a frigid inclination of the body he left him, and hastened to join the general, who was calling lustily in the adjoining room.

There are two towns in Samarcand : one with narrow, filthy streets, and sombre houses of brick or sundried mud, imprisoned by a line of fortified walls and deep moats ; and the other, cheerful and gay, imbedded in eternal verdure. This latter town is situated beyond the ramparts, and extends to the verge of the steppes, which form its boundary on one side. The gardens of all the dwellings communicate by shady walks ; limpid *yaricks*[1] roll their streams along under the shadow of majestic trees ; and the whole town breathes tranquillity, comfort, and, something which seldom greets the eye in these countries, comparative cleanliness.

At the foot of Mount Tchoponata, on the road leading from Bokhara to Samarcand, four huge trees, the growth of many ages, mark the angles of a square called, nobody knows why, Tamerlane's Round-point. Long, poplar-fringed avenues radiate thence in the direction of the four cardinal points, stretching along the Tadjiks' garden.

In the centre of the square are a pump and watering-trough, standing side by side, and all around, a path beaten by the continual tread of animals and men. This place is usually bestrewed with every species of filth—animal and vegetable detritus, rags, half-gnawed bones—which, united with the exhalations of Tadjiks,

[1] Canals.

Uzbecks, and camels, impregnates the air with odors the reverse of fragrant.

On the 5th of June, 187-, the whole square had been neatly swept; the mouth of the well was covered over with a scaffolding of wood, and an impromptu table set up beside the *abreuvoir* and covered with a snow-white table-cloth, fringed with gold; and upon the table a gilded monstrance, and a tripod, supporting the Book of the Evangelists, completed a rude, though not unsightly, altar.

A priest in violet chasuble, ornamented with silver, was officiating, while a soldier in full dress was busily engaged in clearing the altar of mellow golden fruit as it dropped from the overhanging branches, and in chasing the butterflies, wasps, and other insects, of varied hue and hum, that were attracted by the glitter of the gilded monstrance.

A carpet had been spread upon the scaffolding over the well, and on it were standing General Molotoff, the countess, Goreff and his daughter, and Bassalsky and a few other officers of high rank.

Under the shade of the trees stood Relieff, with drawn sword, and a short distance behind him a battalion of infantry-soldiers, who, with their clean gray shirts, and recently-burnished accoutrements glistening in the sun, presented an aspect of neatness and order ever grateful to a general's eye. Joy and satisfaction were depicted in the faces of the men themselves, as they listened reverentially, cap in hand, to the priest saying mass.

In the rear of the battalion were four pieces of cannon, mounted on their carriages; and, turned with the muzzles in the direction of the desert, they seemed to menace the plains beyond.

Close by the cannon, a Cossack soldier was holding by the bridle a magnificent horse, prancing and champing his bit with impatience. This charger belonged to the commander of the expedition. Finally, in the far distance, might be seen the fur caps of the Cossacks, who, little concerned about religious ceremonies, had remained far from the main body of the troops, and held themselves in readiness to form the vanguard of the march.

The divine service concluded, the priest invoked the blessing of Almighty God for the czar and his family; and, having sprinkled the troops with holy water, he blessed the four cardinal points, and gave Relieff and the other five officers of the expedition the cross to kiss. The soldiers then replaced their caps on their heads, and Molotoff advanced to the front.

"Brave comrades," said he, "I have no long speech to make : honor and courage are not to be taught in that way; each one of you possesses them in his breast! Come back victorious, and you shall have the czar's gratitude ; but, should you be defeated, the czar will avenge you! I need not tell you to be brave ; that would be useless—the Russian soldier is always brave! But I will say to you: be resolute, patient, sober, and preserve good discipline, in order to hasten the victory!"

"Long live the emperor!" cried the soldiers.

"Fellow-soldiers," said Molotoff, "may God grant you success!" And, turning to Relieff, he added: "Major, give the order to march."

Before mounting his charger, Relieff cast a last glance around him, and that glance, intended for Lise, was intercepted by the countess, who grew slightly pale. The official leave-taking precluded all further words or demonstrations: all was over. The troops, though they had not yet set out in fact, were already virtually on the march, according to law.

Relieff sprang to his horse, and, in a voice somewhat faltering, yet clear and sonorous, gave the word: "Standards to the front! Form the column of attack!"

The colors soon floated in the sun, and the priest signed them with the sign of the cross. Relieff took up his position in the centre of the column.

"March!" he cried. And the troops started on the line of march.

The sight of a band of men setting out in search of an uncertain destiny is at all times one of sad solemnity. The governor, and those who with him had come to witness the departure, stood for a while silent and pensive, following with their eyes the column, gradually receding, until it had completely disappeared in the distance.

"May God give them the victory!" said Molotoff. "They are commanded by a brave heart. But," changing his tone to one of familiar inquiry, "how the deuce did he get such a strange idea into his head?—Martha, you were in the secret. Can you not give us some some clew to the mystery?"

She shook her head negatively.

"He must have desired to give the Kipchaks a lesson in civilization," said Bassalsky; "he is very fond of giving lessons."

Lise smiled, but Martha knit her brow.

"His counsel is wise, and worthy of attention, though," said she, sharply.

Lise looked at her astonished.

"Monsieur Bassalsky intended no unkindness, madam," she remarked.

"Oh! nor do I either," rejoined Martha, laughing, "mean any unkindness toward Monsieur Bassalsky."

The party took their places in the carriages.

"How the d—l did he come to get into this mess?" thought Molotoff, as he seated himself beside his wife.

X.

THE CAMP.

The evening is close and suffocating. Not a breath of air, not a cloud in the sky, but a dunnish mist floats through the atmosphere, tingeing all objects with a reddish hue, save the azure of the sky, to which it imparts a violet shade. Yellow, wedge-shaped sand-hillocks, resembling mole-hills in appearance, stretch in a straight line as far as the eye can reach, while the intervals between them are marked here and there by ragged tufts of sunburnt grass, which at a distance one might imagine to belong to giants buried, all but the hair, in the sand. The vast, gray, boundless plain is intercepted by a serpentine, silvery line—the river Amu-Darya, coming from a world unknown and death-still, like its own waters. A few black and broken reeds, and here and there a flake of foam floating swiftly by the brink, are the only signs of movement in the liquid mass, which at first sight seems motionless. Not a warble in the air, nor a frolicking fish in the flood; even the mosquitoes themselves are silent at this hour, and do not form the buzzing band which, winding, belt-like, through space, and following the line of the Amu-Darya, has been compared to a second and aërial river. With closely-tucked wings, they hang, drowsy and inoffensive, by their barbed proboscis darted into the reed-stalks along the stream.

Though all around is mute and still, yet thousands of human beings are encamped hard by, and await but the signal to launch forth upon the plain, and awaken the dull solitude with din and carnage.

Nomads from the Mourgab, from Merv, from Khiva, from the gulfs and bays of the Caspian, and from the sands of Khiz-il-Khouma, have flocked together in one vast rendezvous, on the banks of the river which still forms a part of the possessions of the Emir of Bokhara. But yesterday rivals, and waging war against each other, these peoples are to-day united in the common cause; and, obedient to the voice of their emirs and ulemas, rise up in the name of Islam to check the inroads of the common enemy—the Russian.

A long, sandy peninsula extends into the Amu-Darya a little below the sand-hillocks, and may be descried afar by its whiteness in the midst of an impenetrable forest of reeds, fringing it on all sides, save where it unites with the plain. It forms a narrow point, gradually tapering till it disappears entirely in the water; but it again surges into view, and widens by degrees, and finally joins the Russian bank. This double peninsula renders the river fordable at that point.

At the time of our history it is inhabited, though one might be tempted to think only by phantoms, so unbroken is the silence all around. What are those long, flexible shafts, set off with horse-hair plumes, stuck upright in long, parallel rows in the sand? Lances. Other weapons, and bridles with silver mountings and turquoise incrustations are strewed in disorder on the ground; and here and there a blue-painted buckler, adorned with golden coins, glistens in the sun suspended from a bundle of spears. Behind the rows of lances, at the point of union of the peninsula with the Bokharan bank of the stream, is a numerous troop of horses pasturing in entire freedom, and, spite of the heat, all covered with thick blankets. On the approach of a stranger they press closely together, and prick up their pointed ears in a menacing fashion.

A number of braziers are arranged symmetrically by the water-side, near the point where the peninsula sinks beneath the surface; and seated around each one of them, a group of men, in bright and showy-colored robes, and capacious, silk-embroidered leather pantaloons, attentively watch the high-topped, copper tea-kettles gayly steaming on the embers.

These men present a strange, theatrical aspect; and their wide-brimmed, pointed hats of gray felt add to the fierceness of their bony and bearded faces.

A huge colocynth nargileh is passed from mouth to mouth, and smoked in a silence unbroken by a single word. These savage Turcomans from Merv, opposed to holding communion with their neighbors, are even taciturn among themselves. In obedience to the voice of their priests, they have come to succor their fellow-Moslems whom they were but the day before ready to attack; they have come to succor them, but will not consent to fraternize with men whom they have ever been accustomed to despise. They regard all foreigners as enemies; murder and plunder are their chief pleasures; brigands and thieves from the beginning, they are possessed of indomitable courage; they cut out the tongue of any of their number daring to utter the word *fear*, introduced, as they say, into their parlance by the black-headed slaves (Persian prisoners).

Behind the peninsula, the tents, some gray, some black, round or oval, flat or peaked, stretch far over the plain, now clustered in the form of a chess-board, now strung out in a winding row; here in a straight line, and elsewhere disposed in squares.

Some five hundred paces from the Turcoman camp may be perceived triangular tents, or rather huts, hastily constructed with reeds, without any regard to order in the manner of placing them. These are the dwellings of the Kirghiz and Kipchaks. Horses and camels, all ready saddled, roam round the huts at liberty, in eager search of stray tufts of dried-up grass. The horses are very small. Earthen pots containing a sort of ragout of mutton steam away here and there; and feet shod in green or yellow boots, with pointed iron heels, protruding from beneath the huts, give unmistakable signs that these are inhabited by human beings. The Kirghiz usually sleep while awaiting the evening meal. Before one of the hovels a woman, still in the flower of youth (if flowers may associate with filth so loathsome as hers), is engaged in mending a pair of pantaloons; and beside her a couple of naked urchins, with shorn head and low-pending abdomen, gnaw a horse's bone which, each at his end, they hold up harmoniously between them. A dead animal in course of decomposition fills the camp with its pestilential exhalations.

The reeds fringing the Amu are abruptly separated. A man of athletic proportions slowly wends his way toward the Kirghiz camp, with head bowed and back bent, and groaning as he moves wearily along. He carries on his back a bundle of reeds and a goat-skin full of water, both secured by means of a leather strap; his long, black beard, which when he stands erect reaches down to his breast, now sweeps the sand of the plain; and a broad, brown stream of sweat rolls down from his brow, the veins of which are swollen almost to bursting. The hour for repose has not yet come for the Persian slave, nor will it come before the time for eternal rest.

Next beyond the huts of the Kirghiz is the Uzbeck camp, with its two streets, and its quadrangular, almost tastefully-arranged, tents of gray felt. In front of one of the tents a man with a white turban is delivering a sort of speech or harangue to a number of attentive hearers, some seated, some standing, and some leaning against the pickets of the tents.

Suddenly the air was rent by a cry of agony proceeding from the space between the two camps just referred to. A Turcoman had deliberately disemboweled a Kirghiz with his recurved knife, and coolly remounted his horse while another Kirghiz held the stirrup, and the wounded man's companions looked with indifference as, bathed in his blood upon the sand, he writhed in the throes of death.

Still farther, beyond the Uzbecks, the steppe presents a scene of noise and tumult, caused by the arrival of a troop, and the hurly-burly and confusion attendant upon pitching and arranging their tents. The soldiers wear a red uniform with blue collar, not turned down ; and, somewhat dirtier than the Kirghiz, they are less martial in appearance than the Uzbecks. In a word, the new-comers are *sarbares* of the Emir of Bokhara, and form the vanguard of the approaching army.

There are many other nomads assembled in this part of the plain ; horses' heads and the long necks of camels are everywhere to be seen ; and in the distance, where earth and sky seem to meet, clouds of black smoke ascend in spiral columns. Meanwhile the temperature of the air had grown slightly cooler, and the silvery sheen of the water of the river was changed to purple in the rays of the setting sun. Four men drew near, bearing a square carpet, and spread it on the sand by the bank of the stream, and a numerous party of Uzbecks formed in a circle round it. A stripling issued from the crowd and bounded upon the carpet. He was clothed in a scarlet robe reaching to the ankles, and leaving bare his arms and feet ; and from beneath a small cap, perched jauntily on the top of his head, escaped two long, black tresses, in which gold coins interlaced with glass beads formed a variety of fantastic figures. Spite of the almost effeminate beauty of his features and the bright sparkle of his eye, there was in his look an expression of effrontery and cruelty. The fame of Cor-Orlou, the *bardja*,[1] was spread throughout Turkistan, and was even affirmed to have crossed the Hindoo-Koosh Mountains. With a gesture of almost royal authority he drove back some Uzbecks whose eager curiosity had led them to press forward too close to the carpet, and then began his exercises. First moving his feet alternately on the same spot, as a military recruit marking time, he advanced slowly round the border of the carpet, agitating his whole body in oscillations wonderful to behold. At length, making a sudden halt, he bent backward with a graceful sweep until his head rested on the ground, and remained for some minutes in that position, displaying the beauty of his form beneath the loose folds of his ample robe. In the midst of a thunder of applause elicited by this daring feat, the bardja arose, and with a low, majestic step, mingled in the crowd of spectators.

Enthusiasm was at its highest. The youth was overwhelmed with the caresses of the Uzbecks, close to whom he passed; while those farther off caught eagerly at his hands, his tresses, and the hem of his robe, to cover them with kisses. He finally withdrew, and flung himself down to repose on a smaller carpet placed conveniently for the purpose, leaving other dancers of lesser note to entertain the beholders.

Gradually night drew her sable mantle over the plain. Some sheaves of reeds were kindled to light

[1] Dancer.

the way with their vacillating glare; but soon these died out, and all was again wrapped in darkness.

Myriads of stars dotted the sky. A bluish mist overhung the Amu-Darya, and hosts of fishes came frolicking to the surface of the water, attracted by the flames while they lasted.

Meanwhile the peninsula was enveloped in stillness and gloom. Here and there small flickering lights would appear for a moment, and their feeble rays render visible some large shadow moving slowly.

At the very point of the peninsula four Turcomans were reclining on the ground beside the ashes of their already-extinct fire. All at once one of them sat up, and, shading his eyes with his hand, peered through the darkness in the direction of the river. He had heard the neighing of a horse on the Russian bank of the stream, and, looking very intently, he could see some horsemen crossing the ford.

"Hey!" cried he to one of his comrades. "Hussein! look!"

Hussein arose and gazed inquiringly through the gloom. "It is some of our own people," said he; "I recognize Yacoub's black stallion by the white star on his forehead." And he resumed his reclining posture.

A horse just then issued from the water, and his hoofs were already close to the ashes.

"Is that you, Yacoub?" asked the first Turcoman.

"Yes!"

"Have you brought back any booty?"

"No! We perceived a Russian column coming in this direction. This very night it will be quite up in front of you. Of course, we had to fly."

The four Turcomans had arisen while he was speaking.

"The Russians! Where? How many? What for?" they all inquired together.

Yacoub shrugged his shoulders. "Is the sirdar in camp?" he asked.

"He has just got back. He had been over to see the commander of the emir's sarbares."

"I am going to him."

As he was about to start, one of the four men said:

"Wait! Are you not going to tell us—"

"I'll tell the sirdar. You hold yourselves in readiness; you'll have your hands full to-morrow."

"All right!"

"Yacoub!" cried Hussein, "is Haikoullah with you?"

"Your Haikoullah has been killed!"

"Killed! The Russians saw you, then?"

"No; but he advanced too near to the column and was seen, and a bullet brought him to the ground."

"Dead! and what about the twenty tomans he owed me?"

"He will pay them back to you in heaven."

"Have you his horse, even?"

Yacoub did not vouchsafe a reply, but headed his horse toward a reddish-looking tent at the extreme end of the peninsula. The steed walked carefully to avoid treading on the reclining nomads, who made no effort to get out of the way. Hussein was, nevertheless, determined not to be put off; so, holding his hands to his mouth, he trumpeted, at the top of his voice:

"Have you his horse?"

"No!" replied Yacoub.

Hussein stood up, buckled on his arms, and sallied forth in the direction of the steppe, muttering to himself:

"I must go and steal a horse from some swine of an Uzbeck! I can't afford to lose twenty tomans at the opening of the campaign!"

What with the neighing of the horses and the chattering of the two Turcomans, several sleepers were aroused; and in a short time a goodly number were huddled together in a cluster around the ashes, descanting upon the subject of the Russians and the approaching battle.

Yacoub's entire troop came up out of the water.

"Keep sharp watch!" cried the horsemen, as they passed through the encampment; "the Oorooses are drawing near."

"Keep watch! keep watch!" repeated the Turcomans one to another.

Before long the whole camp was on foot. Some thirty individuals were busy smoking their common *shelam* around the spot where Hussein's fire had lately reeked.

"Ooroombay!" said the first Turcoman to an aged individual, still possessing the vigor of manhood, who approached the group; "we are going to spend the night in watching: tell us one of those stories that you tell so well!"

"Oh, yes, do! we all wish to hear you tell a story!"

Ooroombay smiled, seated himself on the ground,

and stroked his beard. "Well, well!" said he; "I will begin."

XI.

OOROOMBAY'S STORY.

"Long, long ago—" he began; and he stopped to reflect.

"Yes, long, long ago," he resumed, in an impressive tone, "the desert, which we call the 'destroyer of life,' was a fertile and cultivated valley—"

"Oh! oh!" interrupted several voices, incredulously.

Ooroombay looked around him with an air of majesty, and went on:

"— was a fertile and cultivated valley. Allah had probably so willed it. The valley was inhabited by an industrious and wealthy people, and governed by an independent king. Timourleng[1] reigned over the universe.

"You will doubtless wonder how an independent king could exist while Timour lived?"

"Indeed, yes; we should like to know how that could be," replied one of the hearers, in a serious tone.

"One day, as our lame sovereign was passing through the valley, the weather being as warm as it has been here this day, he desired to have a drink of *koumiss*.[2] In vain he looked around: there was no habitation in view.

[1] Tamerlane.   [2] Fermented mare's milk.

"'I am thirsty,' said he to the princes in waiting; 'let some koumiss be brought to me from some inhabitant of this country.'

"Twenty horsemen from his suite were dispatched at full gallop. One alone of their number headed his horse at a trot toward a troop of mares which his keen eye descried on the horizon. Timour perceived the tardy gait, and said:

"'That slave is in no haste to satisfy his master's desire. When he comes back he shall feel the weight of my anger.'

"The princes saw their master's brow contracted, and they trembled, and whispered among themselves. Timour maintained an ominous silence.

"Some minutes elapsed; Timour, still thirsty, began to harass his horse in his impatience; and the terrified Mongol warriors looked wistfully at each other. A cloud of dust became visible afar off; a horseman rode up at full speed, and, having abruptly stopped his horse in front of the conqueror, he made a graceful reverence and handed him a drinking-vessel full of koumiss.

"When Timour had slaked his thirst, he looked benignly upon him who had brought him the beverage; but, on recognizing him, his countenance was covered with gloom.

"'Why,' said he, with a voice of thunder, 'were you so slow in executing my orders? It was more by good luck than by any merit of yours that you were the first to come upon a dwelling.'

"'Sovereign master of the world,' replied the horseman, 'the reason of my starting off at a trot was, that, having descried a troop of mares at the foot of the mountain, I was afraid of putting them to flight were I to advance at a more rapid pace. When I reached them, and had taken the milk from one of them, I went in quest of an herb which grows in this valley, and has the property of instantly converting the milk into koumiss. I then returned galloping to your sublime majesty, aware that I should thus save you a few seconds of expectation.'

"Timour's countenance again became gracious.

"'Do you know this country well?' he asked.

"'I was born here, seignior.'

"'It is yours, then, by my gift. You shall reign over this valley, without paying me any fine or tribute.'

"Kouli-Khan, as he was henceforward called, reigned in peace and happiness for thirty years; and, when Timour died, and the princes under his sceptre rebelled and sought to shake off his yoke, Kouli-Khan put down the rebellion in the name of the late sovereign. By-and-by Timour's power fell into decay through the negligence of his descendants, and then Kouli-Khan proclaimed himself king and master of the soil. The possessions of the new monarch extended from the Chinese Mountains to the sea of Aral and the Caspian Sea.

"Kouli-Khan was powerful and respected, and lived to a good old age. Toward the end of his life, Allah, who wills that every human being shall have his share of suffering, caused him to conceive a desire which was soon changed into grief. Kouli-Khan had a son, Prince Yomond, whom he loved as Allah loves the prophet, and who was destined to inherit his father's throne and all his riches. The prince was as beautiful as the full moon, amiable, learned, and brave; but would never consent to marry. Whenever a proposal of marriage was made to him, he left the palace, and was seen no more that day. Not that he was timid, or shy, or disliked female society; on the contrary, his manner seemed to encourage such proposals. Nevertheless, each time the proposals were renewed, he disappeared gayly, charmingly, and affably; but he disappeared. Kouli-Khan had consulted his soothsayers, astrologers, and mollahs; but none could give him a satisfactory explanation of the mystery. The khan was in despair. Yomond was his only son, and the race would become extinct with him. Notwithstanding, the khan was a just ruler, and would not force his son into anything. Thus, Yomond continued in the enjoyment of complete liberty, with the use of his father's vast treasures at will.

"The young prince was much given to the chase. He had had sixty arrows made of gold, and barbed with diamonds; yet he could not consent, in spite of his great riches, to cast so much treasure to the winds. So he made it a law for himself to withdraw every arrow from the wound in the game, which he pursued unremittingly from morning till night. In the course of five years' hunting in this manner he had killed fifty tigers, one hundred and ten wild-boars, more than five hundred *hemions*,[1] and perhaps a thousand wolves, without counting small game, and all without having lost more than three arrows."

[1] Species of horse, ἡμίονος.

Ooroombay here suspended his narration to take the shelam from one of his neighbors, and solace himself with a few whiffs. The group had by this time grown quite numerous with the addition of several other nomads, awakened by the tidings of the coming battle; while a number of horsemen, on coming up to the group, halted, and fixing their lances upright in the ground, leaned over on their horses' necks, and listened to the old man's story with attentive ear.

"Why would the prince not take a wife?" asked one of the horsemen.

"I am just coming to that now," replied Ooroombay. "Pursuing a wild-boar one day, the prince wandered farther from the palace than was his wont, and the animal disappeared in a mountain-gorge. The youthful huntsman, loath to abandon the chase, followed in the track of the beast, but to no purpose; he could not again get sight of him. The passage through the gorge was narrow, but widened by degrees in the direction of a lake, to which it led, inclosed on all sides by rocks of prodigious height. Yomond, despairing of being able to find his game, and overcome by fatigue, sat down by the brink of the lake to take rest. He had seen the place before; but that day the water appeared to him so beautiful, so calm, and limpid, that he was seized by an irresistible temptation to bathe in it. He laid his bow on the ground, and began to divest himself of his raiment. As he was endeavoring to remove his sandals, a slight noise caused him to turn his head. On the smooth surface of the lake, within a short distance of the brink, a woman was bathing, and he observed that she playfully threw the water up over her head, and it fell around her in a continual shower of fine rain, like a silvery cloud. Yomond uttered a shout of surprise and admiration. The long, fair tresses of the bathing beauty, sparkling with the drops of water, resembled a golden carpet spangled with silver, and surmounted with a houri's head. A pearl shell, incrusted with turquoises and rubies, and adorned with a fan of seaweed, was drawn by four pike of gigantic proportions, describing gentle and graceful curves, within a few feet of the edge.

"When Yomond shouted, both lady and shell disappeared beneath the bosom of the water, and reappeared farther off, the lady seated in the shell, and the pike swimming with all the might of their fins toward the opposite shore. The prince, whom nothing ever frightened or astonished, had had time to seize his bow: a dart went whizzing through the air, and in an instant one of the pike had expired, dyeing the water with his blood. A second dart was impelled, and a second pike was mortally wounded. The speed of the shell was visibly slackened, the weight being too heavy for the surviving pike to advance rapidly with it. Yomond plunged into the water, and was gaining on them apace, and the beautiful bather watched his every motion with a look of supplication mingled with terror. Her beauty so dazzled him that he redoubled his efforts, and after a few vigorous strokes he was so near as to be able to surround the shell with his arms. The pike turned round, showing their sharp teeth, ready for the struggle; but with his recurved poniard he left the lady's defenders lifeless by the shell, and seized her in his arms just as she was about to step on the sand.

"Scarcely had the prince touched the object of his eager pursuit, when he recoiled in surprise, discovering that charming form to be cold, soft, and inanimate. A flake of foam was clinging to his hands, and his two arms had left a bluish mark on those of the fair bather. Yomond gazed on her and saw her pale, withered, and expiring.

"'Prince,' said she, in the purest Arabic dialect, and a tone of heart-rending reproach, 'I love you, and yet you take my life!'

"Yomond, in despair, made an effort to speak a word of excuse, but he had not time to open his mouth before a terrifying shout rent the air, and a colossal *génie* appeared at the water's edge. His head towered over the highest eminence on earth, and in his hurried flight black clouds had clung to his long white beard, which resembled a forest of poplars covered with hoar-frost.

"'My daughter!' he cried.

"The prince fell to the earth stunned, and the blood spurting from his ears, and the mountains trembled to their base at the sound of that terrible voice.

"The genie, in order to be able to lift up his child, now closing her eyes in death, drew in his stature, and in an instant it was reduced to the height of a medium-sized tree; but a tear, which he had not had time to retain and enchant, fell from beneath his eyelid with a dull sound and mingled with the waters, which were suddenly lashed into foam. The genial contact of the warm and briny liquid restored Yomond's senses, and the shell floated anew upon the bosom of the lake.

"The young maiden, too, began to revive.

"'Do not chide me, father!' said she, with a feeble voice; 'I love him!'

"The genie took her up in his arms, and, pressing his lips upon the marks left by the prince's hand, all trace of them disappeared.

"'Unhappy child!' said he, 'I had warned you against venturing on the earth inhabited by these wicked and brutal men! How the heartless wretch has bruised you!'

"'But your touch has healed me again, father!'

"'True; but you well know the lot that is in store for you: either to be changed into foam before the year is out, or link your destiny to that of the miserable worm that lies yonder.' And the genie advanced and pushed the prince rudely with his foot.

"This insult caused the prince to spring to his feet. He had never known fear; his swoon had been due to the sound of that supernatural voice, which had stunned his faculties for the moment, but by no means frightened him.

"'Genie though you be,' cried he, seizing his poniard, 'I shall make you swallow your words!'

"The genie burst out laughing, and eyed the youth scornfully from head to foot. But his daughter bestowed a kindly glance upon the prince.

"'Father,' said she, 'he is handsome and intrepid! Allow me to take him!'

"'Hearken, atom of dust!'

"Yomond again would have sprung forward; but

he felt he could not move. The water that laved his limbs seemed to press upon them in a compact mass, and hold them fettered, as it were, in a vise. He perceived that the struggle was hopeless.

"'It is not generous of you, since you are the stronger, to insult me,' said he. 'I regret the injury done your daughter, and of which I was involuntarily the cause, for she is beautiful, and I admire her. I followed her, and I had the right to do so in my own domain.'

"The genie laughed a second time; and his laugh, accompanied by tears, was awful to hear.

"'Your domain!' sneered the giant. 'Look around you!'

"Yomond turned his head. The lake had disappeared. Before him was the billowy ocean, vast and boundless; and, behind, mountains now bare and rocky, now clothed with an unknown vegetation.

"'Be it so, then!' returned the prince. 'But I love your daughter. Give her to me. I will marry her.'

"'Give her to you? Poor, proud worm! Yes, you shall marry her, since Allah wills it thus; but I shall give you to her, and not her to you! Do you even know who I am?'

"'I know not; but it matters little. I am not your slave.'

"'You are in my power, and you are six hundred thousand *tasches*[1] distant from your country. I am the prince of the subterranean waters; to me you owe the richness and fertility of your valley; and here is

[1] About three hundred and seventy-five thousand miles.

the proof of your gratitude! I am a good genie; but a short time ago, this very day, I beheld the face of Allah, and held converse with his holy Prophet.'

"On hearing these words, Yomond, who was a devout youth, prostrated himself before the genie: the water, which had held him fast while he was bent upon rebellion, offered no hinderance to the accomplishment of that act of adoration. The prince felt himself free. Looking up, he thought the expression of the genie's countenance was less harsh and scornful than before.

"'You fear Allah!' said the genie. 'Now, hearken to me! When Allah in his wisdom endowed us with power and strength, he willed that everything produced by us, and proceeding from us, should be weak. Thus, I could crush you with a breath, and you, by simply touching my daughter, could reduce her to foam! Allah alone is great. Before you can marry my daughter, I must first enchant her; and I have not the right to enchant her until you have sworn to conform to the conditions which I shall require of you.'

"Yomond cast his eyes upon the fair bather, and, beholding her radiant, superhuman beauty, he nodded acquiescence.

"'Terrible is the oath I require of you! You shall swear by the head of the Prophet and the mercy of Allah!'

"Yomond shuddered; but he took the oath nevertheless.

"'Here, then, are my conditions,' said the genie. 'You shall have no other wife but her. You shall only behold my daughter on such days as a marriage shall be proposed to you; and never more than one day at a time. When a marriage is proposed, you will not fail to repair to the brink of the lake where you first saw her. You will never reveal to any human creature the mystery of her existence.'

"'I swear it!'

"'On these conditions, we three may yet be happy. But, should you break your oath, that very instant will my daughter cease to live; you shall be accursed by Allah; and I shall withdraw from beneath your valley, and it will become an arid and sandy desert horrible to behold. Therefore, upon your oath depend your eternal salvation, my daughter's life, and the weal of all your subjects! Remember!'

"'I am altogether willing to renew my oath this moment!' cried Yomond, in a burst of enthusiasm.

"That was the third time he had sworn.

"Then he found himself transported to a magnificently-illuminated hall, side by side with a maiden of great beauty. He recognized the lady of the lake, not as the impalpable, supernatural phantom that had so charmed him, but as a woman a hundred times more seductive. The genie was no longer visible. After a lapse of twenty-four hours, Yomond found himself back again at the edge of the lake.

"He lived that life for seven years and was perfectly happy, and scrupulously kept his oath, notwithstanding the prayers and supplications of his father, and indifferent to the charms of a hundred other women who had been offered to him as wives.

"About that time Tchandor-Khan, chieftain of the Turcomans, had a beautiful daughter. The Turcomans were then, as they are now, proud, courageous, and free as thought. Their secular independence—"

"If you would maintain that independence, you must defend it, instead of giving ear to idle tales!" cried an imperious voice behind the group of Turcomans.

The nomads turned rapidly round to chastise the insolent person who thus apostrophized them; but they hung their heads at sight of a splendidly-attired horseman, covered with a sort of steel network, fitting close to his form, and the meshes of which shone like silvery spangles on his purple bashlick.

"The sirdar!" whispered the crowd.

"I will finish your story, old man," said the sirdar. "Yomond's weakness was the cause of his country's ruin. Mozzafar's weakness and apathy have allowed the Russians to enter Samarcand; and, if the Turcomans follow such examples, they too may become the slaves of the unbeliever. Up, Tchandors, Tekkes, Salors! In one hour from this time the sirdar will await you on the Russian bank of the Amu-Darya."

He crossed the river at full gallop, and was followed over by a numerous detachment. The group of Turcomans had been dispersed, each one having gone for his arms and his horse. The two hindmost horsemen of the sirdar's escort were about to ford the river.

"Well, Hahib," said the officer, "what have you for Seignior Mohammed?"

"Nothing as yet. Allah preserve him!—This evening, perhaps—in the thick of the fight—"

Both horsemen disappeared in the darkness. The clear waters of the river were much troubled on that night. For the space of two hours horses and men crossed the ford. Then all was still once more—the peninsula was again silent and solitary; a few gnawed bones, a pipe forgotten, heaps of still warm cinders, and Hussein's horse wandering, like a troubled spirit, in expectation of his master's return, being the only signs left of the passage of man over that desolate spot. In the Kirghiz and Kipchak camps the same noise and merry-making as before continued unconfined, and the gleam of the watch-fires illuminated the plain for a considerable distance.

XII.

THE BATTLE.

The night was drawing to its close, though darkness spread its thickest shades over the steppe but a moment before the dawn of morning. The stream was no longer turbid at the ford; the dying embers of the camp-fires were faintly reflected in the greenish and peaceful water, and silence—absolute, profound, oppressive silence—reigned all around.

Toward five o'clock in the morning the white profiles of four soldiers were visible on the Russian bank of the Amu-Darya. The men cast a hurried and inquiring glance through the obscurity, then descended into the stream, and advanced cautiously. When they had reached the centre, one of them uttered a perfect imitation of the heron's cry, intended probably as a signal, for just then two horsemen issued from their hiding-place behind the sand-hummocks and followed the soldiers across the ford. The very horses seemed to be aware of the necessity of prudence, for not a neigh was heard, and the splash of their feet in the water could not be perceived by the most practised ear.

When the horsemen had got to the middle of the ford, the four soldiers had already gained the opposite bank.

Then a column of troops, numbering about a thousand men, went down to the river in the same direction as the horsemen, the soldiers holding their guns over their heads and walking cautiously on tiptoe. When the horsemen had landed on the peninsula, they turned their horses completely round to watch the column crossing the ford. The white clothing of the soldiers, contrasting with the deep green of the water and the darkness of the night, caused the troops to resemble a legion of spectres in shrouds, their noiseless march favoring the illusion. All was calm and silent. The Kirghiz and Kipchak camps were wrapped in sleep, and a feeble glare still issued from their fires, not yet quite extinguished.

"The savages suspect nothing, major," said one of the horsemen. "Our attempt will be crowned with certain success. Up to this morning I was apprehensive that we had advanced too far."

"What could I do, captain? You know I was obliged to obey the orders of my superior. Before advancing so far as this, I dispatched a courier to Tashkend. Yesterday evening, no longer ago, I received a dispatch from the governor-general, informing me of the arrival of a regiment of infantry and eight guns to reënforce us. They are to be here before daybreak."

"Why did we not await them?"

"I ordered the attack, the night seeming favorable for a surprise. The Kipchaks will not even suppose that we would dare, with such a limited force, to attack them; by daylight we shall be nine thousand strong."

"What do you judge their strength to be, Major Relieff?"

"Twenty-five thousand, more or less, according to our native spies."

"Not so many as I thought. If the reënforcements come in good time, we shall be one to five, and the victory will be certain."

"I have ordered the four pieces of artillery to remain on our side of the river, and open fire as soon as the last man of the column has crossed the stream. That will be the signal of attack. The Cossacks will ford the river after the fire begins, and guard this tongue of land to cut off the retreat of runaways by the ford. I hope we shall drive those brigands back into their solitudes. In case the worst should come to the worst, the artillery, which is not to cross the river, will cover the retreat of our troops. Do you approve of my plan, captain?"

"By all means."

The infantry had already landed on the opposite side; and, although there were still a few stragglers lingering in the water, the main body of the army was forming into column.

Relieff's horse knocked his foot against a gnawed bone, and stumbled on a heap of cinders.

"The site of a camp!" said the major. "What does this mean?"

He was not allowed time to pursue his investigations, for a white cloud, like a cotton-blossom, appeared through the gloom; a detonation was heard, and all at once the plain was filled with noise and tumult. A second detonation followed the first; the Uzbeck camp was on foot in an instant, and howls of surprise and rage rent the air in a hundred places at the same time.

"Forward, march!" shouted Relieff.

The Kipchaks and Uzbecks flew to arms, or in search of their horses; but too late, for the Russian column was already in the midst of the camp. The reeds cracked under the soldiers' feet, and the huts, riddled with bayonet-thrusts, fell to the ground with a dull crash. Cries of agony, wailing, and lamentations, and the clanking of arms, were alone heard for a few minutes, and the Russians were masters of the Kipchak camp.

The number of the slain was, however, small; a woman lay bathed in her blood close by a hut, and ten or fifteen men, surprised during sleep were stretched upon the ground with broken skulls.

"Forward!" cried Relieff.

The column was again formed into attacking order, and marched in the direction of the plain. Meantime, the artillery was thundering away, and the shells, whizzing over the soldiers' heads, fell and burst in the midst of the nomads' camp.

In the open space between the Kipchak and Uzbeck encampments, the runaways had formed in a group together, ready to defend their lives; and the Uzbecks, warned of the danger by the cannonade, were busily preparing to repulse the enemy.

The Russian troops advanced steadily, and were soon engaged in an encounter with the Kipchaks, which lasted a full hour, and ended in the rout of the latter, who fled, leaving one hundred of their fellows dead upon the sand. The passage was now open to the Uzbeck camp.

The steppe was lighted up by the first rays of the morning sun. Relieff looked around him; forty Russian soldiers lay side by side with the Kipchak slain. The struggle had, indeed, been desperate, considering the inequality of arms.

The major raised himself up in his stirrups, and surveyed the plain. The Bokharan bank presented a scene of agitation; the Uzbecks were busied forming in order of battle, and behind them a red line was in view extending across the plain. The emir's army was advancing in columns. The Russian bank, on the contrary, was quiet and deserted, save where the artillery was still in position, and keeping up an uninterrupted shower of shells.

Relieff knit his brow, and again looked anxiously toward the horizon bounding the plain. As far as his eye could reach, he distinguished nothing but the enemy's hordes advancing in masses toward the river.

"Ho, ho!" said he to the captain, "they are numerous." Then, turning to the soldiers, he said:

"The bandits are in large numbers; we shall have

hard work yet, boys, before the day is over!" Then, with a firm voice, "Forward, march!" he cried.

"Long live the emperor!" shouted the soldiers.

Suddenly Relieff felt the captain plucking him by the sleeve. On turning round he saw the Cossack squadron advancing at full gallop, hotly pursued by a numerous band, whooping and yelling, and throwing handfuls of dust into the air.

"The Turcomans!" said he. "Where did the demons come from?"

The fact is, the Turcomans, some three thousand in number, had been lying in ambush behind the hummocks waiting till the Russians had pushed sufficiently forward through the encampments. Then rushing upon them, like an avalanche, they forded the river, in spite of the artillery, which still continued shelling the Uzbeck camp, drove back the Cossacks before them, and advanced toward the steppe for the purpose of cutting off the retreat of the column.

At the same instant, according to a preconcerted plan, another band of Turcomans, about five thousand strong, issued from the southern side of the plain with the intention of completely surrounding the Russians. This band was headed by a horseman clothed in purple, and waving the green standard of the Prophet triumphantly in the air.

The Uzbecks were caracoling on the plain, and the red line of the emir's army was fast approaching the Amu.

Relieff saw that the battle was lost. He took in the whole situation at a glance: should the two Turcoman divisions succeed in effecting a junction, not a man of the column could escape. It was necessary, therefore, to cross the ford at all hazards and retreat toward the Russian bank, in order not to give the nomads time to accomplish their intended manœuvre.

To do this, but little time remained; the Cossacks were now within five hundred paces, and the shouts of their pursuers might be distinctly heard. Relieff could already perceive the gilded crescent on the purple horseman's standard at the head of the second division.

"Captain," said he, "you take command of the column and give the order to retreat; when within a hundred paces of yonder Turcomans" (Relieff pointed to the band occupying the peninsula), "you will open fire and then form in square. Then, attacking the brigands, cut your way through them and cross the river. Once under cover of our artillery, you can hold out for a few hours until the arrival of reënforcements.

"But what about *you*, major?" asked the captain, amazed.

"Me? I am going to die!" And, without leaving the captain time to reply, he gave the order, "Halt!"

The column halted.

"I want a hundred volunteers fearless of death."

Not a move in the ranks.

A general shout arose from the column as from one man:

"We are ready!"

Relieff was deeply moved.

"Brave soldiers!" he exclaimed. "Of course, I

was wrong; no Russian soldier fears death." Then he gave the order, "Let every tenth man in each rank step to the front!"

The men told off by tens, and each one to whom the number ten fell stepped forward without a murmur, almost joyously. A small band of a hundred men was thus formed in a few brief moments, and under the eye of the enemy, now rapidly advancing.

Just then the Cossacks came up with their column, leaving their pursuers but a few paces in the rear.

Relieff extended his hand to the captain.

"Farewell!" said he.

"Major," replied the captain, dryly, "I must stay by you."

"Impossible!"

"I shall never consent to—"

Relieff interrupted him with a stern voice:

"I am your superior, captain, and I order you to obey."

Then, in an undertone, he added: "Show that you can *live* for Russia, as I can *die* for her! Each of us has his mission to fulfill."

The Cossacks gathered around Relieff; the nomads hesitated an instant, observing the column about to open fire upon them. The major addressed a few words to the Cossacks, and, escorted by them, galloped off in the direction of the second troop of Turcomans. As he passed close to the platoon of volunteers:

"Fire!" said he, "and do not cease firing, although your bullets should reach *us!*"

The little band formed a square, and followed Relieff. The Turcomans, who had forced the Cossacks to give way, were now face to face with the main column. A tremendous volley was heard, and the action became general.

Meantime the major had come up with the second troop. With the back of his sabre he struck down the Prophet's standard, and the fifty heroes penetrated into the midst of the Turcomans.

The platoon of one hundred men, intended to impede the junction of the two divisions, kept up a steady fire, for they saw that Relieff and the Cossacks were determined upon a last and desperate struggle.

The desert then became the scene of a sublime spectacle: all around, the motley host of nomads; two white points, like two glades through a dense forest, visible on the plain; and the small band of volunteers and the main column engaged in combat with the Turcomans on the peninsula. Relieff and his followers were completely surrounded by the nomad ranks, and the sheen of the sabres was all that could be seen of the encounter.

A vast hecatomb of men and horses was soon formed around Relieff and his Cossacks, though both leader and men were as yet unscathed.

The dead bodies served as a fortification to protect the Russians; and Relieff felt his bosom swell with honest pride as he gazed on the numbers of the slain around him, and thought of the multitudes of Turcomans yet to fall before he should be obliged to abandon the contest. The desperate struggle lasted half an hour. The neighing of the horses, the yells of the Turcomans, the moans of the dying, and the incessant firing of the musketry, mingled in a grand and horrible chorus. Vultures flitted in the air, floating over their approaching repast, while the artillery boomed uninterruptedly on the opposite bank of the river.

Harassed by the shells, the Uzbecks and sarbazes advanced but slowly, yet the vast circle was rapidly closing around the Russian column.

At length the last Cossack fell, his breast pierced by a lance; and Relieff remained alone, with a few insignificant wounds, though his horse had been killed under him. Heaps of slain lay all around, and immediately beside him were three horses gasping in the last agony of death. Relieff, with a sabre-stroke, shivered the shaft of a lance intended to transfix him, and sprang upon the pile of expiring horses in order to survey the plain beyond. The band of volunteers had disappeared; the hundred Russians lay dead upon the sand. The Uzbecks were evidently endeavoring to join the Turcomans surrounding Relieff.

The main column was crossing the placid, silvery stream, followed by a small band of Turcomans, and the artillery, seeing that it was useless to continue shelling the Uzbecks, pointed their cannon toward the river to cover the retreat of the remnant of the Russian troops. Casting a last glance toward the Russian horizon, Relieff thought he saw a long line of bayonets glistening, and he distinctly perceived eight pieces of cannon approaching the bank of the river.

He uttered a shout of joy. With a haughty glance he counted the heaps of slain around him; his visage was covered with dust and blood, and his brow bore the impress of triumph, mingled with satisfaction that he had done his duty nobly. Heaving a deep sigh of relief, he signed himself with the sign of the cross, exclaimed, "Martha, farewell!" and rushed forward. A strange scene then took place. The Turcomans opened their ranks to make way for him, and lowered their lances in token of respect as he passed. Amazed at his escape alive, he looked up, and saw the purple horseman galloping toward him. He saw the Turcomans reverentially fall back, and then he thought he saw a poniard menacing the horseman's breast, and, guided by his natural instinct, he shouted in the Uzbeck dialect, "Take care!"

The horseman turned round quickly, and Relieff felt a violent shock. His brain reeled, and he fell inanimate to the ground.

There was a frightful tumult on the plain; the sarbazes and Uzbecks had effected their junction with the Turcomans, and on the opposite side of the river twelve pieces of cannon were thundering away.

The grand struggle was soon to begin.

XIII.

THE PRISONER.

THE desert was gloomy and silent, and the faint glimmer of twilight lent a violet hue to the red sand. In the distance a castle, once a fortress for the defense of the road from Bokhara, perched on a bleak and craggy rock, stood with its fantastic outlines clearly marked on the horizon.

Ten horsemen slowly wended their way toward the castle: a djigweet in front, two Turcomans, three Uzbecks, and three Kirghiz, and, surrounded by them, an individual mounted on an old, worn-out gray horse.

It was impossible to distinguish the features of the last horseman. His hair was matted with blood-clots; his face begrimed with dust and blood, and his apparel, once white, now changed to a mass of colorless rags.

From the apparent absence of motion in the body, and the livid hue of as much as could be distinguished of the face, one would have supposed it to be a corpse. Yet a nervous twitching, faintly visible now and then, showed that life was not wholly extinct. Numbers of gadflies flitted around the horses, harassing them with their stings; and, when at times they approached the prisoner's face, he made feeble efforts to keep them aloof with his breath. Each motion he made elicited a chuckle from the nomads.

"They bite, eh?" said a Kirghiz; "that's nothing, you will get used to it."

"Savage swine!" cried the prisoner, in a burst of indignation.

The Kirghiz laughed outright. "You are not in good-humor," said he; "just wait, I'll give you something to rouse your spirits," and with his leather whip he lashed the captive's face until the blood spurted from it.

"You will kill him," said one of the Turcomans; "he is not very strong as it is. Why keep him tied now. There are nine of us here, and he is alone and unarmed!"

The Kirghiz shook his head.

"You don't know these Russians! You don't know what they can do!"

The Turcoman eyed him scornfully from head to foot.

"Were it not for the orders of my chief, I should long ago have put an end to his sufferings with my poniard," said he.

The prisoner fixed his eye upon him with a grateful and supplicating look.

"How he licks his lips at the idea of death, the unbelieving dog!" said the Kirghiz.—"No, no, giaour! You shall have something better than that," he added cracking his whip.

"Hey! Ooroombay!" cried the Turcoman to the old story-teller, who was one of the ten, "just tell Hahib that, if he desires us to have the ransom-money for this prisoner, he had better loosen his bonds and give him something to eat, or he'll die on the road."

"We shall soon be at the halting-place; let him wait until then," said Hahib, without turning around, in reply to the Turcoman's indirect question.

The prisoner heaved a deep sigh, and appeared very much depressed. Relieff (for he it was) had recovered from his swoon to find himself bound on a horse's back, and on the way across the plain.

Let us review the intervening events. When Relieff warned the purple horseman of the danger, the Uzbecks had effected their junction with the Turcomans. A sabre-cut from an Uzbeck horseman inflicted only a slight wound on the major's head; his *képi* having deadened the blow, yet it felled him senseless to the ground; and, but for the interference of the sirdar, who remonstrated on the handsome sum they could obtain for his ransom, he being a superior officer, the Uzbecks and Turcomans would have dispatched him off-hand, and carried away his head as a trophy. This danger past, another of a different nature offered, and had liked to prove more formidable than the first. The Uzbeck that had wounded the major claimed him as his property; a Turcoman, too, urged his right to him; and a Kipchak who had strayed into the Uzbeck ranks said that, in all fairness, he should be awarded to him, as an indemnity to his nation for the losses they had sustained in the recent encounter. The prisoner would have been cut into pieces but for a compromise proposed by the Turcoman sirdar, namely: that three Uzbecks, three Kirghiz, and as many Turcomans, should—if it were possible to restore him to life—escort the prisoner to a secure place, preparatory to entering into negotiations for his ransom or selling him as a slave; and that the proceeds in either case should be equally divided between the nine.

Relieff's wounds, when dressed, were ascertained to be neither mortal nor by any means of a serious character; so he was bound to a horse and conveyed away to the desert.

Another hour's journeying brought them up to the uninhabited castle. Relieff was unbound, taken down from the horse, and cast upon the ground; and the contact of the sand somewhat revived his drooping energies. He asked for some food and drink, and a bone was thrown to him to pick and a vessel of water brought to slake his thirst; and the escort concerned themselves no further about him. Relieff stretched his aching limbs, and, weariness overcoming him, he fell into a profound sleep.

Meantime, the nomads had seated themselves in a circle under the arched entrance to the antique fortress. One of the Turcomans, suddenly descrying in the plain a cloud of dust coming toward them (in the desert every man is an enemy): "They may be coming to take our prisoner from us," cried Hahib, springing to his feet to run for his arms; "if so, we shall have a hard rub."

The cloud grew larger apace, and a number of horsemen could be distinguished riding in hot speed toward the castle.

"There are too many of them," said a Kirghiz; "it would be sheer folly to attempt a defense!"

"Well, then," exclaimed a Turcoman, "all we have to do is to make short work of the prisoner. So long as we can't have him for ourselves, they shall not have him either."

"Very true," replied a second Turcoman.

On this the nomad, poniard in hand, and followed by one of the Uzbecks, approached the spot where Relieff still lay sleeping. The major's ragged clothing had left a portion of his breast exposed to view, and a small chain, with a carnelian medallion attached.

The Uzbeck, being the first to notice this, rushed upon the sleeper, and with a quick jerk snapped the chain and seized the medallion. Relieff awoke with a start, and, seeing the three sinister faces above him, he made up his mind that his last hour had come, and hastily closed his eyes again.

Meanwhile the Uzbeck, having examined the medallion, uttered a cry of astonishment, and arrested the Turcoman's uplifted arm that held the poniard.

"The prize is a richer one than we thought, even. The prisoner is a great chief, and in communication with the Emir-al-Oumra."

"All the more reason for not leaving him to fall into the hands of our pursuers."

While these words were spoken, Hahib and two other nomads had come forward, and the former fixed his eyes attentively on the medallion.

"If we could manage to hide him somewhere, how would that be?" suggested the Uzbeck.

"Well said!" cried Hahib; "just the thing. The bug-hole, you know!"

"Would it not be better to kill him at once? He would suffer less!" remonstrated the Turcoman.

"What do we care for his suffering?"

"Well, but he will die at all events," objected the Uzbeck. "You recollect the last fellow we put down into it? He did not survive three hours."

"Pshaw!" returned Hahib. "This is a sturdy blade that we have here. By putting him in there, we have at least a chance of preserving him; while, if we kill him—"

The Turcoman lowered the hand that held the poniard.

"Do as you please," said he.

Relieff foresaw that some frightful ordeal was in preparation for him; and, although he was resigned to meet his death, uncertainty as to what death he was to die filled him with terror, and chilled the blood in his veins.

There exist in Central Asia certain subterranean prisons, which could only have been invented and preserved by Asiatic despotism and indifference, a sort of wedge-shaped well with very narrow openings. Having once entered, it is impossible for any person to come out again unaided. Scraping the earth with the hands, or climbing up the concave walls of those dungeons, hewed out of solid flint, with but a small aperture above to admit light and air, would be alike impracticable.

"Do you know where it is situated?" inquired the Kirghiz.

"Yes, yes, up in the old citadel.—Come," said Hahib, pushing Relieff with his foot; "up, and follow us."

Relieff, as has already been said, was resigned to death; but the thought of the bug-hole filled him with horror, and he was determined on resistance. Making a desperate effort, he raised himself to his full height, to prepare for a struggle with his torturers, and hasten the end; but his very first movement revealed his enfeebled condition, and showed him that his strength had entirely abandoned him. He stumbled and fell to the ground with a groan. Yet such was the menacing expression of his eyes that Hahib recoiled.

"He will not come," said he; "let us drag him along, comrades!"

They seized Relieff, who offered but feeble resistance, and carried him off, guided by Hahib.

Meantime the noise of horses' hoofs resounded distinctly. At the foot of the fortress the major suddenly perceived a numerous troop of mounted men, winding along the slope of the eminence. At the head of the troop he distinguished the purple horseman whom he had seen in the *mêlée*, only the steel mask was now removed from his face, and Relieff recognized Safar-Hadgi.

"Safar!" he shouted.

A blow with the whip-handle muffled the word in his mouth, and his call was evidently not heard, for the horseman did not look up.

"So you know the sirdar?" asked Hahib.

But the major's lips were so bruised by the blow that he could not answer, and his tongue, numb with pain, refused its office.

Still the troop was fast approaching, and the nomads hastened their steps, in order to lose no time in concealing their victim.

They soon came to an old worm-eaten door, one-half of which was still hanging on its hinges, and the other lay on the ground, beneath a heap of rubbish, the accumulation of years. A rustling noise was heard within—thousands of lizards retreating to their holes at the approach of the strange visitors. Close to the door lay the dead body of a dog, grinning hideously and showing his teeth, as if to defend the entrance to that weird, untenanted abode; and issuing from a sombre, gaping hole, a few paces distant, was a decayed rope, one end of which was attached to the dead animal's head.

"Here it is," said Hahib.

Relieff was laid down at the entrance to the cave.

The cords that had bound him were unloosened, and a rope passed under his armpits. At that moment the instinct of self-preservation, ever present when danger is at hand, gave for a moment new forces to the unfortunate man, and he bounded backward.

"Stubborn fellow!" said Habib, chuckling, and with his iron heel he struck Relieff a fierce blow on the back. When the latter was suspended over the hole, he called out for help. A burst of laughter was the only response; and he felt himself descend, first regularly though rapidly, and then dropped to the bottom.

He fell on a soft substance, which remarking, he endeavored with the aid of his hands, following the outlines of the bulk beneath him, to discover what it was. Suddenly he uttered a shriek, and felt his hair standing on end; and, terrified, he shrunk back to the wall. In the centre of the dungeon he could perceive, by the faint glimmer of light admitted through the aperture above, a half-decomposed corpse, lying in a pool of greenish slime. The major fixed his glance on the dead body, which seemed to move in every fibre; and, attracted by its whiteness, he gave way to his curiosity, and approached to examine the cause of what appeared to him to be an optical illusion. What was his horror on beholding myriads of small, black, rugged heads, attached to white, flexible bodies, preying with avidity on the decaying flesh!

In order to refrain from further contemplation of the sickening spectacle, the wretched man turned his eyes upward to the entrance of the pit. Half-way up a number of spiders were busily engaged in reconstructing their webs, which had been torn away by the prisoner in his downward passage. As soon as their labor should be completed, the hole would be closed up with their network, and the light almost completely shut out from his dismal cell. Now and then they would suspend their toil, and fixing their large, goggle-eyes upon him, they seemed to say, "You have come in here, but you shall never go out again!"

By-and-by, Relieff thought his prison grew darker. Had the spiders already completed their web-curtains, or was it that the hour of sundown had arrived? He knew not; but there was no manner of doubt of the growing obscurity around him.

All at once he felt an itching, which soon changed to an intense burning sensation, and extended over his whole body. Carrying his hand convulsively to several parts of his skin, he perceived a spirituous, nauseating odor, more sickening still than that emitted by the putrid mass at his feet. He looked around him in bewilderment, and saw the gray of the walls changed to a sort of reddish hue; millions of bugs, issuing from countless crevices, were advancing, as it were, in a solid mass.

Vainly did he attempt to crush them. The burning of his skin and the smell grew so insupportable that the prisoner, yelling with pain and despair, endeavored to beat out his brains against the wall; but just then his strength failed him, and he fell full into the slimy pool side by side with the dead body. His shouts seemed to shake the very walls of the dungeon as he rolled frantically in the loathsome glair. At length his voice was so completely smothered that he could scarcely utter a sound. Relieff felt as if he had been plunged into a caldron of boiling oil.

"O Death!" he implored, piteously.

XIV.

LISE.

It was one of Countess Molotoff's rout-evenings. The blue *salon*, already familiar to the reader, was brilliantly illuminated; hosts of liveried serving-men hurried to and fro with trays; and in each of the four corners groups of officers and civil functionaries were engaged in animated converse. Fifty guests had that evening responded to the invitation of the governor's wife. Close by the principal door of the hall stood Molotoff, Goreff, and several superior officers, communing gravely; and seated on the lounge or around the table were the few ladies of the garrison, with their eyes riveted upon the ceiling, and making praiseworthy endeavors to conceal from each other, and from the whole company, how heavily the hours hung upon their hands. Martha went from group to group, doing the honors of her household with that gracious affability and dignified refinement of manner which rendered her so seductive. Her radiant beauty shone forth in all the plenitude of its splendor, no little enhanced by a gorgeous dress, a very *chef-d'œuvre* of modish Parisian elegance, and a profusion of diamonds sparkling on her arms, on her neck, and in her hair.

Yet, spite of that affability and sprightliness, more apparent than real on the present occasion, a certain expression of sadness lurked in her eyes, usually so bright and cheerful, and a slight pallor had taken the place of the wonted glow of her cheeks.

Bassalsky, as a matter of course, was among the guests. Seated with his back against a table, he followed Martha's every movement, waiting till a momentary relaxation from her hospitable solicitude should afford him an opportunity to approach her. It so fell out that he had to wait the greater part of the evening. At length, believing a favorable juncture had arrived, he arose to join her. On perceiving him, she sought to dissimulate an irresistible movement of impatience; yet she did not withhold her hand.

"The truth at times issues involuntarily from our mouths," said he, bowing. "It is almost tantamount to temerity to say that this evening you are divinely beautiful; but—"

The countess interrupted him.

"Really, Monsieur Bassalsky, you ought to have found something more novel to impart to me. Before long you will force me to hate my beauty. It is the theme of all your conversations."

"Madam—!"

"Oh! dear me, yes! I am beautiful! I know it very well; and I know, also, that you are of the same opinion: you have been telling me so for nearly a year. Should Monsieur Goreff, who has not yet told me so, take it into his head to give me that information, I might perhaps feel flattered; but I am sick and tired of your admiration."

"I am unfortunate in my mode of conveying my sentiments, that's all. Pray don't blame me for that."

The countess looked at him with an ironical expression.

"What about Mademoiselle Lise?" she inquired.

Bassalsky felt somewhat confused.

"Madam!" he murmured.

"Come, now, Monsieur Bassalsky," pursued the countess, severely. "I gave you a mission to fulfill, and so far you have discharged your duty with tolerable fidelity. You have paid your court to Lise, and that with so little apparent reluctance that I was in hopes you would begin to realize what a darling girl she is, and that you had banished all your foolishness from your head."

"But, madam," exclaimed Bassalsky, "you seem to have forgotten our agreement—what you told me?"

"We have nothing to do at present with things that I may have told you heretofore. Answer my question: 'What are your intentions?' Mademoiselle Goreff has frequently spoken of you to me, and, I may add, in very flattering terms, too. She has a great deal of esteem for you; while I—"

"You are cruel; but you are aware that you alone—"

"Nonsense, sir!" returned Martha, with a contemptuous laugh. "Do not have the presumption to pay court to two women at once, and especially to two women like Lise and myself. I know that your attentions to Mademoiselle Goreff have been of a nature to induce her to suppose you are in love with her. Then, after pouring your impassioned strains into her ear the whole morning, you come to me with your adoration in the evening! Such conduct, sir, is neither gracious nor politic."

"But, madam," rejoined Bassalsky, rolling uneasily on his chair, "you know that you have to say but a word, and I will never open my lips again to her."

"That is precisely the reverse of what I ask of you!" returned Martha, sharply, her cheeks suffused with a flush of indignation.

Completely chap-fallen, Bassalsky could only stammer out:

"O madam! I do not deserve such severity as to be forbidden to speak to you!"

The countess, feeling she had gone too far, said, in a milder yet no less resolute tone:

"At all events, I forbid you from continuing your attentions to me. They are in every respect out of place. Through kindness toward you, I have hitherto forborne from appealing to my husband to put an end to your assiduities. I suggested an expedient to explain the cause of your presence continually in the palace; but it has never been my intention to give you any encouragement. Besides, I indulged in the hope that a few weeks of intimacy with Mademoiselle Goreff would make your task easy; and, more than that, I am delighted to see that my hope has been realized, for you appear to be on excellent terms with the young lady. So far, so good! But, then, why persist in importuning me with your homage? If you desire that we should remain good friends, cease your declarations of passion to me, and tell me frankly what you think of Lise."

Bassalsky sat with downcast eyes, not knowing what reply to give.

"There, tell me: do you love her?"

"O madam! I think—I suppose—"

Once more Martha gave signs of impatience; but she restrained herself, and went on:

"You will have but yourself to blame for anything disagreeable that may happen to you. My husband has already asked me the reason of your constant visits. I answered that you were paying court to Lise; and, in saying so, I believed it to be the truth, for I will never stoop to falsehood. If, then, your intentions be not openly avowed, I shall be forced to beg of you to make your visits less frequent. You have had ample time to know Lise's disposition.—By-the-way, what was it that somebody was telling me? Is it true that she saved your life yesterday when you were out walking together?"

Bassalsky was completely abashed.

"It is true," said he, in a whisper. At that moment Lise chanced to be crossing the room.

"We have just been talking about you, dear," said Martha, beckoning to her to come over.

The friendly relations between the two ladies seemed to have undergone a marked improvement, for Mademoiselle Goreff now approached the countess, smiling, and her smile was one of cordial friendship.

"About me?" she asked. "And, pray, what have you been saying about me?"

"I was asking for the particulars of the events of yesterday. It would appear that you saved Monsieur

Bassalsky's life. Just tell us the whole story, will you not?"

Lise gave a hearty laugh.

"Oh, it was so funny, I assure you! We were admiring the sunset outside the gates, Monsieur Klotz, Monsieur Bassalsky, father, and I. I had noticed this gentleman walking away from where we were standing; and all of a sudden a hissing sound reached my ear, and at the same moment I saw a snake erect upon its tail, and ready to spring upon Monsieur Bassalsky, who had probably trodden upon it as he passed. I ran to the snake, and, with a lucky blow of my riding-whip, broke its backbone, just as it was within an ace of reaching our friend, who did not see it at all. It appears the reptile was of a species whose bite is mortal."

"Why, you are simply a heroine!"

"And I have not told you the best of the story yet," pursued Lise. "Monsieur Bassalsky, as he stood half-stupefied, gazing on the fragments of the serpent, stammered out something like—'Do you know that you have just saved my life?' And he spoke with such childlike astonishment that I could not resist a laugh. 'I should rather think so,' said I; and then, for the first time, he thought of thanking me."

All this time Bassalsky felt somewhat confused. He recalled the adventure of the day before; and then he looked at Lise, and she appeared so ingenuous, so pretty, and so seductive, that he went and took her hand and raised it respectfully to his lips.

"Yes," said he, "the awkwardness of a man surprised to see courage and beauty united in the same woman caused me to express my astonishment in a stupid manner yesterday. I beg to apologize for it. And I only regret that I did not sooner learn to admire all the perfections united in you, mademoiselle." And turning to Martha, and fixing his eyes earnestly on hers, he said, in an impressive tone:

"You judged rightly, madam; I acknowledge it!"

"Now we are genuine good friends; let us shake hands on it!" cried the countess, offering her own to be pressed.

Mademoiselle Goreff listened, with a certain degree of astonishment.

"How solemn you two people are!" said she.

Martha kissed her.

"It is all to please you, who are so fond of solemn people!" said she, laughing. "Besides, I have re-remarked that Mademoiselle Goreff, who has an utter detestation for flatterers, is nothing loath to receive Monsieur Bassalsky's compliments."

Lise blushed.

"We can scarcely refuse to accept the thanks of a person whose life we have saved, although they be exaggerated," she replied.

Just then Molotoff came forward, and, seeing Lise, smiled graciously.

"You should have told your cousin Relieff," said he to her, "to let us hear from him. He has completely forgotten us, though we are all his friends. I have some important papers to transmit to him, and I don't know where to find him."

"You informed us lately, general," interposed Bassalsky, "that you had received a dispatch from Relieff, in which he apprised you of the complete rout of a band of ten thousand Kipchaks."

"Yes; but that was a month ago. I am aware that he received an order from Tashkend to push on to the Amu-Darya, where he was to join a regiment sent by the governor-general for the purpose of suppressing a league formed against us. But I have no idea of his precise whereabouts."

"Doubtless he keeps up a direct correspondence with Tashkend," suggested a superior officer.

"That is what I complain of. Since he is no longer obliged to send his reports to us, he neglects us entirely, and leaves us in anxiety about him, poor fellow:"

"Oh!" exclaimed Bassalsky, "there's very little danger to be apprehended fighting those savages; it takes four of them to fire off a gun!"

"It is easy to see you are not there," broke in Martha, sharply.

The countess laughed as she spoke; yet there lurked a dash—the merest touch—of resentment behind the laugh. Lise alone observed it, with her woman's instinct.

"My dear Martha," said Molotoff, "you were to a certain extent the cause of his being sent. So far, no great prejudice has come of it," continued the general, "for I received orders this morning from Tashkend to inform him of his promotion to the rank of lieutenant-colonel, as a recompense for the brilliant encounter with the Kipchaks."

"What luck!" cried Bassalsky. "Promoted twice within two months!"

"He has earned it well," replied Molotoff, dryly.

The marked severity of the general's tone completely abashed the young officer.

"I never meant to say the contrary, your excellency," stammered Bassalsky, timidly.

"That is just as it should be," replied the general, turning from him and taking his wife's arm.

"You seem to me a little pale this evening, my dear," said he, with a look of fondness; "I trust you are not ill?"

"No, dear," she replied.

"Really?"

She betrayed a slight movement of impatience. "My dear, you are always watching my looks. You are too fond of me."

"How could it be possible to be too fond of you?"

"Indeed, yes!" murmured Martha, with a tone of undefinable weariness.

She disengaged her arm, attempted a smile at her husband, who stood gazing on her ecstatically, and, leaving him, joined a group of guests.

Bassalsky had approached Mademoiselle Goreff.

"Will you allow me to pay you an early visit to-morrow morning?" said he.

"With much pleasure," replied Lise, presenting her hand.

XV.

THE NEWS.

The next morning Molotoff entered his wife's boudoir while she was still at her toilet; and she was unable, on perceiving him, to repress a movement of surprise and disappointment.

His countenance was overcast with an air of gloomy thoughtfulness singularly contrasting with his usual beaming, mild, and good-natured expression; and his demeanor was constrained and undecided. The presence of the maid who was dressing the countess's hair caused his brow to contract.

Martha turned round inquiringly, as if to learn the motive of the matutinal visit, which constituted, it is presumed, an infringement of the rules regulating their daily interviews; but the marked change in her husband's deportment filled her with disquietude.

The general sat down beside his wife, took her hand, and pressed it to his lips.

"Martha," said he, in French, "I desire to speak with you."

"Dear me! what an air of solemnity!" she replied, endeavoring to smile. "Go on; I am listening."

"I desire to have a chat with you all alone."

"If you speak in French, it will be absolutely the same thing. Katharine will not understand a word."

"True; but her very presence will embarrass me. Be good enough, my dear, to send her out for a few minutes."

Martha repressed a sigh.

"Be it as you please," said she, with an attempt at sprightliness.—"Katharine, leave us."

When they were alone, the general slid to a kneeling posture, crossed his hands on his wife's knees, and with eyes teeming with tenderness—

"Martha, what have I done to you?" he asked.

The sad, plaintive tone in which he spoke caused the countess to shudder.

"I do not understand you," said she, stammeringly.

"What have I done to forfeit your favor?" he pursued, in the same tremulous voice.

Martha, whose apprehensions probably pointed in another direction, had by this time recovered her self-possession. Placing her hand on her husband's shoulder, she replied, with a somewhat forced smile:

"Nothing in the world, dear. Really, you allow the most absurd ideas to enter your head!"

"Tell me, then, my darling, why this marked change in your manner toward me? For the last two months I have scarcely ever seen you except at table or at our official receptions. When I beg for a moment's converse with yourself alone I am informed that you cannot grant it, either because you have a headache, or are tired, or have a new dress to try on. For two whole months, Martha," he went on, glancing wistfully at the ponderous drapery which separated the boudoir from the adjoining chamber, "this is the first snatch of privacy I have enjoyed with your own dear, charming self. To hear your voice where it can reach no other ears than mine, and see your face, and bask in the beams of your eyes when no other eyes than mine can behold them! That—that is my life, my ambition, my— O Martha!" And, seizing her slipper, he pressed it to his lips in one long, fond kiss, as if his whole soul were centred in a last expiring effort.

"My dear Alexander, just let me tell you that I suspect you of being ever so little jealous," said she, archly; "yet you know how unreasonable that is, and that I love you as much as my egotistical nature will allow me to love any one besides myself!"

"Not even M. Bassalsky?" ventured Molotoff, slyly.

Martha laughed, and this time right heartily.

"I told you you were jealous, my poor Alexander; I told you so! I was almost sure of it!" she rejoined, chidingly.

"I am not altogether jealous, you know; but I have noticed his assiduities to you, and considered them insipid and unbecoming."

"No more so than did I, I can assure you; but I have put a stop to them. Besides, M. Bassalsky is now paying court to Mademoiselle Goreff, as, I believe, I told you before—"

"Yes, yes! but yesterday evening!—"

"Oh! if you had only heard how I rebuked him yesterday evening, you would not regard him as very dangerous to your happiness! Besides, I must tell you once more, he is really and truly in love with Mademoiselle Goreff."

"And how does Lise take it?"

"I am rather of opinion that she is favorably impressed with him, which, I must confess, astonishes me; for it seems to me that Lise's gravity and sedateness can never sort with Bassalsky's characteristic levity."

"Why not bring about the match? Lise has a handsome fortune, and Bassalsky is rich and of good family."

"I have good hopes that we shall succeed in marrying them."

"Oh! very good!"

A gentle knock at the door of the boudoir interrupted the conversation, and the maid announced that M. Goreff awaited his excellency in the breakfast-room.

"Ah! to be sure!" exclaimed Molotoff. "I had totally forgotten my invitation to the venerable *savant*. Shall we have the honor of your company at breakfast?"

"Certainly, if you are good enough to wait for me."

"What a proposal!"

"Well, then, I must let you go; for I have to complete my toilet."

And the general hastened away to apologize to his guest for his apparent discourtesy.

No sooner had the general left the boudoir, than the mask of sprightliness which the countess had assumed for the occasion disappeared as if by enchantment, and she burst into a flood of tears. Burying her face in her pocket-handkerchief, she sobbed bitterly.

"Oh, dear me, how miserable indeed am I!" she repeated over and over.

The maid, accustomed to see her mistress imperious, exacting, often ironical and even sarcastic, but never before yielding to emotion, could scarcely believe her eyes when she returned and found her in tears.

"Oh! oh!" she exclaimed, in a hushed voice; "what can be the matter!"

But Martha, true to her haughty instinct, hastily dried her eyes, and cast a withering glance at the girl. "Did I call you?" she asked, fiercely.

"No, madam; but I thought—"

"You are no longer in my service."

And the sentence was irrevocable. Tears and entreaties proved unavailing; poor Katharine was forced to quit the palace that very evening.

Martha could never brook the presence of even a passing witness of her weakness.

In another wing of Tamerlane's time-honored palace a very different scene from that just described had taken place at the same hour.

Bassalsky had repaired to Mademoiselle Goreff's apartments. Blooming and pretty in her morning robe of white muslin and rose-colored ribbons, Lise looked so charming when he beheld her that he felt all the irresolution suddenly subside which had tortured him the whole of the way from his quarters to the palace.

His sentiments toward the young lady were pretty difficult to analyze. He could not be said to be distractedly in love; yet their associations during the past few weeks had been of so friendly a nature that, little by little, they had grown indispensable to him. Lise was very pretty, and Bassalsky liked her immensely; but liking and loving are not precisely the same. The young man thought within himself that Lise would be a perfectly suitable match for him, and an agreeable companion to introduce in society—nothing more; in a word, married life with Mademoiselle Goreff presented itself to his mind under very flattering colors; nevertheless, he would certainly not have died broken-hearted had some insuperable obstacle to their union offered on the following day.

Mademoiselle Goreff was one-and-twenty, had seen a great deal, and was of a serious and contemplative turn of mind. She had observed that Bassalsky refrained from those compliments of which the other officers were so despairingly prodigal; and for that reason she courted his society. Then, Martha's contrivances helping, the mutual relations of the two young people gradually took a character of confirmed intimacy. Bassalsky possessed considerable wit and talent, was well-informed, and of polished manners; he was, besides, brave and adventurous, and, on the whole, rather a good sort of man. As an officer, aside from a slight tincture of foppishness and an overdose of levity, his soldiership was remarkable. In fine, he might very well find favor in the eyes of a woman, and he pleased Mademoiselle Goreff. In St. Petersburg or Moscow, where Bassalskys might be found in swarms, certain it is that Lise would not have noticed him; but at Samarcand the captain was of a different stamp from his comrades, for the most part soldiers of fortune.

Yet Lise was not head and ears in love either. But she had come to the conclusion that she might as well as not unite her lot to that of a man to her liking; inasmuch as, during the five years elapsed since her majority, she had met with none she liked better.

With this state of things in view, the reader will not be astonished at the coldness of the interview between Lise and Bassalsky.

"Mademoiselle," said the officer on entering, "I have come to ask the favor of an interview in private."

"I am prepared to hear you," Monsieur Bassalsky.

"Mademoiselle, I love you, and it would afford me happiness to call you my wife. Will you consent to our union?"

"If my father consents, I will."

"Let us wait upon your father."

"Come along!"

And arm-in-arm they repaired to the *savant's* apartments, where they learned that he was breakfasting at the governor's.

"Let us go to the governor's."

"Come along!"

With the same measured gait they crossed the Talari-Timour, and told a servant to announce them.

Molotoff and Goreff were at a game of whist; and Martha had taken up her needlework.

Bassalsky approached the countess, and apprised her of his intention to ask Lise's hand in marriage.

"Bravo!" she exclaimed.—"Alexander," said she to her husband, "come here!—Here," she whispered into Lise's ear, "I'll be the *svacka!*"[1]

[1] Match-maker.

Molotoff answered :

"Wait, my dear, till I have finished this—"

"I'll wait for nothing!" interrupted Martha, with a stamp of the foot by way of emphasis. "Quick! quick!"

The governor laid his cards on the table.

"You too, Yegor Alexandrovitch!" added Martha.

When the *savant* and the general were by her side, seated in easy-chairs to which the countess had waved them, she said to Goreff :

"Yegor Alexandrovitch, I have the honor to ask your daughter's hand in marriage for Monsieur Bassalsky!"

The amazed *savant* stared at the countess.

"Why, madam, I know nothing—"

"Oh! no restrictions! plain *yes* or *no!* Your daughter consents ; my husband consents ; all we want is your consent—and that I demand. Monsieur Bassalsky is rich and of good family ; he loves your daughter, and your daughter loves him. They will be engaged now, here, on the spot, if you will allow ; and my husband will immediately write to Russia for the necessary papers. We await but a word from you."

"What think you, general ?" he inquired, comically. "If the match is a suitable one for my daughter, I am agreed."

Molotoff smiled.

"As for me, I believe the match to be well assorted."

Goreff nodded his head affirmatively.

"Very well, then," said he ; "I consent."

"Bravo!" exclaimed Molotoff. "I'll go and write forthwith to St. Petersburg, and I shall have the reply in six weeks at latest. Let us have the betrothal arranged this very day, and two months hence we can have the wedding—the first Christian marriage-ceremony ever solemnized in this country."

Then, turning to Bassalsky, he said : "From this day forward you are my aide-de-camp, and you will come and take up your quarters in the palace. You will thus have a better opportunity to pay court to your *fiancée*."

Lise had thrown herself into her father's arms ; and Bassalsky and the countess were conversing together when Klotz entered the room.

"General," said he, "a courier from Tashkend."

"Let him come in," exclaimed the governor, eagerly. "Ah! perhaps he is the bearer of tidings from our friend Relieff."

A non-commissioned officer entered, and handed a sealed packet to Molotoff.

Martha grew pale.

Molotoff hurriedly broke off the red-wax seal, and opened General Kaufmann's dispatch.

"Victory, gentlemen!" he shouted. "Our brave troops have completely dispersed the league formed against us by the Emir of Bokhara."

"God save the emperor!" cried all present.

"After the retreat, however," continued Molotoff, "the enemy again formed in order of battle, some sixty thousand strong, and gained the desert between Samarcand and the Amu-Darya, whither our troops were unable to pursue them. We have orders to place the town in a state of siege, and send out reconnoiterers to the environs. The Bokharans' losses in battle were about thirty thousand."

Suddenly Molotoff interrupted his reading, and his countenance became clouded. In a faltering voice he resumed:

"Every medal has its reverse. Gentlemen, we have been rather too hasty with our rejoicings. The victory has been dearly bought! We have lost one of our best comrades, and one of the bravest officers in the Russian army—Major Relieff!"

The governor was interrupted by a piercing cry. Martha had arisen from her seat, and, erect, motionless, her eyes staring wildly—

"What is it?" she gasped.

Molotoff was himself profoundly affected, so he did not at first observe the change in his wife's countenance. Indeed, it escaped the attention of all but Lise, who sat next to her, and seized her vigorously by the arm. Vain were all endeavors to calm Martha's agitation. She saw nothing, heard nothing; but with a tremulous, half-stifled voice asked once again, "What is it?"

"Relieff has fallen on the field of honor, and with him one hundred and fifty brave hearts who sacrificed their lives for the safety of the Russian army. Honor to his memory, gentlemen! We shall this evening pray God for his soul!"

Martha had listened attentively to the end; then, stretching forth her hand, she uttered a muffled cry, and fell swooning to the floor.

All present, save Molotoff, gathered solicitously

round the countess. He alone hesitated an instant; a terrible suspicion had, for the second time, stung him to the core.

Suddenly, drawing his hand over his brow, he advanced to where his wife lay, placed her on a chair, and, gazing for a moment on her wan and death-like visage, he was seized with a violent sobbing-fit.

Goreff, Lise, and Bassalsky, had withdrawn precipitately.

"Sad omen this for our marriage!" said Lise, in tears, to her betrothed.

"Alas, poor Serge!"

XVI.

THE SLAVE-MARKET.

SEID-MOZZAFAR-DINN was walking in his garden with his vizier Chakrullah and our old acquaintance Mirza-Mohammed. The emir was apparently in excellent spirits, and graciously addressed his conversation in regular turn to the minister and the chief of police.

"So, vizier," said he, "you think the Emir-Al-Oumra will give his consent?"

"His reply would lead me to suppose so. He informs me that his letter will be followed in a few days by a special embassy to be dispatched to your majesty."

"Mohammed," said the emir, "you will see that a vigilant watch be kept on the immediate surroundings of the reis's house, where the Princess of Khiva, my future wife, is stopping. That begging dervish, just now sirdar of the Turcomans, is, I am told, frequently seen prowling about here. O Mohammed! Mohammed! I must indeed have a high respect for you, to have pardoned the failure of your attempt against him!"

Mohammed prostrated himself on the ground.

"However, there will very soon be an end of all this," pursued Mozzafar; "and I hope we shall then have a reckoning. He can no longer be of any use to me, and we shall see if he still dares to brave me to my face.—Vizier, have you received a reply from the Russian commandant in Tashkend?"

"I am daily expecting it."

"Look you here, Mohammed, for some time past nothing succeeds with you. That officer whom I wanted the other day, and you could not find in Bokhara, is to be sold this very day by auction at a *Moultani's*[1] shop. Your police is badly organized, Mohammed! If my anger is once raised, woe to you!"

Mohammed prostrated himself again, and the emir addressed Chakrullah.

"What think you of that Indian? He managed first to conceal his prisoner, and he now boasts of the protection of the law. Yesterday it was in my power to have him taken from the Moultani's house; to-day, because he has exposed him for sale in public, I am obliged to respect his property. Henceforth the prisoner is inviolable, as far as I am concerned: the seller and buyer are alike beyond my power; and I am under

[1] Indian's.

the necessity of paying in ready money for that man, whom I want, and paying one of my subjects for him too! Do you not think it is absurd?"

"Absurd!" replied the vizier, sententiously.

"Revolting!" chimed in Mohammed.

"I must have an interview with the reis on the subject. But, for the time being, nothing can be done! I shall have to purchase the prisoner, for he is indispensable to me. He is a powerful chieftain; I can use him as a hostage, and demand a large ransom for him. Peace will be made on more facile terms when I have him in my power; and, should all else fail, I can at least wreak just vengeance upon those accursed giaours.— Mohammed, hasten to the sale, and purchase him, although you should find it necessary to go ten thousand tomans!"

"You shall be obeyed at once, sire."

"Call at the *haznadar's* on your way, and tell him to hand you the sum. But do not come back without the prisoner. Do you understand? Ah, hearken!" added the emir, calling after Mohammed, "that Moultani is a dangerous man; so keep your eye upon him .... and at the very first opportunity that offers .... you understand?"

"Great is the wisdom of your majesty!"

The square occupied by the reservoir of the *Divanbeghi*[1] is the chief rendezvous for the people of Bokhara.

---

[1] Named after the *divanbeghi* (secretary of state) of the Emir Imacouli-Khan.

"It is an almost quadrangular space, in the centre of which a deep reservoir has been sunk, one hundred feet in length by eighty in breadth. It is surrounded by cubic stones, with eight steps descending to the water's edge. A few elm-trees, planted here and there, shelter with their shade the inevitable 'tea-shop,' with its *samovars*, resembling immense casks of beer. These last, manufactured in Russia, expressly for the use of the people of Bokhara, enable the tea-venders to furnish to all comers an excellent cup of green-tea. Three sides of the square are devoted to stalls where bread, fruits, sweetmeats, and meats, both hot and cold, may be found at all hours of the day. The famished crowd, pushing and crushing with a bee-like buzzing, treats us to a most curious spectacle. The fourth side of the parallelogram is formed in a sort of terrace, serving in place of a pedestal to the Divanbeghi Mosque, in front of which, beneath thinly-planted trees, public story-tellers, dervishes, or acrobats, celebrate in verse or prose, while actors by their side reproduce them in pantomime, the heroic exploits of the prophets and illustrious warriors."[1]

Reservoir Square was crowded, for it was one of the days set apart for the sale of slaves. One of the shops on the terrace was open to visitors, who had gathered in vast numbers near the entrance. In the interior of the shop were one hundred or so Persian slaves, chained by the neck, and lying pell-mell along the floors. A Moultani, with the usual head-dress prescribed for their use, in order to distinguish them from the true believers, a red mark on his forehead, and his

[1] Vámbéry.

yellow, repulsive face turned toward the assembled multitude, was descanting in pompous terms on the rare merits of his human *stock*, as he wielded a long, leather strap, which he sent cracking from time to time among the slaves, by way of preventive chastisement. In the centre of the shop or stall, the most conspicuous place, being visible from all the corners of Divanbeghi Square, had been chosen for the site of a temporary stage. A man, attired in a magnificent scarlet-silk robe, with visage painted and beard dyed, was chained by the neck to a post, bearing the sign, "Tura Ooroos."[1] He was fettered hand and foot to the platform by means of other chains, as he lay on his back, with his face turned toward the public.

The man was no other than Relieff. The chains with which he was loaded hindered him from making the slightest movement; but his eyes sent forth flashes of indignation, which served to excite the boisterous laughter of a second Moultani, who was exclusively attached to his person, and stood by his side on the platform.

Just at the moment when Relieff had fallen exhausted by the bites of the hideous parasites, his guardians observed that the sirdar's troop had ridden past the citadel without stopping, and went and delivered him from his dungeon. They dressed his wounds, and bound him once more on a horse, and he arrived at Bokhara half dead and completely insensible. Once in that city, the nomads became aware of the impossibility of keeping him for any considerable length of time. The news of the capture of a Russian officer of

[1] Russian chief.

importance had preceded them, and they well knew how much the emir's despotism and rapacity were to be feared, as well as the fanaticism of the people. On the other hand, they had not the money requisite for the prisoner's maintenance; besides, Relieff was in so precarious a condition that his torturers themselves saw the absolute necessity of taking proper care of him, and that, in the absence of suitable treatment, he might die, and thus cause them to lose the sum they hoped to obtain for him. Accordingly, Hahib suggested that he should be intrusted to a slave-dealer, to be put into good condition, and set up at the next sale.

Hahib's suggestion was adopted, and a bargain was struck with a Moultani, who agreed to advance the necessary amount to effect the prisoner's recovery, on condition of receiving twenty per cent. of the proceeds of the sale, which would leave him no very paltry profit, since he assured the nomads that he expected the prisoner would bring, at the lowest reckoning, three thousand tomans.[1]

Relieff was taken to the Indian's house without any further delay, where assiduous attention, proper food, and humane treatment, soon restored him to health and strength. He felt his spirits gradually revive, and with them the hope that before long he should see his captivity ended.

The dealer, whose calling Relieff had never suspected, managed to gain his confidence. He made him believe that he had purchased him of the Turcomans; that he liked the Russians, and despised the Mussul-

[1] About six thousand six hundred dollars.

mans as being persecutors of his religion; and promised to put him in possession of means of communicating with his friends.

"I paid one thousand tomans for you," said the Indian, "through pity for the deplorable condition to which the savages had reduced you, and because your torturers pretended you were a great chieftain, and that you could purchase your release from captivity. Of course, you can understand that it is not in my power to be charitable on a very extensive scale—as I should like to be," he added, with a hypocritical smile. "So I hope you will deal fairly by me; for I have spent a great deal of money to effect your recovery."

The Indian could not possibly have chosen surer means to deceive Relieff. Skeptical by nature, the major scowled when he heard the Moultani make a parade of his kindly sentiments; but no sooner had the dealer come to the subject of ransom than the cloud disappeared from Relieff's countenance, and he offered to pay ten thousand tomans for his liberty, if necessary. The Moultani's eyes glistened; but, after a moment's reflection, he said: "Yes; but if the emir comes to know you are here, he will have you taken away, and I shall have nothing—nothing!"

"The emir must not be apprised—"

"Then how am I to furnish you with means of communicating with your friends? I am only a poor Indian."

After several days of caviling and vacillation, the Indian felt convinced that no better course could be pursued than to sell his prisoner by auction, as he had promised to the Turcomans. Indeed, as it was, he found it no easy matter to conceal a man whose presence in Bokhara was a secret to none, and for whom the emir, in his eagerness to secure him, had had diligent search made for a month past. Therefore, to attempt to keep him any longer was altogether preposterous, with the existing system of espionage in Turkistan. Besides, the Turcomans themselves kept close watch upon the dealer's movements.

Thus the Moultani was constrained to relinquish his ambitious views of lucre; yet, sagacious and crafty as he was, he took good care to disguise his determination to Relieff, and continue luring him with the most seductive promises. His aim was now to keep the prisoner concealed, by all means, until the day of sale, when, as already hinted, he would become inviolable by law.

The day immediately preceding that fixed for the sale, the Indian came with beaming countenance to inform Relieff that he had at last discovered an expedient for putting him in communication with Tashkend. Then, producing a bottle of wine—a rare commodity in Bokhara—he offered to pledge the prisoner in a cup on the prospect of his early deliverance.

Relieff unsuspectingly accepted the proposal, and quaffed the beverage at a single draught. The wine had been impregnated with a powerful narcotic. Relieff immediately fell into a profound stupor, from which he only recovered next day to find himself combed, rouged, and tricked out for the public eye, and exposed for sale on the platform in Reservoir Square.

Pen could not depict the rage that filled the major's breast, or the maledictions which he heaped upon the treacherous Moultani's head. That barbarous exhibition, to which he would have preferred death itself, caused the lofty and independent spirit of the Russian officer to suffer horribly. In his indignation, bound as he lay, and unable to move hand or foot, he imagined he felt strength sufficient in his arms to crush the vile herd that stood examining him with eager curiosity. Forced by his chains to hold his head straight, his eyes were suffused with tears of rage, and his lips quivered convulsively. A man with his face painted, and decked in a gay costume, but chained and furious, was a wonderful source of merriment for the gawky loungers of Bokhara. Within a few paces of the platform, Ooroombay, with the Turcomans and Kirghiz of the escort, stood in a group, pointing with the finger to their late prisoner, and laughing in an insolent manner.

Meanwhile, the Indian appointed to show the prisoner to the chapmen as they came along was engaged in earnest converse with an aged man wearing the green turban distinctive of the descendants of the family of the Prophet.

"It is as you say, seignior; he killed one hundred Turcomans himself alone. He was wounded; he traveled eight days strapped to a horse, and was six hours in a bug-dungeon. It is not yet two months since he went through all that—and look at him now!"

The Moultani advanced to Relieff, and separated the locks of his hair, to point out a recent wound.

"See the marks still," said he. And he opened

the prisoner's robe, so that the purchaser could plainly see the traces left by the insects on the major's breast; though, truth to say, their prolonged preservation was mainly due to artificial means.

"Hem, hem!" ejaculated the chapman.

"The ransom will be a royal one! And, in the mean time, you can have him working, for he is right strong: just feel those muscles—that neck!" And the Moultani, as he spoke, stroked the prisoner's arms and face with his hand. Relieff could not brook the touch; he made a sudden movement that caused his chains to clank sonorously against the floor of the platform. The Indian burst out laughing.

Relieff's rage now knew no bounds. He cast a fierce glance at the old man.

"If you purchase me, old idiot, I will brain you one day or another; for to you I owe the foul touch of this ignoble wretch!" he howled in the Uzbeck tongue.

"Oh, oh!" exclaimed the descendant of the Prophet. "He's not over-gentle!"

"Pooh!" replied the Indian. "That's only the effect of the surprise. He has been quiet and resigned for a month; but the trick the dealer played upon him has made him furious." Then he whispered some words in the old man's ear, to which the latter replied with an affirmative nod of the head.

"How much do you suppose you can give for your ransom, dog?" inquired the purchaser, pushing the major with his foot.

Relieff had recovered his calmness, and, gazing scornfully on his torturers, he wrapped himself in a disdainful silence, with the firm resolve not again to break it.

"He will not answer you, seignior!" cried the Moultani; "he's as stubborn as a mule. But, hold! here comes the dealer."

"No, no! never mind him: I'll buy, if you lower the price."

"Impossible, seignior, to take four thousand tomans."

"May I be your victim! Four thousand tomans! You surely don't mean it?—I'll give you three thousand. A pretty good sum, too!"

Ooroombay, who had come up to the platform, together with the other Turcomans, conferred with these in a hushed voice, and beckoned to the dealer to approach.

"We'll never do any better than what's offered," said he; "sell—go on!"

"Wait! Perhaps I can get—"

"Yes; but quickly, then. My comrades are losing patience, and the old man may back out."

"No, no! Just wait. I know my business."

At that moment two troops of horsemen came riding up toward the terrace from opposite directions of the quay. Safar-Hadgi was at the head of one of the troops, composed of Turcomans; and Mirza-Mohammed was gesticulating in the midst of a group of Tadjiks and civil functionaries, forming his suite. On catching sight of the nomads, Mohammed put spurs to his horse, and was soon in front of the platform, and his followers behind him. The Turcomans still advanced, but at a walk, without any evidence of haste, or of having noticed the breakneck precipitation of the Tadjiks. When the Moultani recognized Mohammed, he seemed anxious to close the bargain.

"Come, now, your last bid! I'll be easy with you," said he urgently to the old man.

"Thirty-five hundred tomans," replied the latter; "I told you so before."

"Four thousand, and I purchase the prisoner in the name of the emir!" cried Mohammed, looking haughtily around upon the assembled crowd.

The Moultani bowed to the very ground, without any thought of disputing a bid which he knew he was to take as a command. Accordingly, he was preparing to hand over the prisoner to the chief of police; but, before he had time to do so, the Turcomans had reached the spot, and Safar-Hadgi, reigning his horse close up to the platform, cried:

"I bid five thousand tomans!"

A slight pallor was visible on Mohammed's face; but it disappeared promptly. Feeling secure of the emir's protection, and relying upon the numbers of his Tadjik escort, he tossed back his head, and, with a haughty air, said:

"The sirdar has doubtless not heard the announcement I have just made: the emir purchases this prisoner!"

"Five thousand tomans bid!" repeated Safar.

Mohammed turned to his suite.

"It is hard," said he, in a subdued tone, "to make these mad-brained devils understand.—Six thousand tomans!" he cried.

"Eight thousand!" returned Safar.

"It is not courteous of the sirdar of the Turcomans thus to set at naught my master's will!"

"Your master is not mine!" said the hadgi. "So, let him pay for what he desires to purchase, as I am prepared to do."

"Very well! The emir shall be made aware of all this!"

"What is that to me?"

Mohammed felt he must needs bid higher still.

"I bid ten thousand tomans for the prisoner!" cried he, hoping that his pertinacity would drive his opponent to withdraw.

"Eleven thousand!" replied Safar.

"Ah! this is going too far!" howled Mohammed, goaded to bravery by the menacing countenance of his terrible master, which he fancied he saw flitting before his eyes. "The emir is lord of the soil, and may take whatever he deigns to purchase!—Seize the prisoner, my lads!" cried he to his Tadjiks. "These savages may come and take him from the palace if they can!"

Some few of the Tadjiks obeyed their chief's order, and rushed upon the platform; but the Moultani, who had come so close to the realization of a handsome profit, uttered a despairing cry, and Ooroombay, whom nobody had been thinking of, stood erect by the side of Relieff, and shouted, in a voice of thunder:

"Turcomans! our property is in danger!"

At a signal from the sirdar, the horsemen of his troop surrounded Mohammed's escort, and awaited the word from their leader to give battle.

"Mohammed!" said the sirdar, "one single step,

and neither you nor your followers shall leave this place alive!"

When Mohammed saw himself surrounded by Turcomans, whom the Persians dread as they dread fire, he was completely distracted and lost all presence of mind. The thought of Mozzafar's anger caused him to forget the existence of another and more immediate peril.

"Be it so!" said he. "Take that slave, but remember, it is not against me, but against the emir, that you have dared to strive."

The Persian was in act to retire, and the Turcomans were making way for him to pass, when Safar motioned him to stay.

"Wait," said he; "we have one more account to settle together—pay that man eleven thousand tomans!"

"I?" vociferated Mohammed.

"What! have you lost sight of the money belonging to me?"

Mohammed reined up his horse to the side of the sirdar's, and, in a voice rendered tremulous with mingled supplication and rage, he murmured:

"Seignior! you hold a receipt of mine, and—"

"Swine!" cried Safar, "do you think I have any design to rob you of your money? Pay; and all here present will be witnesses to the payment."

"Well, but—"

"After all," said Safar, chuckling, "you need not pay, if you prefer not. Return to your emir."

The menace lurking beneath the nomad chief's irony caused the Persian to tremble.

"I'll pay!" said he, eagerly—"I'll pay!"

He took a long purse from his belt and counted out the sum, which was received by the Moultani with sundry reverences and genuflections. Then, darting a wrathful look at the Indian, he turned bridle, and, followed by his Tadjiks, passed out between a double row of Turcomans formed to make way for him.

"Now," said the sirdar, when he was alone with his followers, "let this giaour dog, who killed a hundred of my best horsemen, be taken to the camp! The miserable existence he will have to drag out with me will cause him to regret he did not die, for he shall learn how Safar-Hadgi avenges his comrades."

"Your words are words of wisdom, sirdar!" shouted the Turcomans with one voice.

Relieff had recognized Safar-Hadgi from the commencement of the scene and thought for a while that Heaven had sent him a deliverer; but the final speech of his former friend blighted his last hopes, and he closed his eyes in despair.

XVII.

MOHAMMED.

The way from the square to the palace appeared short to the Persian. The most sombre thoughts took possession of his mind. Indeed, his position was nowise enviable: placed between the anger of his sovereign and Safar's denunciation, equivalent in itself to a death-sentence, he felt himself, as it were, inextricably entangled in the meshes of a net. He tortured his brain to find an issue, but discovered none, and the drapery veiling the door of the hall where the emir sat appeared to him like the curtains of the gates of hell, as he perceived it waving ponderously before his eyes. He had then recourse to a strange expedient. Timidly drawing aside the drapery, he entered, and flung himself with his face to the ground.

Mozzafar, who knew his favorite of old, suspected he was the bearer of bad news, and knit his brow.

"Where is the man I ordered you to purchase?" he inquired.

"Alas!" sighed Mohammed, still prostrate on the floor.

"Another failure!"

"Sire," murmured the Persian, breathless with affright, "permit me to lay faithfully before you the reason which prevented me from executing your sacred orders."

"Speak! It is the last favor I shall grant you!"

Mohammed raised his face, livid with terror, and gave a stammering relation of the scene described in the foregoing chapter. As he proceeded with his recital, the cloud on Mozzafar's brow grew darker and darker, and his eyes darted vivid flashes.

When Mohammed had finished—

"So this accursed dervish is ever to cross my path!" exclaimed the emir; "I shall find nobody to rid me of him! You could not have the insolent slave massacred, chopped into pieces?"

"Sire," ventured Mohammed, perceiving that his master's wrath had been turned away from his own person, "he is sirdar of the Turcomans, and was surrounded by his own troops, and you know that the greater part of the nomads are encamped in the vicinity of your capital."

This speech exasperated Mozzafar.

"Slave!" he vociferated, "I know not what hinders me from having you beheaded!"

Mohammed again smote the flag with his forehead.

"Sire," said he, "your slave is but an abject thing!"

"Why, dog, did you not carry out my orders? From all you have just reported, I can see no excuse for your disobedience! Whether your zeal for my person is diminishing or not, I cannot tell; but one thing I see clearly: your intelligence is becoming sensibly obscured."

"Sire—"

"Silence! You should have offered that dealer twenty thousand, thirty thousand, fifty thousand tomans! With no choice between the offers, I suppose he would have granted the preference to his sovereign."

"But, sire, your majesty did not authorize me to go beyond ten thousand tomans!"

"I have told you already that, since you have grown rich, you have lost your wits! Who was to force you to pay the dealer any sum you might have promised him? *He* is not a sirdar of the Turcomans, and he would have trusted his emir. The sale once over, what would have been easier for you than to have had him hanged?"

Mohammed could find no other reply than a plaintive moan, and once more smote the flag with his head till it rebounded again.

"You are the cause of considerable damage to me, and you must be punished for it. I should have had you put to death, but a certain weakness which I cannot overcome inclines me to clemency, and I'll grant you the privilege of purchasing your life at the price of fifty thousand tomans, which is my estimate of its worth! So, you will hand over that sum to my haznadar this very evening."

Avarice was so deeply rooted in Mohammed's breast that it proved this time stronger than his love of life. He arose to his knees and exclaimed:

"Such a sum, sire!"

"You have it not at command, perchance?" said the emir, with a chuckle; "so much the worse for you, then, for, if it is not in my treasury before sunset this evening, your head falls!"

"You are determined upon my ruin, sire!"

"Your ruin, dog! Does not all you possess in the world come from me? I take it back again now, for I am not satisfied with you. Enough! Prepare to pay, or to die!"

Mohammed bowed his head.

"Sire, your mandate shall be obeyed."

"Now, hearken!" added Mozzafar. "If, after the expiration of one month, Safar-Hadgi is still free and at liberty to brave me to my teeth, I shall order your death; and this time my decision shall be irrevocable. I swear it by the beard of the holy Prophet!"

The emir raised the drapery and issued from the

hall, casting upon the still prostrate functionary a last look teeming with wrath and menace.

Mohammed quitted the palace and directed his steps homeward; his breast boiled with sombre rage, and his fiendish nature longed to find some one on whom to take vengeance for his recent humiliation. All at once a dark and cruel flash lighted up his eye, as he perceived Hahib, who was awaiting him in the court-yard.

"Ah, Hahib!" said he, in a honeyed tone, "welcome! You are just the very man I wanted to speak to! Step into my apartment." Before entering into the interior of the house, he gave some orders to his servants in a low voice; then, followed by the former slave of the emir, he passed through a number of rooms, and at last stopped in one looking upon the court-yard; there he asked Hahib:

"Were you present at the slave-sale?"

"Yes, seignior," replied Hahib.

Mohammed looked at him and laughed.

"You have scarcely fulfilled your engagement: Safar-Hadgi lives and is as powerful as before," said he.

Hahib hung his head.

"Allah protects him; but let an opportunity offer!—"

"It is very slow in coming."

"I am following your instructions, seignior."

"What instructions, Hahib?"

"Did you not say: 'Don't try to assassinate him; wait till you see him engaged in a *mêlée* or a combat?' Then you added: 'He is a just man, and has, in all probability, warned the reis that, should he not die in battle, the blame can be laid upon no other than me—'"

"Yes, yes!" interrupted Mohammed; "but what else did I order you to do?"

"To watch his movements," replied Hahib, "and report to you, should I catch him in any breach of the law of Mahomet; but, during the two years that I have been in his service, I have seen nothing. He is a saint, seignior, and an upright man."

"Oh, oh!" chuckled the Persian, with the kindliest of smiles; "you are beginning to take a liking to your master."

Hahib made no reply.

"You would feel happy to be released from your oath; is it not so?"

"Oh, yes! seignior," exclaimed the slave; "he has saved my life, and, though I seek to injure him, it is much against my will. I obey you, but the path of the traitor is repugnant to me."

Mohammed seemed to reflect.

"Hahib," said he, abruptly, "do you happen to possess fifty thousand tomans?"

The bewildered Hahib recoiled.

"You are pleased to jest with your slave, seignior."

"So, you have them not at command?"

"Assuredly, seignior, no!"

Mohammed struck his hands together, and a sudden change came over his countenance. His tone shifted from the honeyed to the gruff, his voice quavered menacingly, and his lips contracted into an ominous smile.

"Hearken, Habib!" said he; "the emir is discontented with me, and has inflicted upon me a penalty of fifty thousand tomans: I, in turn, am discontented with you, and, as I cannot wring money from you, I must needs have recourse to other means to stimulate your zeal."

The thick carpet which covered the floor of the room in which this scene was enacted, deadened the footsteps of persons passing over it; so Habib, whose back was turned to the door, did not hear those of two men who had entered at the call of the chief of police.

One of these men, a gigantic Tartar, placed himself at the left hand of the slave; the other, an Indian, with a cruel and repulsive look, at his right. Mohammed smiled.

"Do you recollect your agreement?" he went on. "By the emir's orders I was to have your feet cut off; but I refrained from doing so, in consideration of your oath to obey me blindly: do you remember that oath?"

Habib shuddered.

"Yes, seignior," he said, stammering.

"No, I think you have forgotten it, and I feel the necessity of refreshing your memory. I will this day take an installment from your skin.—Down with him, and take off both his thumbs!" ordered Mohammed. And the fearful order was executed under the gloating eyes of the fiend in human shape.

"Your zeal will now be more ardent in future, perhaps," said the chief of police, chuckling.

"Oh, a curse upon you!" exclaimed Habib, rolling over and over on the floor—"a curse upon you!"

"Now," added Mohammed, "the emir has granted

me one month to dispose of Safar; I will give you fifteen days. If at the end of two weeks your task is not further forward than at present, fear my certain vengeance."

"Take my life at once, then," replied Hahib; "for I will obey you, fiend, no longer!"

"You forget your oath. But never mind, you will reflect. I leave you at liberty, but do not think of taking flight. You may reveal the whole secrets to the sirdar; it will cause him no astonishment, for he knows me well," added the Persian, with a cynical laugh. "He will only drive you from his presence, and then the trifling pain which has just now been inflicted on you will be nothing in comparison to the tortures which will be in store for you."

"O cursed, cursed wretch! And yet I had thought you so generous, so benign!"

Mohammed burst into laughter.

"Stupid brute!" said he, "think what pleases you; but obey me, for you are in my power. Forget not that I can at any moment claim you from the sirdar as a fugitive slave from the emir's palace."

Hahib still lay writhing in pain.

"Up, and away, unless you wish your torturers to return!"

"You shall be obeyed," murmured Hahib. And he went away with faltering steps.

When Hahib had gained the street, he cast a look of burning wrath upon the Persian's house, and muttered to himself, "My oath shall be fulfilled, but my revenge will follow immediately after!"

XVIII.

SAFAR-HADGI'S HOUSE.

We trust the reader will permit us now to go back a short way, in order to follow Safar-Hadgi's movements from the time when, after issuing from the mosque, in company with the reis and other ulemas, he set out for Khiva and Merv, to organize the Turcoman league, whose dispersion has been related in another chapter. When Mohammed had said to Hahib that Safar was a just man, and would not hold him responsible for an accident, he had judged rightly. Indeed, the hadgi, on delivering the accusing document, signed by the Persian, to the reis for safe-keeping, had said to the latter:

"Should I disappear, or should you not hear of or from me, you will take this paper to the emir. But if you should receive tidings that I have been killed in battle, return it to that Schiite dog."

And when, after his successful mission, he had again passed through Bokhara, on his way to the Amu-Darya, he modified his instructions still further, requesting the reis not to give the document to the emir until he heard from him, Safar. On both occasions the reis made a solemn engagement to obey.

On the evening of his departure, Safar-Hadgi had met Hahib a few miles out of Bokhara. The slave was stretched upon the sand exhausted, and giving evidence of acute suffering. Pious and humane, as it behooves every good Mussulman to be, Safar alighted from his horse. Hahib told him a part of the truth. He informed him that he was one of the emir's slaves, and had fled from the palace to escape a terrible punishment that his master had ordered to be inflicted upon him in a moment of anger, aroused by the insolence of a certain dervish that same morning. On hearing that, Safar reflected that he himself had in a measure been the cause of the man's misfortune, and he took pity on him. He proposed to Hahib to go along with him, and the slave consented with alacrity.

The nomads in Turkistan always travel with two horses. Safar allowed the slave to mount his spare horse, and thus to accompany him first to the Emir-Al-Oumra, and afterward to Merv. Faithful to his orders, the Hahib watched his master's actions, but abstained from all attempt at violence against him. When, in the course of their journey, they were one day attacked by a band of robbers, Safar, at the risk of his own life, saved that of his servant; yet, fanatic as he was, and hence persuaded that his oath bound him to be his master's enemy, Hahib, on another occasion, endeavored to assassinate him during the heat of the battle. We have seen how the attempt proved fruitless, and the fatal blow was averted. Little by little, however, Safar's uniform kindliness to, and mild treatment of, his slave made an impression upon the latter. Hahib was a primitive being, in the full acceptation of the term. He was at first firmly convinced of the necessity of fulfilling his oath, but two months in the service of the hadgi wrought a change in his sentiments. Though still resolved to obey Mohammed, he felt he would be delighted not to find an opportunity, nor indeed did he seek one from that time forward. The slave's uncultured mind was struck with the contrast between the emir's cruelty and the benignity of the sirdar, and he gradually became attached to his master. But the dire vengeance wreaked upon him by Mohammed had the effect of giving another turn to the slave's ideas. He felt the necessity of prompt obedience, but vowed, at the same time, that, his duty (as he called it) once fulfilled, he would be revenged on the fiendish Persian for his own injuries and those of his innocent master, whom he felt himself bound to betray.

On leaving the chief of police, Hahib repaired to the Turcoman camp, situated near the gates of Bokhara. He lay down upon the sand in the vicinity of the sirdar's tent, with the intention of watching his movements. As already hinted, Safar-Hadgi had correspondents throughout the whole Turkistan territory. Supreme chief of one of the most powerful associations, his friends were numerous in every city and in every province. Thus he was enabled, when setting out on his expedition against the Russians, to commission one of his confidants to purchase a house for him in Bokhara, either in the square, or in one of the streets running along the wall of the reis's garden.

He became possessor of a small dwelling, the garden of which adjoined that of the chief of the ulemas; but, strange to say, never had the sirdar of the Turcomans crossed the threshold of the house, nor did any person in all Bokhara suspect that it even belonged to him. The house, to all appearance, was deserted. A begging dervish had, indeed, been observed to enter it furtively; but, inasmuch as dervishes have the privilege of going wherever they please in Bokhara, that circumstance had excited nobody's curiosity.

Although Habib had had his beard cut in the Turcoman fashion, and had completed his disguise by begriming his face, he ventured as little as possible about the town, lest some of the emir's servants should recognize him. One day, however, having been sent for by Mohammed, he met on the way a dervish whom he had frequently seen issuing from the sirdar's tent. The man seemed desirous to conceal himself, and Habib, suspecting a mystery, determined to follow him; but the dervish, as if aware of being watched, entered the mosque. As Habib had an instinctive dread of public places, and as the incident occurred at a time when he was rather well-disposed toward his master, he relinquished the pursuit. As he lay down by the tent, the dervish's countenance flitted across his mind, and he had a secret presentiment that connected with that face was a mystery, the unraveling of which was perchance indispensable to his very existence.

We shall leave Habib lying in wait, and penetrate beneath the hadgi's tent. It was a large, square tent, of the finest felt manufactured in Turkistan. Mossy carpets covered the floor, and quilted hangings, scarlet and yellow, were so arranged as to form three distinct compartments. Piles of cushions on the floor of the first of these showed it to be the sirdar's reception-room. The floor of the compartment to the right was covered with wolf-skins, and a Russian iron bedstead —an article of great luxury among the nomads—stood close to the side of the tent. At the foot of the bedstead, Relieff, loaded with chains, was lying on the skins, just as he had been thrown there by the Turcomans who brought him from the slave-market.

The sirdar, it will be remembered, had ordered him to be transported to his tent. Gloomily, but tranquilly, there he lay, his thoughts fixed on death alone, which he wished for with eager impatience.

The drapery was moved aside, and Safar-Hadgi made his appearance.

Relieff turned his head, and, seeing who it was that entered, put on an expression of disdain, shrugged his shoulders, and turned his eyes away again. Yet the sirdar's countenance was by no means stern or threatening: far from it—a benevolent smile lingered on his lips.

"Judge me not lightly, friend," said he, in the Russian tongue; "I am not the master here: I was obliged to treat you harshly, in order to save you from death and from slavery."

Relieff had had, when in Samarcand, an opportunity to learn and appreciate the hadgi's disposition, and a fugitive ray of hope entered his breast. Yet he had passed through so many trials that he did not make his feelings known; he appeared rather not to have heard what was said.

"You saved my life," continued Safar, "and that I shall never forget. I shall do everything in my power here to lighten the burden of your captivity. Hitherto I have been obliged to appear to hate you. Besides, my title of sirdar only gives me the authority of a warrior-chieftain while the contest lasts. The slightest mark of pity observed in my bearing toward you would have been the signal for your death, and made me an object of suspicion. You must not forget that my people ever bear in mind that I have lived a number of years among yours."

Relieff now turned his eyes toward the hadgi, and listened to him attentively, but did not yet break silence himself.

"Brother," said the sirdar, drawing nearer to him, "you are in chains and suffering. Patience!"

He took a file from his pocket, knelt down beside the prisoner, and endeavored to cut the chains that fettered his feet.

"Thanks, Safar!" said Relieff; "I give you my thanks!"

The file began to make an impression on the iron.

"I am going to deliver you from your chains," pursued Safar, "and you shall no longer feel their weight. But you must promise me you will not take them off. Should my servants enter here and see you free, your life would be in jeopardy. You must promise, too, that you will follow my instructions."

Relieff raised his eyes in a look of gratitude.

"I thank you, Safar! I will do everything you tell me to do. There are noble hearts in all nations; I acknowledge that. If you restore me to liberty—"

At these words, Safar's countenance became clouded. For a moment he ceased filing the major's chains.

"Liberty!" he exclaimed. "Oh, no! Do not harbor such wild illusions! I can mitigate your sufferings as a slave. I desire to spare your life, but I cannot, and will not, give you your liberty!"

Relieff made an abrupt movement, as if he would withdraw from the contact of the hadgi.

"What would you do with me, then, villain? Why lure me with hopes that cannot be realized? Rather take my life!"

Safar laid his hand on Relieff's arm, and took up his file again, heedless of the prisoner's agitation.

"Hearken to me, Ooroos," said he. "Much do I owe to you, but still more do I owe to my religion and my country! When you spared me in Samarcand, you said, 'What can a pygmy like you do against my country?' You were right; I acknowledge it now; events have come to prove it. I am little, and your country is great. You could, without danger to it, set me at liberty. You had the right so to do. But I have seen you in the combat! My country is weak, and I am sensible of the immense injury you are capable of doing to it! You have a strong arm, loyal heart, and vast mind; you are, and ever will be, an enemy to my people; and I have not the right—at least so long as we are at war—to restore you to liberty."

"Mean subterfuges!" cried Relieff.

"Why should I resort to subterfuges? Are you not in my power? No, brother. You yourself, loving as you do your religion and your country, what would you do in my place? Answer!"

Relieff meditated. His pride was touched by the flattering comparison drawn between them by the sirdar, a man of sterling worth. Meanwhile, Safar plied the file incessantly. The major's hands were already unshackled. Silently, the hadgi fell to cutting those of the feet.

"You reason justly," said Relieff. "But why, then, free me of my fetters? Would it not be better to put an end to my life at once?"

"No, brother! To-morrow, or the day after, at furthest, I will have you sent to Khiva. You will find an asylum in the palace of the Emir-Al-Oumra, my former master and my friend. You saved his daughter from slavery. You will find in him rather a friend than a custodian. When the war is ended, you shall be free!"

"When the war is ended! Will it ever end? Your fanatical and unbelieving Mussulmans—"

Safar interrupted him:

"I do not insult your religion! Why do you insult mine? It is ungenerous!"

Relieff clasped the hadgi's hand in his.

The last chain had fallen off.

"I shall leave you an instant, brother," said Safar. "I am going out in your behalf. Will you promise not to leave the spot you are now in until I return? I exact that promise, for on it your life depends!"

"What is the good of preserving life without liberty? But, be it so! It is your desire, and I give you my promise!"

The sun had already disappeared below the horizon. Hahib, in spite of the pain he was suffering, did not once remove his eyes from the door of the sirdar's tent. He recognized the dervish beggar who came out. Hahib sprang to his feet, and followed him cautiously.

The dervish left the camp, passed through the city-gates, turned his steps along by the walls, gained the mosque, and entered it. This time, Hahib entered too. Mingling in a small group of believers, who were engaged in prayer in one corner of the sanctuary, he kept his eyes riveted on the dervish, not one of whose movements escaped his vigilance. Long was the dervish's prayer. The slave was on the point of losing confidence in the success of his efforts, when the holy mendicant, after a final act of humiliation, arose, cast a searching glance around him, and moved in the direction of the door, followed by his pursuer at a suitable distance to guard against being seen by him. Once in the square, the dervish looked in every direction to satisfy himself that he was unobserved, then approached Safar-Hadgi's house, and entered it, though not until he had cast a last inquiring glance all around.

The moment the door was shut, Hahib crossed the street like a flash, and attempted to penetrate into the house; but the door was unyielding. The main entrance was securely closed. So great was the slave's anxiety to probe the mystery, that, heedless of his still poignant suffering, he scaled the garden-wall, and crept stealthily to the window of the dwelling. In Bokhara the houses have but one story. Night had come, but the moonlight enabled him to view the four rooms into which the house was divided. Bare and unfurnished, they were evidently not inhabited.

Emboldened by his good luck, so far, the slave entered by one of the windows, searched through all the rooms, in every nook and corner; inspected the garret and the court-yard, but in vain. He found no human soul beneath that solitary roof. The dervish had disappeared! Yet Hahib did not give up all hope. He explored the garden, examined the walks, searched under the bushes, and beneath the thick brushwood; but the object of his search was nowhere to be seen. All at once he thought he heard a voice in the air overhead. The sound proceeded from the top of a stately sycamore growing close to the wall surrounding the reis's garden. He looked up. The mendicant was sitting on a branch of the tree, holding converse with an invisible being. A sweet and melodious voice replied, and that voice seemed to issue from the reis's house. Fain would Hahib have caught a glimpse of the unseen speaker, but the wall was too high. So, he lay down on the ground for the purpose of hearing. Strange! He listened attentively, but the sounds reached his ear confusedly, he could distinguish none: was the wind blowing unfavorably, or was the dialogue held in a strange tongue? He knew not.

Yet his eyes were intently fixed upon the dervish, whose features he had hitherto been unable to discern; for prudence counseled that he should remain at a respectful distance. Suddenly, a moonbeam darting through the foliage illuminated the dervish's visage, just then turned toward the slave.

Hahib recognized Safar-Hadgi.

XIX.

THE TURCOMAN PRINCESS.

As soon as Hahib was possessed of the information he desired, the artificial strength which had sustained him hitherto began to abandon him, and the pain, which had seemed to be lulled while the excitement lasted, then returned with renewed violence. Spite of his sufferings, however, Hahib was aware of the danger that would threaten him should he be discovered ; so, calling up all his energy, he crawled along in the direction of the inclosure over which he had climbed, and the situation of which he carried perfectly in mind. He reached the foot of the wall without any hinderance, but on attempting to take the same way as before, and climb over as he had then done, he saw that the task was altogether impossible. His little remaining strength had been exhausted ; he repressed a sigh of pain, and fell swooning under a raspberry-bush, whose spreading branches concealed his body from view.

The reader will, doubtless, have guessed that the soft voice which Hahib had heard answering Safar was that of Emineh. The daughter of the Emir-Al-Oumra, it will be remembered, had been placed by Mozzafar in charge of the chief of the ulemas. To attempt to obtain an interview with Emineh appeared hopeless, for the reis, a pious and austere old man, would certainly not have consented to compound with his religion. Safar and Emineh had, however, by common accord, resolved upon overcoming all obstacles. We cannot explain how Safar discovered the sycamore whose branches waved over the reis's gardens, nor how the maid herself had found out in the same garden a small copse, situated upon an eminence immediately under the sycamore; one thing, however, is evident, namely, that they had succeeded in securing repeated interviews from the time of the hadgi's return from his expedition.

Eminch and Safar loved each other. Their love had sprung at once from the common danger to which they had been, and still were, exposed, and from the contact, so rare among Mussulmans, of men with women. While still in Samarcand, Eminch, when at the risk of cruel punishment she would steal away from the palace of Timour, to offer up her prayers in the mosque, and endeavor to forget the hardships of slavery, had observed Safar on several occasions. Further on the emir's daughter became aware of the impression which she had produced in the Turcoman's mind, and then, for the first time, she conceived a sentiment for him that was something more than sympathy.

The hadgi had made no mystery to her of his engagements, but he had explained to her that among Mussulmans, and particularly in the sect to which he belonged, such vows were not irrevocable, adding that a pilgrimage, the good-will of the Shereef of Mecca, or a large gift of money, would be sufficient to procure his release. Then the Emir-Al-Oumra, to whom he had made known his projects, approved of them in every respect. Eminch and Safar might, then, hope for happier days, but for the time being they were bound to secrecy, the Islam law being extremely stringent with respect to the purity of conjugal life. On the evening in question Safar was the bearer of good news.

"I received a letter from your father," said Safar; "an embassy with instructions to demand your surrender has set out from Khiva, and will be here before the end of the week. Our happiness will soon come, for my army will not quit Bokhara before the arrival of the embassy, and will hold Mozzafar in check, should he dare to refuse to give you up to your father."

"Allah is good, Safar, and ever protects those who fear him."

"Yes, my well-beloved, I hope that the time of affliction is over, for you, at least; as to me, I have still a mission to fulfill, a country and a religion to defend against the inroads of unjust conquerors; but I shall, at least, if Allah wills it, have a peaceful spot, where I can, from time to time, enjoy repose by your side. My beloved one, do you remember the Russian officer who gave us our liberty?"

"Do I remember him? Not a day passes over that I do not bless him, and call down upon his head the blessing of the Prophet."

"The hazards of war have made him a prisoner; he is here in chains and covered with wounds. I remembered his generosity toward us, and I have taken him under my protection."

"Well done, Safar!"

"It is my intention to send him to your father, who will be his safeguard until the end of the war, when I shall restore him to liberty."

Emineh was pensive.

"Does that disposal meet his views?" she asked, abruptly.

Safar smiled. "It is not quite as he would have it, but he must needs be resigned."

"Why do you hesitate to set him free at once, and allow him to return back to his people?"

"He is a man of courage and great energy, and a renowned chieftain among the Oorooses; to let him go would be prejudicial to our cause."

Emineh shook her head.

"Did he delay to reflect when he was setting us at liberty, or did he bind us to any conditions?" asked she.

"True, my beloved, but he only consented to let me go because he thought I was not dangerous to his country. On the contrary—"

Emineh interrupted him:

"Allah alone is great, Safar; our country will be powerful if God so wills it; otherwise he can destroy it with a breath. God will find other means to chasten us, and this man will be powerless against us, if such be the supreme will. No, Safar, act according to the dictates of your conscience and stop not half-way in your generosity!"

"Such is your will?"

"I pray you."

"Your will shall ever be sacred with me. You shall be obeyed: to-night the Russian officer shall have his liberty."

"Thanks, Safar; God will reward you. And I will love you all the more, if that be possible."

Their voices were soon mingled in a low, mysterious murmur. They spoke of their hopes and their plans. Some time afterward Safar wafted a last kiss of salutation to the emir's daughter, descended from his tree, and left the garden.

We left Relieff in the sirdar's tent, bound by his promise to remain there faithfully. He stretched out his weary arms, and breathed freely. A feeling of comfort, which had long been unknown to him, pervaded his whole being, and he fell asleep.

The noise of voices in the adjoining room aroused him from his slumber. Some Turcomans were conversing in the sirdar's reception-room. Relieff could not understand anything of what they said, save the word Ooroos, which, from its frequent repetition, led him to conjecture that he was the subject of their discourse. Night was come, and, as the darkness increased around him, the sound of the voices gradually died away. A faint ray of light shone through Relieff's compartment, and Safar-Hadgi, with a lantern in his hand and a bundle on his shoulder, was once more by the side of his prisoner.

"Brother," said Safar, "I bring you your liberty!"

At such unexpected tidings Relieff could not repress a cry of astonishment and joy.

"Not so loud—not so loud! you are not yet out of danger! We have just decided in council upon your removal to Khiva. But I may be watched."

He took the bundle from his shoulder and threw it upon the bed.

"Put on those dervish's clothes which I have just taken off. Haste!"

Relieff, not yet altogether recovered from his surprise, divested himself of his own garments. While putting on those of his disguise, he sought to question the sirdar; but the latter placed his finger on his lips in token of silence.

"An angel has interceded for you. By-and-by you shall hear it all. Silence!"

When the major was ready, Safar examined him and corrected a few imperfections in the garb. He then took him by the hand.

"Now," said he, "follow me; and utter not a word."

The sentinels recognized the sirdar, and respectfully made way for him and his companion to pass. They soon reached the limits of the encampment. Before them lay the desert, as far as the eye could reach.

A few minutes' walk brought them to a favorable spot beyond the reach of noise from the camp, and completely wrapped in darkness.

Then only did Safar break the silence.

"The emir's daughter, whom you delivered at Samarcand, has insisted upon your being set at liberty. To her alone are you indebted."

"So, then, I am free—free to return to Samarcand.—entirely free?" inquired Relieff, unable to believe in his happiness.

"Quite free—thanks to Eminch!"

"Nobly does she pay her debt!"

"Now for mine!" rejoined Safar. He broke a

chain suspended from his neck, and handed to the major the medallion already familiar to the reader.

"Take this talisman," said he. "It is the seal of the Shereef of Mecca."

"But—" Relieff was about to object.

"Take it. Your disguise is insufficient, you may easily be recognized; but, even should you be, this talisman renders you inviolable to all Mussulmans. I do not believe I commit any breach of duty by intrusting that seal to a Christian, when that Christian is an upright man, as you are."

Relieff took his hand and pressed it cordially.

"The medallion will be needful to me, for I shall have here to contend with the emir, and I cannot long keep out of his way. To-morrow I shall dispatch three of my servants after you. Give me your promise that, after you have reached Samarcand, you will repair each night to Timour's Round-Point. You will surrender the talisman to the person who pronounces the words 'Safar and Emineh.'"

"Unless I die, you shall have it before eight days from this time."

"When one of your people gives what you call your word of honor, does he ever fail to keep it?"

"Never!"

"Give me, then, I pray you, your word of honor that you will not reveal to any one of your people the name of him to whom you owe your deliverance. All Christians are not like you. When peace shall have been made, a Russian might reveal it to a Moslem, and were my name to be used in connection with this event, I should be suspected, dishonored, and perhaps tried."

"Oh, with all my heart! I give you my word of honor that your name shall never come out of my mouth."

"You are free. But, before we separate, permit me to demand of you a last favor. I am told Mozzafar has made peace with the Russians. You will be able to tell when you reach Samarcand. Do you think you can conscientiously inform my messenger? This I beg of you as a favor, and by no means as a condition of your liberty."

"The Russians, Safar, declare war and conclude peace in the face of the world. If I learn any news at Samarcand, I will communicate it to your envoy."

Safar then took a purse from his bosom.

"A horse I cannot give you; dervishes rarely travel in that way, and your departure might attract attention. But you will have to purchase an ass. Take this money."

Relieff did not even think of refusing. He took the purse.

"Safar, farewell!" said he.

"Farewell, Relieff, till another battle comes!" returned Safar.

And the two friends, of different races and born in enmity, locked each other in a fast embrace. Relieff disappeared in the darkness.

The first face that appeared to Safar when he awoke was that of Habib. The cool morning breeze brought back consciousness to the slave. He raised his head, looked around, and, having satisfied himself that the house and garden were deserted, and all danger had disappeared, he set off to the house of the chief of police. Mohammed was absent, having been sent for by the emir. Fearing his absence should be observed by his master, he requested one of the Persian's servants to say he would soon renew his visit, and returned to the camp.

Although pain has little effect on savage natures, Hahib's suffering was so poignant that the change in his countenance did not pass unnoticed by the sirdar. The hadgi was attached to the slave by reason of the kindness he had shown him. It was in a tone, then, of sincere interest that he inquired:

"What is the matter, Hahib? Are you sick?"

The slave was ashamed to receive such a mark of kindness; so he replied, stammeringly:

"I fell and hurt my hands yesterday."

"I am sorry for that, for you were just the person I should have desired to send on a particular mission."

"Oh, no matter about my hands, seignior. I feel very little pain now, and certainly none to prevent me from doing anything you may have for me to do."

"So you feel happy in my service, good Hahib?"

The slave bowed profoundly, to conceal his pallor, and murmured:

"Are you not good and kind to me, and am I not deeply indebted to you?"

Safar directed him to take one of his best horses and set out for Samarcand; gave him the watchword to serve as the signal by which Relieff should know him; and got his promise to bring back the medallion.

"Perhaps you are not familiar with the surroundings of the city? However, any one you meet can show you where the Round-Point is," said Safar.

"I know Samarcand, seignior, having been there frequently with the retainers of the emir's household."

"Then you will have no trouble in finding your way. Do not lose a day, or even an hour, Hahib; for that talisman is my safeguard, and I should be in the greatest danger, particularly if my enemies should learn that I allowed it to go out of my possession for a single instant. The person I am sending you to may not meet you on the very first night after you arrive; but let not that give you any anxiety: he is not so well mounted as you will be. You must start this very evening. Do not forget that I rely upon your fidelity. If you are faithful in this instance, I shall be repaid for all I have done for you."

Hahib flew to Mirza-Mohammed and told him all, not omitting even the watchword, or his master's apprehension lest the object of the secret mission should be suspected.

Mohammed at once inferred that Safar was in communication with Eminch, and that the seal of the Shereef of Mecca was no longer in the hadgi's possession. Radiant with joy, he hastened to the palace, having first instructed Hahib to go on to Samarcand and to bring the medallion to *him*.

The slave followed him a long time with his eyes.

"Ah!" he exclaimed, soliloquizing. "I have kept my oath, and we are even! You and I for it now!"

XX.

THE IMPEACHMENT.

THREE days after Habib's departure, and the day after the dispatch of a second messenger whom Safar had deemed it expedient to send on the same errand, a great flourish of trumpets was heard at the entrance to the Turcoman camp. An embassador from the emir demanded an audience of the grand council of the nation.

A few brief remarks on the internal but by no means complicated machinery of Turcoman administration may here find their place, in order to aid the reader in the comprehension of the events now to be narrated.

The Turcomans are perhaps the only people of Asia who have adopted a republican form of government. They have neither kings nor rulers: with them all men are equal. In time of peace they are governed by a council, whose members are chosen from among the most renowned of their warriors, and their wealthiest veterans; and when an expedition has been decided upon, a *sirdar*, or war-chief, is elected. The sirdar-elect is invested with absolute power, of an exclusively military character, which ceases when the hostilities are ended. Even during the campaign, all administrative affairs are under the direction of a council elected at the beginning of the expedition, and presided over by the senior member. The decisions of the council are without appeal: even the sirdar himself, who is a member, by right of his functions, must in all cases submit to its authority. Its sittings are announced by a muezzin from the top of the council-tent, which is invariably pitched in the centre of the encampment.

The muezzin, having been notified of the arrival of an embassy, promptly convoked the council. When the president had ascertained that all the members were present, he requested them to be seated on their cushions, and gave orders to admit the envoy. Mirza-Mohammed, for he it was, entered alone, leaving his suite without the tent. Bending in a profound reverence, he raised his hand to his forehead and then lowered it to his breast, as prescribed by etiquette, and then stood erect.

"Elders and chief men of the Turcomans," he began, "my master, Seïd-Mozzafar-Dinn-Khan, Emir of Bokkara, has sent me to demand of you justice against one of your members, whom he charges with adultery, treason, and sacrilege."

Profound silence followed the Persian's introduction. The three crimes enumerated were the gravest provided for by the Islam law, and those punished with the greatest severity. The stupefied Turcomans looked at each other inquiringly. Safar-Hadgi, who was present at the council, grew slightly pale.

The president arose.

"Point out the guilty one!" said he, in a stern voice.

"He is here with you!" exclaimed Mohammed. "The most powerful of all of you—the sirdar!"

A scene of indescribable tumult followed. The Turcomans arose and gesticulated furiously. Safar-

Hadgi alone remained seated, and apparently quite composed.

The president called the assembly to order, and turned his eyes upon the hadgi; but, observing his placid countenance and disdainful air, he said to Mohammed:

"State the precise nature of the accusation."

"I charge the sirdar with the crime of adultery with the Princess of Khiva, already betrothed to our prince; with the crime of holding secret intelligence with the Russians; and with the sacrilegious appropriation of the seal of the Shereef of Mecca. Therefore I demand, in the name of my master, that the sirdar be immediately delivered to me, to be publicly tried in the emir's tribunal, and punished according to law for adultery, treason, and sacrilege!"

The Turcomans, who had resumed their seats, were gazing steadfastly at their chief.

Safar arose, and, looking scornfully at the Persian, said:

"Whence this unheard-of audacity, Mohammed? Has your life indeed become burdensome to you?—I will not, in the presence of this man, stoop to refute his absurd accusations. The emir is not my sovereign; his tribunal I disdain, and I refuse to be arraigned before it. To you alone, my comrades, and at present my judges, will I consent to make my defense."

Mohammed chuckled, and replied:

"You hope for the protection of the reis, on whose credulity you imposed; but he has been informed of your conduct, and will see you no more, he says."

The president knit his brow.

"It is not your consent that we demand," said he to Safar, "but your defense, and that we must have, however unwilling you may be to offer it. The charges brought against you are of too grave a nature to be treated thus lightly. Our ally complains that he has been insulted; and, if you would not have us deliver you up to his justice, establish your innocence. Such is my command as president of this sovereign council, and my request as your comrade. Painful would it be for us to have to abandon him who has so often led us to victory."

Safar drew himself up to his full height, and assumed an air of pride and disdain which awed the whole assembly.

"Since distrust has entered your breasts, be it so. I will give the explanation you demand; but before you, and you only. I am not amenable to the emir's government; and I claim the right of being judged by you, inasmuch as I am no longer among comrades, but among judges."

"We are prepared to hear you," said the president, sternly.

"Oh, no!" replied Safar, in a tone of irony. "The justification cannot be complete so long as a doubt hangs over the head of the accused. I require a stay of proceedings for one week, to enable me to refute the calumnious charges preferred against me. Comrades, I demand of you that delay."

The president shook his head with visible signs of dissatisfaction, shared by the majority of the members of the council. Mohammed perceived this growing distrust. Indeed, he had calculated upon it. He knew that Safar had no immediate means of justification; and he had hoped that, the indignation of the fanatical Turcomans once aroused by his startling revelations, the hadgi would be forthwith arrested. Of course, the moment Safar should fall into his hands, he was a dead man. Nothing could avert his doom; for the reis, after due investigation of the facts, had promised to abstain from interference with the hadgi, and to let the law take its course. Mohammed's triumph would thus be assured. If, however, Safar succeeded in communicating with the chief of the ulemas, although unable to proclaim his innocence, it were easy for him, with the desire of revenge, to prevail upon the reis, with whom Mohammed was in no very good odor, to put the emir in possession of the document signed by the chief of police. All these reflections crowded upon his mind, and so filled him with fear that he lost sight of his prudent reserve.

Advancing toward Safar, he exclaimed, violently:

"You are awaiting Hahib's return, are you not?—or perhaps you expect some foreign friends to come and deliver you? No, no; you shall be handed over to me this very hour; then defend yourself before the emir, if you can!—Turcomans! in the name of my master, you must—"

The president stopped him short.

"Must!" he repeated. "That word, to which you are accustomed, sounds disagreeable in our ears. Your master may *demand* justice of us, but *must* is unbecoming.—Comrades, I am of opinion that we should grant the sirdar the delay he requests. What say you?"

"So are we," replied the Turcomans, unanimously; for, like their president, they were galled by the insolent tone of the Persian.

"But—" articulated Mohammed, and he was interrupted by the president.

"Hear the decision of the council: On this day week, at the same hour, the sirdar, accompanied by all of us, will appear before the emir's tribunal. If he be found guilty, he shall be handed over to Mozzafar; but, remember, should we find him to be innocent—for we, too, shall be his judges—your master will have a terrible account to settle for the insult offered us in the person of our chief."

Mohammed had recovered his calm self-control, and his fruitful imagination suggested another expedient.

"Turcomans," said he, in a humbler voice, "I deeply regret having made use of an offensive term. I meant to say that my master desires to see justice done; and he knows how hard it would be for you to guard so important a prisoner in your camp."

"What do you mean to convey?" asked the president.

"I demand that the sirdar be taken to prison, since you have decided that he shall not be tried before a week. He can there await his trial without an opportunity of holding communication with any one. If he were to remain here in the camp, what certainty is there that this man, but yesterday your chief, would not succeed in bribing those lately under his command, and effecting his escape?"

Safar-Hadgi would have interfered, but the president, with an imperious gesture, motioned him to be silent, and enjoined upon him to take no further part in the debate.

"Be it so!" replied he to the envoy. "The sirdar shall be taken to prison this very evening. We will be answerable for him. He shall be guarded by a hundred Turcomans, in such house as the emir may see fit to point out as his residence for the ensuing week, and no person shall speak to him save in our presence. Does that satisfy you?"

Mohammed saw that his prey was on the eve of escaping, and he resolved to strike a decisive blow.

"What most astonishes me," said he, "is that Safar-Hadgi allows himself to be dragged off to prison, when a single word from his mouth would be sufficient to overthrow my accusation! Here, as in Bokhara, the shereef's seal, which we have all seen in his possession, shields him under its all-powerful protection. Why will he not have recourse to it?"

The blow was well directed, and Safar grew frightfully pale. But, fortunately for him, the Turcoman council, like all other tribunals in the world, would not revoke its decision. Yet this last speech of the chief of police inspired the nomads with certain misgivings concerning their sirdar, as was evident from their whisperings and the distrustful expression with which they eyed him.

"The emir will be the accuser and we shall be the judges, in one week from to-day," said the president. "For the present, our decision has gone forth, and we will not recall it. Go, then, and make it known to your master. Before sunset our sirdar, with an escort of a hundred horsemen to guard him, will repair to the place which you will designate. But let not a hair of his head be touched before the day of the trial has come, for, guilty or not, should any evil befall him, warn your master that the Turcomans will not leave one stone upon another in his palace or his city. You may now withdraw. Your mission is at an end."

At a signal from the president, the Turcomans rose to their feet—the usual form of dismissal. To utter a single word further would be a flagrant breach of propriety.

Bursting with rage, Mohammed left the tent.

When he found himself alone with his old comrades, Safar asked permission to speak, and, thanks to the prestige he still maintained among the nomads, he was enabled to obtain a hearing with comparatively little trouble.

"Comrades," said he, "I would not justify myself while that man was present, because I scorn the calumny of a slave of the emir, my personal enemy. I am here, alone and a prisoner, before you, and I will now endeavor, in a few words, to show you that I am innocent of the crimes imputed to me, as I hope to do hereafter with proofs in the face of the Mussulman world."

"Speak! speak!" cried the Turcomans.

"Yes," said he, "it is true: I have repeatedly seen the Princess of Khiva in secret."

He was interrupted by a confused sound of angry voices, which soon swelled into open tumult. With the president's aid, however, Safar succeeded in restoring order.

"But," he went on, "the Princess of Khiva is not,

nor will she ever be, the wife of Mozzafar. An embassy from her father, the Emir-Al-Oumra, is now on the way, and will be here three days hence to demand the surrender of his daughter. Has not the Prophet said that a father's will is sacred? The Emir-Al-Oumra gave her into my charge at the time of my last journey to Khiva, and his embassador will confirm my words," added the hadgi, addressing the president. "Had I not, then, the right to see her?"

"If your statement prove true, we will waive this head of the accusation," replied the president.

"Yes," continued Safar, "I have sent emissaries to the Russians. Do you know why? To convict Mozzafar of treason, for I am apprised that he is treating secretly with the government of Tashkend, and means to abandon the league. Oh, it was a deep-laid plot! Happily, you are not blind tyrants, and you are willing to be guided by the truth. In a few days, perhaps to-morrow, the embassador will be here; and my messengers too will, I hope, have accomplished their mission before the time appointed for the trial. It only remains for me now to touch upon the third and last head of the accusation—that of sacrilege. I deny having ever been guilty of that frightful crime, the most heinous of all, since it is alike offensive to both God and man. It were easy for me to refute this calumny; but the sirdar of the Turcomans, in the midst of his countrymen, cannot stoop to subterfuges. I shall walk with head erect, or my head will fall. Allah is almighty to decide!"

Silence reigned in the council-tent. One by one the Turcomans moved out, and each, as he passed by the sirdar, recited the following verse of the Koran :

"Allah alone is just, and the balance of his justice was forged by the angels' hands !"

XXI.

THE WEDDING.

Two months had brought about a complete change in the aspect of Samarcand. The city had been declared in a state of siege. Predatory bands of Kipchaks, Kirghiz, and Turcomans, remnants of the army destroyed on the Amu-Darya, infested the neighboring country, and were, at times, bold enough to approach the very gates of the capital. Repeated attempts to suppress them had proved fruitless ; the more so, as the marauders were under the protection of Mozzafar, whose possessions were contiguous to the Russian territory. It at length became apparent that one of two alternatives must be adopted—either to drive the emir from his capital, or make peace with him. The latter course was preferred, and the preliminaries of a peace were said to be under discussion at Tashkend.

A marked change was also noticeable in Tamerlane's Palace : no more routs nor *soirées* were given. The great arched gate was seldom opened ; and when, at rare intervals, the governor and his wife drove through the streets in their carriage, the officers of the garrison and the citizens were surprised at the emaciated countenance of the general and the pale features of the countess.

On the evening of the day on which the sirdar was impeached, however, Samarcand breathed an air of festivity and rejoicing. A motley and eager crowd was gathered around the approaches to the palace, and stood gazing in wonder at a wooden structure erected in front of the walls and surmounted by a cross. Though betraying signs of hasty construction, it had some pretensions to elegance of form. Along the way leading from the palace to this impromptu church (the first Christian sanctuary ever seen in Turkistan) was spread a narrow carpet bordered on either side by tastefully-arranged vases of flowers.

We must now beg the reader to follow us to the blue *salon*, whither he has so often accompanied us heretofore. Martha occupied her favorite seat, but so changed was her appearance that it was almost impossible to recognize her. Her haughty smile had given place to a nervous contraction of the lips; her hands were transparent, her eyeballs sunken in their sockets, and surrounded by a large, black circle. She was still beautiful, but the cast of her beauty was no longer the same. Before her stood Lise, in her bridal robe.

The church opposite the palace had been constructed at Bassalsky's expense; and the wedding was to take place that same evening, all the necessary documents having been received from St. Petersburg.

"Yes, Lise, my angel," said Martha, "it is true, I confess it. It was indeed I who drove you to this marriage; but I consider it to be my duty to ask you once more, though at the eleventh hour: have you seriously reflected?"

"Very seriously," replied Lise, laughing. "I know my future husband's defects, but they don't frighten me in the least."

"How courageous!"

"You are always chiding me for my coldness! You are right; I am of a cold, reserved disposition. Hitherto I have not known, and I hope I never shall know, what you call dash, enthusiasm, and passion. To these are due almost all the follies of youth, and sometimes evil actions also."

Martha lowered her eyes. Her wild nature had been tamed by continued grief. Lise went on:

"I am in the habit of weighing all my own acts; and this one, which is incontestably the most important of all, has had two months of thoughtful consideration. Had I observed any cloud threatening the future, I should not have hesitated one instant in breaking up the match. But, although I know Monsieur Bassalsky—and be assured I know him well—"

"Are you quite sure you know him?" interrupted Martha.

"Shall I describe his character to you?"

"Yes, do!" replied the countess.

"He is a frivolous, presumptuous coxcomb, and somewhat less in love with me than he has been, or still is, with you."

Martha made a gesture expressive of doubt.

"Yes, yes!" insisted Lise, with a laugh.

"Well, but—"

"His love, like all his other sentiments, is superficial. He marries me because he is charmed at the idea of being talked of throughout all the Russias. People will read in the newspapers: 'The first Christian marriage celebrated in Samarcand, on the southern confines of the empire, was that of Monsieur Bassalsky, a brave and distinguished officer.' That announcement will even be brought to the emperor's notice, and perhaps be mentioned in Paris. Here he will be the hero of the day! Under similar circumstances, he would have married his grandmother's first-cousin! How could you expect him to be otherwise than delighted at his union with a tolerably pretty woman, who is, after all, a very good match for him?"

"What, Lise!" exclaimed Martha. "You know all that, and yet you marry him?"

"Certainly. His defects are the guarantee of my happiness. People of a wavering disposition are easily influenced. He respects me already, and he will respect me still more when he knows me better; for I shall carry his name with dignity. I think he has some affection for me as it is, and by-and-by esteem will come, and our existence will be calm and tranquil, perhaps a little cold, but exempt from catastrophes. I am twenty-one years of age, and have never been in love with any person; I have chosen a man who will never domineer over me; and, as I have no desire to domineer over him, we shall be perfectly happy."

Each word from Lise's mouth was a sting in Martha's breast, and caused her to wince. But she was so downcast, and Lise had gained such an ascendency over her, that she merely sighed, and said:

"I had no idea you could reason so well."

"My fondness for travel, adventure, and change of scene, is no more decided than is my determination to lead a peaceful married life. In a word, I marry Monsieur Bassalsky precisely because I am persuaded that he is not passionately in love with me, and that he never could be with any one."

"How do you know?"

"He has proved it with such an adorable creature as you, *chère comtesse!*"

"Flatterer!" said Martha, kissing her. "So you are to become Madame Bassalsky this evening?"

"It is a *mariage de raison*, brought about by myself, instead of by my parents, as is usually the case. I am not the daughter of a *savant* for nothing!"

Martha reflected a moment.

"Yes, there may be some truth in what you say; but do you know your own mind as well as you might? Let me tell you, my dear girl, I was once like you, and thought I was studying my interest when I contracted a *mariage de raison*, which to me appeared quite in harmony with my disposition. Well, now, tell me, Lise, do you know of any woman more unhappy than I am?"

Lise looked at her with an astonished expression.

"Why, certainly! Yes, a great many, dear countess!"

Martha clutched her by the arm.

"You can't see? You don't observe anything?" said she, with clinched teeth. "Oh, and I had so often thought I read in your eyes that you understood all, and I loved you for it!"

"Dear friend! It was no secret to me that you

loved my cousin, and that you regretted his death. I pitied you from my heart; but I have too high a respect for you to believe that you ever swerved from the path of duty, and I hope that your grief will one day be soothed."

"Unfeeling creature! No, I have never forgotten my duty; but we had been engaged, and I broke my plighted faith to him in obedience to the voice of reason—or of pride! One day I perceived (alas! too late) that I had been the cause of my own unhappiness; and, on discovering the true nature of my feelings toward that man, I took alarm, and sent him to the sacrifice!"

"How you exaggerate!"

"How I exaggerate, say you? Perhaps you think that, placed as I am between the bleeding shade that haunts me night and day and the hideous reality from which I have no respite day or night, I do not suffer? I knew a kind, tender-hearted, and devoted man, who loved me spite of everything, even to death, and I abandoned him to destruction, to sell myself to a whining, pitiful, old idiot!"

"O countess!"

"Ah, did you but know the sort of existence I lead with that old fondler of a husband, who has blighted my youth, and how I loathe his doting affection! I sacrificed the one I loved, in order to satisfy my longing for pomp and ostentation! Oh, that man! I detest him! I hate him!"

The horrified Lise placed her hand on Martha's mouth.

"Do not give expression to such thoughts," she

exclaimed; "they are revolting to my cooler reason! Duty is before passion. If you do not love your husband, you ought, at least, to respect him as your friend! He, too, is kind and devoted!"

"That is precisely what I find fault with. My thirst for domination is now sated. I feel the need of a ruling spirit to govern me and hold me in check— such a one as he whose blood is upon my head! My husband can but repine, and kiss the hem of my robe. Now, do you imagine it is very agreeable to wipe one's slipper on an old doter's head? It is well enough for once; but just think of it for a whole lifetime!"

Appalled at the depths of that sombre and haughty spirit, and bereft of speech, Lise gazed at the countess.

"And yet I pity him!" went on Martha. "How often have I opened my lips to tell him that I loved Serge and detested him! But pity restrained me from uttering the cruel words. He loves me at heart, after all, and that love preys upon my life! Then I descend to falsehood. When he asks me the cause of my sufferings, which I can no longer conceal, I tell him I am sick, that the climate does not agree with me, and what not. And he offers to resign his post, and bury himself with me in Switzerland or Italy. To calm the nerves of a woman who despises him, he would sacrifice the very prospects that once excited my ambition!"

"You have lost your reason!" cried the terror-stricken Lise. "For pity's sake, no more!"

"Now and then his eye darts flashes of anger, and he fixes a threatening look upon me. An outbreak seems imminent; and I bridle up exultingly at the prospect of putting an end to my martyrdom. But, no! The very next moment he is on his knees before me, and I feel a burning tear upon my hand. He begs to be pardoned for his unkind thought, the coward; and I, like a coward, too, go on dissembling!"

"Dear friend, allow me to speak reason to you," said Lise, imploringly. "Listen to me. You know you have often told me that my words were comforting to you."

"I will listen to you, my angel," replied the countess. And she kissed Lise on the forehead. "But no one can heal the wound that is eating into my heart."

"I will try, at all events. Now, why this constant remorse? You sacrificed Serge to your ambition, as you say. Of that there is no certainty; yet, after all, three years have since elapsed, and you had no compunction of conscience two months ago. As to his death, I do not see why you should lay it at your own door. To be sure, you were the cause of it; but only indirectly. If a man who had had a house built were to feel remorse because a mason had been killed by falling from the scaffolding, you would consider that somewhat exaggerated, would you not?"

"Indirectly, did you say? Ah, I see; you were not aware of the circumstances. It was not his wish to go away; but I had recourse to unworthy stratagem to send him on the fatal expedition!"

"True; but it was your duty so to do. You loved him, and you wished to have him removed from where you were."

Martha seized Lise's head between her hands, and, holding it back—

"No!" she cried. "I destroyed him because I was jealous of you!"

"Of me?"

"Yes, of you! Do you comprehend *now?*"

Lise rose to her feet, and, with a commanding gesture, rendered the more impressive by the grave and solemn tone which accompanied it—

"Martha!" said she, "one crime cannot atone for another. Your conduct, then, toward your husband is all the more culpable; and your conscience will accuse you with the misfortune, not of one man, but of two!"

Overawed by the earnestness of Lise's tone, the countess sunk back on the lounge.

"But I cannot," said she, faintly.

"You must!" interrupted Mademoiselle Goreff. "That will be the expiation!"

At that moment the two women were startled by a loud peal of laughter from the adjoining room. The drapery was raised, and Molotoff entered. Close behind him was Bassalsky, whose fit of boisterous hilarity had not yet subsided.

"Those Tadjiks," cried he, at the top of his voice, "are gazing at our little church as if they thought its sudden appearance in the heart of their city was a sign of the end of the world!"

Such ill-timed mirth provoked Lise and increased Martha's sadness. Bassalsky paid no heed, but went on:

"The time is up!" said he to Lise. "I have come for you."

Molotoff always entered his wife's room with a

timid and embarrassed air. His eyes seemed to implore a smile, and search for it on the lips of his idol with that expression of timorous anxiety peculiar to amorous old men.

Melted to pity at his dejected and rueful countenance, Martha made an effort to smile, and putting out her hand, "Are you not going to kiss me to-day, Alexander?" said she.

Molotoff, equally oblivious of the decorum of the situation, and of Lise's and Bassalsky's presence, rushed across the room, kissed his wife with unbridled fury, kneeled and kissed her robe, and stood up again with joy beaming in his eyes.

"Come!" said he to the bride and bridegroom. "Now for the path of bliss!"

Then drawing Lise's arm through his, he whisked her off, saying to Bassalsky in a decidedly sportive tone: "*Monsieur l'aide-de-camp*, I am usurping your rights this evening!"

When the door had closed behind them, Martha buried her face in her handkerchief and burst into a fit of sobbing. "I cannot! no, I cannot!" she repeated over and over.

A numerous congregation was assembled in the church. The special mass usual on such occasions being ended, the pope [1] turned round from the altar, and, before proceeding to the nuptial ceremony, ran hurriedly over the question prescribed as an indispensable formality: "Does any person oppose the union of Captain Bassalsky with Mademoiselle Goreff?"

[1] Priest of the Greek Church.

"I oppose it!" cried a voice that came ringing from the door of the sanctuary.

In an instant all eyes were turned in the direction of the entrance, and the amazed assembly beheld a mendicant dervish advancing toward the altar.

"I oppose this marriage!" he repeated.

"Who is that madman?" cried Bassalsky. "Out with him!"

But the dervish put his hand upon the officer's shoulder, saying: "Captain Bassalsky does not recognize his old friend?—nor you either, comrades? Have the sufferings and hardships of captivity so changed my countenance?"

"Relieff! Alive!" exclaimed Molotoff. And the general clasped him in his arms.

XXII.

THE SPY.

THE sentiment which elicited Molotoff's cordial welcome to his former aide-de-camp was the soul-felt satisfaction afforded him by the major's opposition to the marriage. For a long time past, the suspicions that preyed on the governor's mind had been diverted from Bassalsky to Relieff; yet the resistance now offered to Lise's union with the officer was by Molotoff imagined to be conclusive evidence that Relieff was himself enamored with his cousin. The uxorious general would never have dared to appeal to his wife to clear up the doubt; but he had arrived at the conviction that she was profoundly affected at Relieff's sad fate. Was this love, or simply a nervous woman's whim?—he could not tell; but he felt how hopeless and fruitless it would be to contend with a dead man's shade. Keen, indeed, were his sufferings; but his kind and loving heart told him he had no right to upbraid his wife with this passion from the invisible world.

Now, however, matters had assumed a different aspect. Molotoff had to sustain the struggle against a living man who loved another woman than his own wife. With what he knew of his wife's disposition, he hoped that the circumstance just referred to would wound her pride, and give place to the return of better days for him.

Like all amorous old men, the governor was extremely selfish in regard to matters concerning his love; so, quite oblivious of the awkward situation of Lise and Bassalsky, whose wedding had been so abruptly deferred, and heedless of the general bewilderment of all present, he set to embracing Relieff lustily and repeatedly, and then invited him to the palace, to change his costume and recite the story of his adventures.

We have said elsewhere that the governors of the several military districts of Turkistan enjoy all the attributes of sovereignty. Again, the home government has adopted the wise policy of enjoining on those functionaries such display of representative pomp and pageant as may be calculated to inspire the natives with awe; while the strictest respect for the individual interests of the conquered peoples is enforced by the colonial laws.

Neither Lise nor Bassalsky dared to interfere with Molotoff's effusive demonstrations; but Relieff, feeling that the scene was prolonged beyond the limits of decorum, respectfully disengaged himself from the general's embrace, and said to Mademoiselle Goreff:

"As soon as I have reported to his excellency, I shall be with you, my dear cousin, and we shall have a long talk. So, pray await me.—As for you, sir," he added, addressing Bassalsky, "I shall be ready to-morrow to give you any explanations you may choose to demand."

"Very well, sir. I shall expect you to-morrow."

Goreff seemed to recollect all at once that he was the bride's father.

"And when—?" he began stammeringly.

"You shall hear all, this evening, Yegor Alexandrovitch."

The old *savant* attempted a gesture of contentment, and muttered:

"Oh, indeed!"

This was as much as to say, "Inasmuch as my daughter's marriage exercises no manner of influence on the Turanian and Iranian races, it is little short of a matter of indifference to me."

Relieff next addressed the audience:

"Although at first sight my authority to do so might be questioned, I oppose this union, for weighty reasons, which I shall make known to the proper persons. Should those reasons, however, prove insufficient, the ceremony will but have been postponed for a few days. Excuse me, then, gentlemen—and you, father—and be assured that I have acted in accordance with a profound sense of duty and of right."

Molotoff's approval of Relieff's conduct was tacitly conveyed by his manner of welcoming the latter; and the bride's father also appeared to assent to the intervention; so the pope saluted, and the assembly began to disperse amid a general outpouring of excursive comments upon the great and unexpected event of the evening.

Meantime, the general had withdrawn to his apartments arm-in-arm with the major. Taking a servant aside, he instructed him to go to Relieff's quarters—where everything was still under seal—for one of his uniforms, which he had left behind on setting out with the expedition, and replace the major's epaulets on the tunic with a pair of lieutenant-colonel's, which he was to purchase in the city.—In every Russian town, and every town conquered by the Russians, the complete insignia of the various ranks are at all times to be found on sale.

When they reached the general's dressing-room, the latter insisted upon it that Relieff should then and there proceed to his toilet and ablutions; and, as soon as he saw his guest comfortably installed in the bath, he sat down by his side and requested him to begin his recital.

Relieff submitted with a good grace; and while he related his hardships and sufferings, Molotoff more than once felt his eyes moistened with tears.

The major, mindful of his promise to Safar-Hadgi, drew on his imagination for a story to explain his deliverance.

"In consideration of a suitable bribe," said he, "one of my guardians furnished me with a complete dervish's outfit, and in that disguise I was enabled to cross the desert, and arrive here without the occurrence of any disagreeable incident. Heaven protected me, for I did not meet a single human being the whole way. I reached Samarcand this evening, and, supposing that you thought I was dead, I directed my steps toward the palace; but the crowd at the entrance was so dense that I found it impossible to pass through it. Indeed, before long, I found myself carried to the door of the church. On looking in, I saw you, and advanced. . . . Your excellency knows the rest."

"I was so rejoiced to see you once more, my dear fellow," said Molotoff, "that I had forgotten until this moment to inquire what were your reasons for opposing the marriage."

"If you will allow me, general, I will not tell you that; it is not my secret."

"Oh, just as you please! Only, as you are probably unaware that Monsieur Bassalsky is my aide-de-camp, if you have any serious charge to prefer against him—"

"No, general. Considerations of a personal character, purely personal," interrupted Relieff, with much animation. "Besides, my cousin may not admit them."

"Keep your secrets, my dear fellow! keep them!" broke in Molotoff, merrily rubbing his hands.

Relieff now came out of the bath and donned his novel uniform. Observing Molotoff's sly glances, he viewed himself in a mirror and smiled.

"Some lieutenant-colonel has been good enough to lend me his uniform," said he.

"Not at all; you're mistaken. It is your own uniform. I had it brought from your old quarters."

"Well, then, some one must have changed it during my absence, for I am not a lieutenant-colonel yet, that I'm aware."

"You think not, eh?"

The amazed Relieff stared at the governor, who took a childlike delight in the success of his surprise, and embraced the new colonel, congratulating him at the same time on his promotion.

On this the steward came to announce that the collation ordered beforehand by his master awaited him. Relieff was melted to tears at the extreme delicacy of attention with which the minutest details tending to minister to his comfort and satisfaction had been anticipated by the general.

When the collation was ended Molotoff arose, and with a somewhat tremulous voice said: "Now let's go and see my wife. She must have heard of your return, and be anxiously awaiting your visit. She had like to have died when she heard you had been killed, and she remained inconsolable from that time forward."

Usually when Relieff heard Molotoff mention his wife's name an involuntary shudder passed over him; but this time he was prepared for the allusion, and so was enabled to reply composedly:

"I have given my promise to Lise and her father to call on them. To-morrow I will present my respects to the countess. Pray, excuse me for to-day."

"As you please, my dear fellow," said Molotoff, inwardly rejoicing at Relieff's apparent indifference.

Though only seven o'clock, night was already fallen when Relieff took leave of his cousin, and, with a light heart, shaped his way toward one of the city gates. Spite of his weariness and the varied emotions he had passed through, and notwithstanding his present happiness, the new colonel was not forgetful of his engagements with the sirdar. On reaching the fortifications he was astonished to find the gates shut, being unapprised of the state of siege. He called to a soldier on guard and made himself known as a superior officer; but, not being in possession of the password, he was not allowed to go out. In a state of despair he renewed the attempt at all the other gates, but met a positive refusal at all of them, and officers and men were no little amazed at his request.

Relieff returned to his old quarters, where everything was prepared to receive him.

The colonel enjoyed still another moment's delight at finding himself once more in his own place, after so many adventures. He seated himself at his desk, and began to write, as he had done at the opening of the present history—to Russia; but, by the time he had traced a few lines, Nature resumed her sway, and, overcome by fatigue, he laid down the pen, and flung himself on his bed.

On hearing of Relieff's return, Martha's first sentiment was one of genuine pleasure; but by-and-by, when she had had time to reflect, the feeling of joy gave place to one of jealousy and distrust. Indeed, she had the same thought as her husband, namely, that Relieff's opposition to the marriage was an evidence that he loved his cousin; and, consequently, that she—the countess—had been deluding herself with false hopes.

Then came an interval of suspense. She knew that her former *fiancé* had arrived, and she was in hourly expectation of hearing his name announced at her apartments. The evening passed, however, and he did not come. About ten o'clock, the general entered his wife's boudoir; and, thanks to her present resentful mood toward the colonel, he met with a cordial reception. They talked long. Molotoff apprised her that Relieff would pay her a visit the following day; and at length the countess dismissed him in the most gracious manner possible.

That night was a wakeful one for Martha. Anger and jealousy distracted her troubled thoughts; and, then, the recollection of the few hours—the first in two months—spent in intimacy with her husband inspired her with a feeling of disgust. Nor was it before a late hour in the morning that she succeeded in closing her eyes in a heavy slumber, disturbed with painful dreams.

About nine o'clock the same morning, Lise called to see her; but the maid gently drew aside the drapery of the chamber-door, and, observing her mistress to be still sleeping, would not dare to awake her, nor did the young lady choose to be urgent. It was eleven when Martha awoke, with a heavy head and agitated nerves; and Relieff was not announced until after breakfast.

Before she went to receive him, Martha glanced at her mirror, and found herself to be ugly, older-looking, and jaded. That woman, whom we have seen despising Relieff, had now become distractedly in love with him. So, determined not to be seen by him to less advantage than heretofore, she called her maid, powdered her face, applied the slightest touch of *rouge* to her cheeks, and adjusted the folds of her robe. The whole operation consumed but a few brief minutes; yet, when she opened the *salon* door, Molotoff had just entered, and was already chatting with the colonel.

Martha was now no longer that self-commanding woman so skillful in concealing her emotion. At sight of Relieff, she grew pale; and her disappointment at finding him accompanied by her husband was betrayed by a gesture which she was unable to restrain. The former *fiancés* exchanged a glance of love mingled with regret; and the conversation became general, but devoid of animation, almost cold.

Molotoff's cordial warmth of manner was chilled by Martha's presence: Relieff felt ill at ease between the old man who had received him so kindly, and the woman he adored; and the countess, in a faltering voice, wavered betwixt the timid and the aggressive. Indeed, her patience was all but exhausted; she burned for an interview with the colonel alone; and the governor gave no signs of an immediate withdrawal.

The frigid and ceremonious visit lasted two hours, during all which time Relieff had avoided catching Martha's eyes, for he could feel the general's riveted upon him. He had observed the countess shudder while he was relating the story of his adventures; and while that circumstance filled his soul with delight, it strengthened him in his resolution not to give way to the emotion due to a first meeting. From the very commencement of the interview he had apprehended that something—he knew not precisely what—was taking place between the governor and Martha; and for no consideration in the world would that loyal and upright heart willingly give pain to the woman he adored, or to the man whom he had ultimately learned to love and esteem.

Meantime, Relieff's mind was made up to quit Samarcand, and he earnestly desired to have a last interview with the countess—an interview of friendship—for the purpose of determining the nature of their relations for the future; for the colonel had resolved that he should never more set eyes on Molotoff's wife. It would be unseemly to prolong his present visit. So Relieff arose.

"I take my departure in three days from to-day, madame," said he, as he tremulously raised her hand to his lips; "but I trust I shall have the honor of seeing you once more before I set out."

"Monsieur Relieff forgets that he used to have his home here. Had he continued to be our friend, he would have remembered that circumstance and spent those three days with us, since his rank prevents his being my husband's aide-de-camp any longer.—Is it not so, Alexander?"

"Certainly," replied Molotoff.

Relieff thought he detected a shade of constraint in the general's tone.

"Unfortunately, madame," he returned, "I have some business to settle here, for I am going first to Tashkend, and I wish then to quit Turkistan altogether. So I shall have very few opportunities, but these I will improve to come and remind you of your kind offer."

"You have some business here?"

"I should think you must have heard of it since yesterday?"

"Oh!" said Martha, "your opposition to Lise's marriage! What instigated it?"

"It would take too much time to explain it, madame; but Lise, who is your friend," said Relieff, laying stress on the word friend, "will tell you all. I am of opinion the affair will be satisfactorily arranged."

The embarrassment which accompanied this speech did not escape the countess's notice. Jealousy, for the second time, stung her to the core.

"Stay to dinner with us to-day," said she, entreatingly.

"Impossible! It just happens that this evening I shall have a great deal to do."

"Were I to beg of you, would you not sacrifice your business to me?" asked Martha, with a fascinating look. "You rather owe me an apology for not having come to see me yesterday. Now, then, I pray you, stay!"

The last words constituted at once a request, a command, and a threat. Relieff would fain have yielded, but probably he just then thought of Safar-Hadgi. He repressed a sigh of regret.

"Impossible!" he repeated.

Martha knit her brow.

"Ah!" she exclaimed.

And, turning to her husband—

"What affairs of moment can a person have in Samarcand?" she inquired.

Molotoff was delighted to have an opportunity of piquing his wife, and hinting at what he fancied to be Relieff's passion for Lise.

"How indiscreet of you, my dear!" said he. "Love-affairs, perhaps."

Relieff, provoked at the insinuation, was on the point of protesting; but Molotoff, as if aware of his intention, forestalled him.

"For that matter," he went on, "very shortly none of us will have anything else to do here. A dispatch from Tashkend this morning informs me that the peace-treaty with Mozzafar has been signed."

"Ah!" exclaimed Relieff, with an air of evident interest; "the treaty has been signed?"

"Yes, with the Emir of Bokhara, who binds himself to abandon the league and notify his auxiliaries to quit the khanate. Should they hesitate in complying with the injunction, he is to cut off their retreat, and act conjointly with us. We hope to be able to raise the state of siege in the course of a week. The day after to-morrow an expedition sets out; and, this time, when we have dispersed the nomads, they will be powerless to reorganize again."

"Is this matter a secret?" inquired Relieff. "Is any one here aware of it?"

"I have just received the news myself; but it is by no means a secret. It will be placarded up about the town to-morrow."

"So, then, I am at liberty to refer to it?"

"Most decidedly so!"

"You are not apprehensive of its becoming known to the enemy?"

"Not the least. If they hear of it, so much the better; perhaps it may induce them to disperse of their own accord."

"Then you authorize me to speak of it?"

"To any one you see fit," replied Molotoff.

"So you refuse?" said Martha, returning to the charge, in her fondest tone of entreaty.

"Alas! madame, I cannot do otherwise."

When alone, Martha bit her lips till the blood came. Galled by Relieff's refusal, stung with jealousy, and humiliated and enraged at the thought of having been deceived by Lise, all her evil passions were kindled anew, and agitated her brain to the verge of distraction. She felt the necessity of going out and taking the air, to dispel the fever which devoured her, and revive her drooping energies; so she ordered her carriage to be brought. After waiting ten minutes— and we know she was not of a patient disposition —she reprimanded her coachman sharply for his tardiness.

"Countess," replied the man, "it was not my fault; Colonel Relieff has just left the stable; he made me saddle Mademoiselle Goreff's horse, as she was going out—"

"Enough!" interrupted Martha. "That will do!" And she threw herself back in the carriage.

The only frequented drive outside the walls of Samarcand at that juncture was the poplar avenue stretching away from the north gate. Indeed, the length of the avenue, and the width of the open space between the ditches and the gardens, rendered the place a most unfavorable one for a *coup de main*. But at all the other gates the inhabitants were afraid to venture abroad, owing to the nomad hordes infesting the surrounding country.

Martha took several turns up and down the avenue while occupied with her sombre reflections.

"He loves her!" thought she. "And that girl has had the audacity to deceive me so shamefully. It is really odious. She will now spend the whole of her days with him; and who knows but that she may even accompany him when he goes away? Oh! but that is impossible; I will never submit to it!"

The habit of domination had so biased the sense of right and wrong in that woman's mind that she sincerely believed she had a claim on Relieff's heart.

"No!" she vowed, inwardly; "that shall never be!"

At that moment the carriage had made the final turn and was advancing toward the drawbridge on the way to the palace. All at once the countess shuddered. She had just observed Relieff beneath the arched gateway riding in the opposite direction to her; consequently they would meet. They did meet, and pass each other. Relieff bent in a low bow; but Martha turned away her head, which surprised the colonel not a little. He repeatedly turned round in the saddle to look after the carriage, until at length it disappeared within the gates, after which he continued on his way at a walk.

Meanwhile Martha, after a lapse of ten minutes or so, ordered the driver to turn about.

"What can he be doing beyond the ramparts at this time of day?" pondered Martha. "I shall soon know."

Before long she caught sight of horse and rider.

As before observed, the deep, soft sand of the avenue deadened the sound of horses' feet or carriage-wheels passing over it; hence Martha was enabled to follow Relieff without attracting his attention. After having ridden a certain distance he reined his horse into a path running parallel to the avenue; which seeing, the countess alighted and entered a garden adjoining the same path. Heedless of the thorns, which tore her dress and lacerated her hands, and oblivious of the danger of wandering so far from the ramparts, Martha cleared her way through the brushwood and followed Relieff step by step.

In this manner she arrived at Timour's Round-Point, where Relieff dismounted, fastened his horse to a tree, and, having chosen out a secluded spot, lay down upon the grass, as if expecting to be joined by some one.

The coachman's words then came back to her mind.

"He is expecting her!" was her first thought. And she boiled with rage. Returning to the carriage, she cried, "To the palace at full speed!" No sooner had she reached home than she sent to inform Monsieur Bassalsky that she desired to see him instantly.

XXIII.

THE ARREST.

"Do you know what is now in the wind, Monsieur Bassalsky?" asked Martha, when the officer entered.

"No, madame; I only know that, unless I have a fair explanation, I shall be forced to tender my resignation, and demand, not only of Monsieur Relieff, but of his excellency, an explanation of what occurred yesterday. I have awaited the colonel in vain the whole day. When I received your message I supposed I should have the honor of meeting him here."

"Well, sir, the colonel will probably run away with your betrothed this evening, and leave you in a ridiculous plight."

"Impossible, madame!"

"Ah! Impossible, is it? Then just go out to Timour's Round-Point."

Bassalsky sprang to his feet.

"Oh! I shall have my revenge! I shall pursue that man and challenge him—such an insult to me!"

"Your position will be none the less ridiculous; for a single word from him was sufficient to put off your marriage, and it will be some time before you can hand in your resignation. As matters now stand he may, by virtue of his rank as lieutenant-colonel, refuse to grant you satisfaction. Ah! he has made a pretty fool of you! Then he has kept you waiting the whole day! Ho! ho!"

"Yes! And Lise, too; she told me to be calm and wait."

"Ha! ha! ha! They are together now at Timour's Round-Point."

Bassalsky ground his teeth with rage, due rather to the thought of his ridiculous position than to his grief at the loss of Lise.

"Ah! at the Round-Point!" he exclaimed; "very well, I shall shortly be there, too! Not alone, either! I am the governor's aide-de-camp, and I can send a patrol in that direction. Ah! I am ridiculous, am I? Oh, we shall see about that! Adieu, madame; you shall hear of me before long!"

"Pray, be calm, Monsieur Bassalsky."

"I am calm, but I will certainly not submit to such outrages tamely. Adieu, madame!"

Bassalsky rushed out and flew in the direction of the gate nearest to the Round-Point. He sent a soldier to announce him to Major Bagroff, the commandant of that post, an officer known in Samarcand as a strict disciplinarian. The young man was somewhat dismayed when he saw Bagroff advancing, for he did not expect to find him on duty; and he knew it would be useless to explain the nature of his errand, for the major would never consent to interfere in such a matter without an order from the governor.

All at once a diabolical idea suggested itself to his mind.

"Major," said he, "we have positive information that messengers from the enemy are to communicate this evening with some of the inhabitants of Samarcand, with whom they are in league. Unfortunately, the traitors' names are unknown to us. The place of meeting is to be Timour's Round-Point. If you will order out a patrol I will accompany you, and I expect we shall surprise them in their hiding-place."

The major made no objection to Bassalsky's proposal, and both officers, followed by the patrol, soon shaped their way to the Round-Point.

The thickly-planted gardens of the Tadjiks, which surround Samarcand like a verdant zone, seemed to add to the obscurity of the night. The soldiers marched along cautiously, cutting their way through the brushwood. The major, who was quite given up to the object of his mission, glanced inquiringly all around, while Bassalsky was engaged in reflecting upon the best course to pursue.

They approached the Round-Point. Major Bagroff, who was all attention listening to catch the slightest sound, distinctly heard the murmur of two voices coming from the open space.

"Silence! we hear them!" he whispered to the aide-de-camp.

He beckoned to the soldiers to halt, and, advancing to a tree, he placed himself so as to be hidden by the trunk, and then made a sign to Bassalsky to join him.

The major distinctly heard a conversation, held in Uzbeck, and was all ears to distinguish each sound, for he understood the language perfectly.

Sooner or later every Russian veteran in Turkistan becomes familiar with the various dialects of the natives.

"I believe you, Hahib," said one of the voices; "but forget not my instructions. Inform him that peace has been concluded, and hand him this letter, this purse, and this medallion. Thank him for me, and tell him I shall be his friend forever."

"Will you pardon me for your captivity, and the harsh treatment you have received at my hands?"

"With all my heart, Hahib. But go; time is flying. Where is your horse?"

"I left it far from here, for, having perceived an Ooroos patrol, I was fearful of being observed."

Bagroff made a sign to the soldiers, and glanced at Bassalsky as if to ask his advice; but the aide-de-camp, who had recognized Relieff's voice, paid no heed to the major's look of inquiry; he had become sensible of the infamy of his conduct, and was pale and bereft of speech.

"Adieu, Hahib," said Relieff once more.

"Adieu," said the other, "and may Allah protect you!"

"Forward! Arrest those rascals!" cried Bagroff, suddenly.

In an instant the open space was filled with Russian soldiers. Hahib cast a look of unspeakable scorn upon Relieff.

"Traitor!" said he.

After the first moment of surprise had passed, Relieff, with a commanding gesture, pointed to a tree.

"Take my horse and fly!" said he.

And he folded his arms. With the rapidity of lightning, Hahib sprang into the saddle, severed the bridle with his poniard, and disappeared in the obscurity.

"Fire!" commanded Bagroff.

A few gunshots reverberated across the plain; but the darkness of the night and the dense brushwood in the gardens favored Hahib's escape.

Meantime the soldiers had surrounded Relieff, and Bagroff, placing his hand on his shoulder, said:

"You are my prisoner, sir!"

Bassalsky came forward.

"We have been mistaken, major," said he. "This is Colonel Relieff, one of our most esteemed superior officers."

"I know the colonel perfectly well," replied Bagroff; "but I have surprised him, by night and outside the gates, conversing with a native whom he afterward aided to escape, being thus guilty of a triple transgression of the martial law while the city is in a state of siege; and, although I am convinced that the gentleman will give a satisfactory explanation, it is my duty to arrest him."

Relieff came to Bagroff's aid.

"The major is right, Monsieur Bassalsky, and I am amenable to a court-martial."

Then, with a bitter smile, he pursued:

"I presume Lise has informed you (for when I left her she was on her way to you) that I am no longer opposed to your marriage. I presume you are aware why I resisted it at first. I am happy to acknowledge my error." And, turning to Bagroff, he added:

"I await your orders, major."

Bassalsky was piteous to behold as he stood pallid and tremulous, and his face bathed in perspiration. He approached Relieff, and whispered in his ear:

"Speak! explain the cause of your presence here.

I cannot allow you to be arrested thus; I should be dishonored forever!"

"Pshaw! How can that affect you?"

"But, after all, what were you doing here?" insisted Bassalsky.

"Ah! that, my dear fellow," said Relieff, laughing, "I will not tell you. I admit your right to arrest me, but not to question me."

Bassalsky, in the greatest despair, advanced toward Bagroff.

"Come, major, for Heaven's sake, no useless severity. The colonel only returned yesterday, and was unaware of the regulations. Let him go."

Bagroff shook his head.

"It will be very easy for the colonel to give a satisfactory explanation. As for me, I am utterly powerless in the matter. I deeply regret that my duty obliges me to arrest him, and make my report, and have a search made at his quarters."

"But you don't understand me. I have been mistaken: I was led to suppose that my *fiancée* had a rendezvous here with somebody, and—"

Bagroff turned away.

"So much the worse for you," said he.

"Oh!" exclaimed Bassalsky, "I will save you. I'll fly to the palace and back. *She* is the cause of all this, and she must repair the evil she has done."

Bassalsky was in the act of starting.

"Pardon me, sir," said Bagroff, "your signature will be necessary to my report, and I summon you to stay for that purpose."

"Well; but, major—"

"His majesty's service!"

"Ah! This is too much! You have no idea of the horrors of my situation. I will sign nothing at all, and—"

"Monsieur, you will place me under the necessity of reporting you!"

"Oh! Merciful Heavens!" exclaimed the young man.

"It won't take long," replied Bagroff, somewhat melted, and perhaps more deeply, too, than he would have it appear.

Advancing toward Relieff, he said, "It becomes my painful duty, colonel, to ask you for your sword."

"Here it is!" replied Relieff; "you are fulfilling your duty. I bear you no spite for it."

Then, after having delivered up his sword—

"Forward, major!" he said; "I shall follow you."

In less than an hour after Bassalsky's departure, Mademoiselle Goreff was announced to the countess.

"Impossible!" cried Martha; "you mistake!"

"Pardon me, madame; the young lady awaits you in the *salon*," replied the servant who had announced her.

"Ask her to come in! Let her come in immediately!" said Martha. Then soliloquizing: "Lise here! What can this mean?—So it *is* you!" she exclaimed to Lise, who had just entered.

"Dear me! You seem astonished," said Lise.

"So you are not at the Round-Point!"

Lise burst into laughter.

"At the Round-Point at this time of night! Why, countess, what can you be thinking of?"

"Good Heavens!" exclaimed Martha, in a fever of anxiety. "Can I have been mistaken?"

Lise was still laughing.

"You appear quite agitated, *chère comtesse*," said she. "How curious! For the last two hours I have been riding about the city in search of some one to impart the good news to, and I have met with nothing but disappointment. I have just now come from my *fiancé's* quarters, where I was informed that he was here. I hasted to the palace, and I not only don't find him, but I find you thunderstruck at my presence! What does all this mean?"

"You have been at Monsieur Bassalsky's?"

"Yes!"

"All alone?"

"Certainly! There can be nothing wrong in that, since we are to be married in a few days. Serge has given his consent, and, regarding myself as the bearer of good tidings, I ordered a horse to be saddled in all haste, and, encouraged by my cousin, who was detained, as he said, by some important business, I galloped to Monsieur Bassalsky's, and behold! the gentleman was not there!"

"Ah!" stammered Martha, all but speechless.

"Yes! But what were you thinking of? What was that you were saying about the Round-Point?"

"Nothing!—Ah! Monsieur Relieff consents to the marriage? Why, pray, did he oppose it at first?"

"That is what I have still to tell you! That concerns you exclusively. Will you allow me to speak in all frankness?"

"Oh, speak! Speak quickly," implored Martha.

"Well! Because— How shall I explain it to you? He was under the impression that my future husband was engaged in a deep intrigue with you, and that you were sacrificing me to appearances! He also informed me of Monsieur Bassalsky's passion for you—which was no secret to me!—and many other things! Then I made my profession of faith to him, and he replied: 'You are the wise woman of the family: do as you see fit.'"

"So he does not love you?"

"Me! Come! come! My dear friend, are you in jest? Why, you know he loves you, and—did I do right?—I told him you loved him too."

"O Lise! dear girl!" exclaimed Martha, sobbing; "how unhappy, indeed, am I!"

"'I am going away,' said Relieff to me, 'quitting Samarcand forever, and I shall probably never see her more; but what you have just said, Lise, soothes my sorrows and wipes away all my tears. I have never ceased to love her; and I was so much afraid of being unable to continue to respect her! I shall see her once more—one last time! Tell her that I wish to cast myself at her feet, and kiss the ground she treads upon; and to thank her for the supreme consolation which she grants me as a solace for my future forlorn condition. *You* may tell her all this. *Do* tell her! *I* respect her too much to express my love to her otherwise than by bowing my knee before her. Tell her, Lise, that I shall go away—that I shall no longer be a burden to her life—but let her know that there exists a man who, at a nod from her, will sacrifice his life, his soul, his very honor! Yes, dear girl, your last words cause me to forget my hardships, my sufferings, and even the grief of seeing her belong to another. She loves me! Duty commanded me to stifle my passion, to drown it in the depths of my heart; and she may, for a while, have thought that I had ceased to adore her! Oh, tell her that never has her image left my heart! She married another, and I experience an immense satisfaction at having sacrificed my happiness to hers. Tell her that she did well, if she is but happy!'"

"Enough!—enough!" interrupted Martha, in a faltering voice. "Do you not see that my life is leaving me?"

"Oh!—true! How pale you are! How you tremble! Good Heavens! countess, what is the matter?"

"The matter is my infamy and my wretchedness!" said Martha, clutching her by the arm. "Do you know what jealousy is, and what it leads to? I have been jealous of you to-day."

"Again?"

"Do you know what I did?"

She was interrupted by a noise from the adjoining room. Bassalsky, livid, breathless, and his hair standing on end, rushed into the *salon*.

"Madame!" cried the officer, addressing the countess, "I hold you accountable for my honor, which I have forfeited by your fault!"

"For Heaven's sake, what is it now?" inquired Lise.

"What is it? She has made me a denunciator and a spy! I have just been the cause of the arrest of Colonel Relieff at Timour's Round-Point. He is accused of holding secret communication with the enemy, and transgression of the martial law. He is in prison; a search is being made in his quarters; and he will be tried by court-martial!"

"O countess!" exclaimed Lise, who now saw clearly into the mystery. And she cast an upbraiding glance at Martha, who shrunk and cowered under its burning significance.

"I have come, madame," went on Bassalsky, "to demand reparation. I am frivolous and inconsistent; but I have never played the spy or the coward. And yet I shall now be supposed to have acted as both."

Martha was still insensible and bereft of speech.

"Be explicit," said Lise to Bassalsky. "What steps is the countess to take? Is there anything she can do?"

"Is there anything she can do? She can have her husband issue an order countermanding the arrest; otherwise I am dishonored."

"But—" remonstrated the young lady.

"*Buts* are out of the question. If the countess will not repair the injury of which she is the cause and I the instrument, I shall insist upon an explanation of the circumstances from the general himself to my comrades. Should the general refuse, then I know what alternative remains."

Martha had risen from her seat as he spoke, and her countenance bore an expression of sombre and determined resolution.

"I have been faulty toward you," said she, bending her haughty head; "but menaces are needless to coerce me to fulfill my duty." She rang, and a servant appeared at the door. "Request his excellency to come here without delay," said she.

Bassalsky in the mean time recounted to Lise the various circumstances attending Relieff's arrest; and Martha, to whom he affected not to address his conversation, listened with eager attention. When Molotoff entered, without giving him time to utter a word, she cried:

"Dear Alexander, for mercy's sake, save Colonel Relieff!"

When the governor was apprised of the particulars of the case, he shook his head with an air of dissatisfaction, feeling pretty certain that concern for Lise was not the only motive his wife had for interfering.

Nevertheless, he replied:

"It is a matter of no great consequence; the state of siege is about to be raised. The colonel has but recently returned from captivity, and can, at all events, allege his ignorance of the laws at present in force. An explanation will follow, and all will be set right." Then, addressing his wife—"You are quite pale, Martha," said he. "I see no occasion for it. Relieff is in no danger, I promise you."

"My general," remarked Bassalsky, "Major Bagroff has sent in his report, and given orders to have a search made in the colonel's quarters."

"Very well! and pray what is there in that to alarm you? The colonel is one of the best and most honorable officers in the service, and a search cannot be dangerous under such circumstances. Besides, I will answer for his safety with my own; so be at ease in your mind."

"Oh, thanks, dear, good Alexander!" exclaimed Martha, flinging her arms round her husband's neck, who now, perhaps for the first time, received her embraces coldly, though in sooth he was little accustomed to them.

"He will be tried by court-martial," said the general, "for the law must be abided by; but, as I said before, he has nothing to fear. This I will guarantee, for I am convinced of his innocence."

XXIV.

THE TRIAL.

THE day appointed for Safar-Hadgi's trial had come. From an early hour in the morning a dense crowd had been gathering round all the approaches to the emir's palace, for the trial was to take place in public. The large court-yard was hung with scarlet and yellow damask, and partially shaded with a white *velum* or awning. At the lower end, upon a carpeted estrade reached by ten steps, there stood, close to the wall, a sofa of scarlet velvet embellished with golden tassels, and near it lay a number of cushions heaped upon the floor.

Facing the sofa, which was to serve as a throne, a scaffold had been erected sufficiently high to command the square without; and upon the scaffold a man in black, with an unsheathed cimiter in his hand, stood gazing with indifference on the motley throng.

A regiment of sarbazes was arranged in double row around the wall inside; while the battlements and embrasures and a palisaded space in one corner of the yard were literally crammed with restless and noisy spectators. In another corner there was a wood cabin with grated windows, and four sarbazes were posted near the door to keep off the crowd.

At ten o'clock a cannon was fired; the sarbazes cleared the entrance, and one-and-twenty mollahs passed in and took seats on the cushions at the foot of the throne. The mollahs were followed by one-and-twenty begs, or chief citizens of Bokhara, with turbans of white and gold, and attired in long robes of scarlet silk bordered with fur.

The cannon was again fired, and the palace-door was thrown wide open. All present now prostrated themselves with their faces to the earth, for the emir was about to make his appearance.

When the heads were raised again the emir was already sitting, or rather reclining, on the sofa. Mozzafar was magnificently arrayed in a robe sparkling with costly gems. Supporting himself with one hand resting on the cushions, he leaned forward, and with the other took a golden sceptre presented by a servant kneeling.

At a signal from his master, Mirza-Mohammed issued from a group of functionaries in front of the throne, and advanced to the centre of the yard. Facing the emir, he prostrated himself and kissed the ground, and then arose and crossed his hands upon his breast.

Mohammed's countenance was radiant with joy and contentment: all his plans had proved successful. The reis, whose credulity he had imposed upon, had yielded to the emir's persuasions to abandon Safar-Hadgi to his fate. He had also consented not to attend the trial, thanks to the contrivance of the wily Persian, who had represented to him how unbecoming it would be for the chief of the ulemas to be present at the execution of a man to whom he had on a former occasion publicly extended his protection, and who had afterward abused his confidence in such an unworthy manner.

Mohammed knew that the sirdar's expected messengers had not yet arrived, and that, consequently, Safar-Hadgi was not in possession of the seal of the Shereef of Mecca. This last circumstance was alone sufficient to seal his doom, were he even to succeed in clearing himself of the accusations preferred against him. Yet Mohammed was shrewd, and the net in which he had managed to entangle his enemy was so cunningly devised that he did not believe in the possibility of the victim's escape. The erection of the scaffold had been suggested by Mohammed in the exuberance of his barbarous exultation, and cordially sanctioned by the emir.

At the last moment, however, an unforeseen event occurred, which might have caused the plans to miscarry. The embassy from Khiva, to demand the surrender of Eminch, reached Bokhara the very same day. But the Persian had been on the outlook, and, having been the first to learn of their arrival, he hastened to meet the embassadors outside the gates of the city, and, by dint of prepossessing attentions and enticing arguments, induced them to defer their visit to the palace until the third day.

On taking leave of them, the crafty chief of police, affecting an air of deep concern, had the caution to hint to the embassadors, with a view to shield his own and his master's responsibility, that the public attention was taken up with matters of grave importance.

"It will be better, seigniors," said he, "not to see my master until after the disposal of this sad affair, the precise nature of which I refrain from mentioning, for fear of causing you pain. The trial comes off to-day."

Fatigued by their journey, the embassadors, for the most part men of years, and little interested in the affairs of the Emir of Bokhara, readily consented to the proposed delay.

Meantime, Safar-Hadgi, seeing that neither of his messengers had returned up to the day preceding the trial, had relinquished all hope, and prepared to meet his fate with resignation. He was not even aware of the arrival of the embassy, so well had Mohammed taken his precautions. His first intimation of their presence was from one of the Turcoman guards, who remarked to him, in a tone of mockery, as they marched to the emir's palace: "The embassadors from Khiva arrived this morning, and you are all in the dark about it, although you pretended they would be the bearers of credentials to you!"

Safar expressed his indifference by a wave of the hand. He knew that the embassadors could no longer save him; for, so long as he was deprived of the talisman, the charge of sacrilege could be easily substantiated.

As he marched along, however, the recollection of Emineh flashed upon his mind, and he shuddered at the thought that the emir might possibly attempt to have her too put to death. Although his own doom was irrevocably sealed, it was his duty at least to make effort to save her whom he loved.

"Comrade," said he to one of the horsemen, "I have a last favor to ask of you: send and request the embassadors to come to the tribunal, and be present at my trial."

"That is needless," replied the Turcoman, bitterly. "The rumor of our shame is already spread over the city. Who in Bokhara does not know that the sirdar of the Turcomans is to be arraigned for judgment to-day?"

"My enemies have an interest in keeping the embassadors in ignorance of it," insisted Safar. "Grant me, I beseech you, this last favor, comrade!"

With a shrug of the shoulders, the nomad yielded to the sirdar's supplication.

"All right!" said he, and he dispatched a trooper with the message to the embassadors. Safar-Hadgi thanked him with a motion of the head, and relapsed into a silence which remained unbroken until he was placed before his judges.

Mohammed was then beaming with joy as he awaited his master's orders with an air of satisfaction and triumph.

"Mohammed," said the emir, "is the accused ready to hear our good pleasure?"

"He is ready, your majesty."

"Let him be brought."

The main gate was opened, and the Turcomans, armed *cap-a-pie*, entered boisterously, and, casting a look of contempt at the sarbazes, formed up in a group before the estrade. The sirdar, who was in the centre of the group and unarmed, glanced at Mozzafar with a defiant air that exasperated the ferocious emir.

"The sirdar is not, then, brought before us as a criminal?" he asked. "Is that according to the Turcomans' promise?"

"It was decided by the council that we also should be his judges, and that our chief will not be delivered up to you unless found guilty," replied the president. "Nothing more than that was promised."

"It is well!" said Mozzafar, repressing his rage. "You will judge him too.—Mohammed, I charge you to inform the tribunal of the heinous crimes of which we accuse this man."

Mohammed advanced.

"Sire, dignitaries, and functionaries, and you, noble Turcomans," he began. Then, complacently stroking his beard, he continued: "In the name of his majesty the emir, I accuse Safar-Hadgi of criminal relations with the Princess of Khiva, betrothed to my sublime master; of holding secret communication with the enemies of our faith; and of sacrilege.—Judges, give ear! The Princess Emineh, daughter of the Emir-Al-Oumra, and whose hand had been demanded by our prince, was given in charge to the most pious reis, the guardian of our holy religion. The sirdar dared to violate the venerable man's dwelling, and, regardless of the respect due to a woman destined to become my master's wife, had the boldness to hold culpable relations with her. I affirm the fact under oath, and I demand that the penalty of death be inflicted on him."

"Sirdar," said Mozzafar, "what reply have you to make to the accusation?"

"None," replied Safar, smiling contemptuously. "I will not deign to dispute with you the question of my life. There is but one point in your slave's accusation to which I would object. I deny that the Princess of Khiva is betrothed to you. The Emir-Al-Oumra, her father, a prince whom I respect and admire, intrusted her to me, and never will he consent to sacrifice her to such a bloodthirsty tyrant as you. The truth of my words will be confirmed by the embassy whom your infamous falsehoods have kept aloof this day, and to whom you will have to render a terrible account of your acts. I shall be dead then, the victim of your hatred! But tremble, tyrant! Your chastisement is near at hand!"

Mozzafar shrugged his shoulders.

"The criminal insults his judge," said he. "That is the natural order of things.—No, sirdar, I bear you no hatred. I only punish you; and I shall prove that you have lied! The embassadors are here, and had they desired to demand the surrender of the Princess of Khiva, who is there in that prison, under accusation as you yourself are, they would have done so before now. You violated the reis's domicile, and the princess, even supposing she were not betrothed to me, ought not to have received you. You confess to have seen her, do you not?"

"I have already said that I had the right to see her."

A murmur of disapprobation escaped from the crowd of by-standers.

"What penalty does the tribunal believe the sirdar to have incurred?" asked Mohammed.

"Death!" said the mollahs.

"Death!" repeated the begs.

"Death!" ejaculated the Turcomans in a low murmur, as they widened the circle surrounding their chief.

Safar made no motion. Mohammed continued:

"One crime was not sufficient for this man, set upon trying the patience of Allah and the Prophet to the utmost. As a perjurer and a traitor, he has held secret communication with the Russians, the enemies of our country and our religion."

"It is rather your master that you ought to accuse of treason, Mohammed!" replied Safar, "as my companions will one day understand when their eyes shall have been opened!"

Mozzafar arose, and cried:

"Dog! do you dare—?"

"I dare," interrupted Safar-Hadgi.—"Proceed, honest Mohammed: of what do you accuse me next?"

"Of sacrilege!" vociferated the Persian. "You one day showed us the seal of the Shereef of Mecca, and one and all, our master foremost, bowed in homage to the sacred sign. This very hour, when your crimes have brought down the sentence of death upon your head, you can still save yourself; for none here will dare to raise a sacrilegious hand against a man who is under the protection of the chief of Islamism. Safar-Hadgi, sirdar of the Turcomans, chief of the Nakishbendies, and beloved servant of the Prince of Mecca, produce your master's seal, and we will prostrate ourselves before you as we prostrate ourselves before the emir."

Safar vouchsafed no reply.

"Your silence condemns you. You dared to deceive us and mock our religion.—Judges and mollahs, what punishment has this man merited?"

"Death!" replied the judges, with one voice.

Mozzafar swayed his sceptre.

"Turcomans, do you acknowledge your sirdar's guilt; and, if so, will you deliver him over to our justice?" he asked.

The president advanced.

"We deliver him up to you," said he. "And we disown and curse him." And, spitting upon the earth, he made a sign to the Turcomans, who immediately withdrew from Safar-Hadgi.

The oldest of the mollahs now arose, and said:

"We, the sovereign tribunal, assembled within these sacred precincts to judge Safar-Hadgi, do find him guilty of the crimes of treason, adultery, and sacrilege, of which he has been accused by Mirza-Mohammed before the throne of the most noble the Emir of Bokhara. And we most humbly beseech our master and king, the emir, to inflict upon him the punishment prescribed by the law of Islam."

"The law," said Mozzafar, arising, "shall be applied in its utmost rigor. The punishment I order is as follows: Safar-Hadgi shall have his eyes plucked out as an adulterer, and his tongue cut out as a traitor, and he shall be impaled for the crime of sacrilege, and his body exposed in public during one month. I have said!"

"Do you acknowledge the justice of the judgment that has been pronounced upon you, or have you any objection to state?" asked the aged mollah who had before spoken.

Safar-Hadgi never winced as the dread sentence was being pronounced, and, but for an occasional anxious glance in the direction of the main gate, he seemed indifferent to all that was taking place around him. The mollah reiterated his question, and this time Safar gave ear, and drew himself up to his full height.

"None!" he replied. "Allah and the Prophet will judge us all, Mozzafar.—As for you, Mohammed, I might cause your head to fall yet, but that I disdain to be avenged of so vile a slave. Mohammed, I pardon you.—Emir, I await your executioner!"

At a signal from Mozzafar, the sarbazes surrounded Safar-Hadgi to take him to the place of execution. But he, with an authoritative gesture, drove them back, and walked toward the scaffold, saying:

"Think you, Mozzafar, that I cannot march alone to death?"

Bravery never fails to elicit the admiration of the uncultured children of the desert. A murmur of approbation arose from the Turcomans, who were grouped in a corner of the court-yard. Mozzafar would fain have caused Safar-Hadgi to be bound and dragged to the scaffold, but he dared not. With an air of calm determination, the hadgi, followed by the soldiers, ascended the steps, and, casting a haughty look upon the assembled multitude, touched the executioner on the shoulder, as he cried:

"Here I am, friend!"

But, to the amazement of all beholders, the executioner, who until that moment had been looking in the direction of the square without, turned suddenly round and fell at the hadgi's feet.

At the same instant the gate was thrown wide open to admit the reis, and the square was seen to bristle with Turcoman lances.

The astonished Mozzafar sat erect upon his sofa; Mohammed, livid with fear, slunk back toward the entrance; high excitement convulsed the group of Turcomans; and the executioner was kissing Safar-Hadgi's feet.

XXV.

DELIVERANCE.

THAT same morning Hahib, after a weary and perilous journey of several days, came within view of Bokhara, and sat down to reflect what course he should pursue. He now had it in his power at once to take revenge upon Mohammed and to save his master's life, for he was the bearer of the shereef's seal. The slave conjectured—and not without good reason, either—that, once Mohammed should find himself in possession of the talisman, his first care would be to get rid of an inconvenient confidant; and then the sight of his mutilated hands aroused in Hahib's breast the deadly hatred which rankled there against the Persian. There was another line of conduct which he could choose, namely, to make a full confession to the sirdar, and throw himself on his protection, and that one he resolutely adopted.

"Were he even to put me to death," he soliloquized, as he shaped his way toward the Turcoman camp, "it would be nothing more than I deserve; but, at all events, I should not die without having had my revenge upon the other."

On reaching the camp, he was apprised of the hadgi's arrest and trial, and he determined upon using all his endeavors for his master's deliverance.

"Comrades," said he to the Turcomans, "I have in my possession the means to save the sirdar and confound his enemies. Will you not lend me your aid?"

The appeal was answered with a unanimous cry of consent, for Safar-Hadgi was sincerely beloved by his countrymen. Hahib foresaw that, unless he was suitably accompanied, his attempts would be baffled by Mohammed's vigilance, so he proceeded to Bokhara, followed by a thousand Turcomans. They found the city deserted, all the inhabitants having repaired to the scene of excitement, save here and there a few old men or children, who timidly took refuge within their houses till the savage troop had passed. The nomads formed up in the square of the grand mosque, facing the reis's garden, and the slave proceeded forthwith to demand admittance to the holy man's presence, where he found himself in a few brief minutes, for the shercef's seal opened every door.

Hahib laid before the venerable old man all the circumstances of Mohammed's treachery and the emir's dark intriguings, and even confessed his own offenses, and finally implored the reis's aid in behalf of the sirdar, so basely calumniated and betrayed.

Now, the Shiite Persian was held in utter detestation by the Sunnite pontiff, and as the latter's reluctant estrangement from Safar-Hadgi, whose meekness and piety had on more than one occasion excited his wonder and admiration, had been brought about by the false representations and subtle treachery of the chief of police, Hahib's appeal for the reis's coöperation found a willing response, without the help of the shereef's talisman. The distressing discovery that he had been made the tool of the designing Mohammed so mortified the chief of the ulemas that his first impulse was to hasten to the palace, and cause the judgment to be suspended; but Hahib remonstrated that, under the existing circumstances, and in view of the emir's malignity, such rash precipitation might rather compromise than insure the hadgi's safety. The following plan was then proposed by the slave, and promptly approved by the reis:

In every city and town in Central Asia, where death is the only punishment prescribed by law for high crimes, executions are numerous, though the office is not exclusively assigned to any particular individual, but open to all applicants. An enemy of the doomed person, a craven flatterer of the sovereign, or any one wishing merely to exercise his arms, provided he demand no compensation, is at all times readily accepted.

In the present instance, however, a practised executioner had been chosen, and was to be paid in proportion to the difficulty of his task. Now, the slave's proposal was, that the reis should purchase the man's consent to allow another to perform the office in his stead. Accordingly, Hahib was shaved and his head dressed after the Turcoman fashion, and otherwise disguised, so that it was impossible to recognize him. Besides, for reasons already hinted, the executioner should not be personally known either to the emir or Mohammed. The reis handed the slave a well-filled purse, and dismissed him, with the promise that he would make his appearance at the tribunal just as the sirdar was mounting the scaffold-steps. Returning to the Turcomans, he explained to them his plan and his hopes, and instructed them to remain in the square and as close to the palace-gate as possible, and to hold themselves in readiness to rush to his aid, should that be found necessary. Then, elbowing his way through the crowd, he was at the executioner's side just as the latter was preparing to ascend to his post, a few minutes before the arrival of the judges.

Their interview was a brief one. Hahib gave as a pretext an implacable resentment for an injustice done him by the sirdar in the distribution of the booty after a battle, and begged the executioner to allow him to take his place. Such proposals being of frequent occurrence, the man accepted unhesitatingly, and, for a consideration of one hundred tomans, ceded his office and his weapons to the sirdar's slave.

We left Hahib kissing Safar's feet.

"Mohammed!" cried the hadgi, drawing himself

up to his full height, "you said you would prostrate yourself before the seal of the Shereef of Mecca! Behold it here!"

He had just received the golden medallion from the hands of the slave, and, as he held it on high, it glittered before the eyes of the astonished multitude.

The Turcomans flocked around the scaffold, and the sarbazes, mollahs, and begs, bent their heads; but Mozzafar, seeing his designs frustrated and his expectations balked, yet unwilling to declare himself vanquished, looked wildly for Mohammed, to give him an order. The Persian was nowhere to be seen. With downcast and troubled mien he had slunk behind the spectators, and was crawling toward the gate. Mozzafar's rage now grew to frenzy. Wounded as he was in his pride and his despotism, and forsaken by his very favorite, he was still determined to continue the struggle.

"The cloak of religion is not sufficient to cover your crimes, sirdar!" he shrieked. "You have yet to clear yourself of the charges of adultery and treason!"

"And you talk of treason, Mozzafar!" exclaimed the sirdar. "You shall learn how Allah punishes traitors!—Comrades," he went on, addressing the Turcomans, who had closed in a menacing circle around the scaffold and the handful of sarbazes who sought to defend it, "here is a letter to me from Samarcand. Hearken, all of you!"

Livid with fury, Mozzafar shouted to the sarbazes: "Kill that man! Slay him!"

But the Turcomans raised their weapons, and the

terrified sarbazes recoiled in dismay to the very edge of the scaffold without daring to obey the emir's command.

Safar-Hadgi unfolded the sheet which Hahib had handed to him simultaneously with the medallion.

"Give ear!" he cried, in a voice of thunder. "Here is what my correspondent writes me from Samarcand: 'Peace has been concluded with the Emir of Bokhara, who agrees to send back the nomadic hordes of Uzbecks and Turcomans to their own country. Hence, should the proclamation which he will issue to that effect, enjoining upon them to retire, be treated with contempt by the nomads, Mozzafar binds himself to act conjointly with us. This is the plain truth, my dear friend, and I impart it to you, for by to-morrow it will no longer be a secret for any one—the treaty of peace will be placarded through the city.

"'Your devoted friend forever.'

"Signed by one of the principal Russian officers at Samarcand."

"Kill that man!—it is false!" howled Mozzafar, rushing down from the estrade to the centre of the group of sarbazes.

"Treason!—Forward, Turcomans!" cried the nomad standing nearest to the main entrance.

The gate was dashed open with irresistible force, and the next moment the court-yard was invaded by the Turcomans, with eyes of fire; the sarbazes were dashed to the ground and compelled to throw down their arms; and emir and minion, mollahs and begs, were huddled together in a cluster by the fierce troopers closing in a circle around them; for Mohammed, just as he was about to sneak out by the gate, was driven back by the avalanche to the very side of his terror-stricken master.

Safar-Hadgi descended from the scaffold and mingled in the ranks of his countrymen.

"Where is your throne now, Mozzafar?" cried he. "I could at a single nod cause your head to fall on the scaffold which you meant for me; but I will not. Never shall my hand be raised against a man on whose brow Allah has placed a crown. Your life is under the protection of the venerable reis! I pardon you, Mozzafar, and leave you to the punishment appointed by Heaven for your crimes!—My children, let us take possession of the Princess of Khiva and quit this inhospitable city, shaking the dust from our feet as we leave it!"

Just then a voice from the gate cried: "Make way! Make way for the Khivan embassy!" And the embassadors were seen advancing, between a double line of Turcomans, toward the throne where the downcast and still agitated Mozzafar had regained his seat.

"Emir of Bokhara!" said the first embassador, "the Emir-Al-Oumra demands of you by my mouth the surrender of the Princess Emineh, his daughter, whom he had given in charge to the sirdar of the Turcomans. Our master has charged us to conduct her back to Khiva."

This harangue was responded to by a wild cry of enthusiasm from the multitude. The Turcomans burst open the temporary prison in which the princess was retained captive, and led her in triumph to the sirdar, who, bending respectfully before her, said:

"Your father desires you to be brought to him, hanoum! I shall shortly be with your father!"

"Allah is great!" replied Eminch; "and he protects all those who put their trust in him!"

"Comrades, follow me!" ordered Safar.

"Pray, seignior," said Hahib, imploringly, "I have still an affair here that claims my attention: if you deign to forgive your enemies, I cannot forget my revenge!"

Hahib had been watching the movements of Mohammed, who was making a second attempt to reach the gate by stealth; and, just as he was about to make good his escape, the slave seized him by the arm and dragged him back to the foot of the estrade.

"Mercy, Hahib!" implored the Persian.

By a movement rapid as lightning Hahib forced the chief of police to his knees, and held him in that position.

"Since the sirdar in his magnanimity has seen fit to leave you your life and crown," said he to the emir, "it is still yours to reward and to punish! Behold before your throne two of your slaves, whom I accuse of grave offenses! Judge and punish, Mozzafar!— Do you recognize me?".

"Who are you?" faltered the emir.

"O tyrant! you do not even recollect the objects of your rage! I am that slave whose feet you commanded to be cut off! Your orders, as you now perceive, are not always obeyed!"

Mozzafar looked threateningly at the chief of police.

"Yes," pursued Hahib, "the order was given to this other slave; but this is not *his* first act of treachery, as the venerable reis can prove.—Chief of the ulemas, speak, that his majesty may gladden his heart by ordering my torture and that of this craven here!"

The reis turned his eyes inquiringly to the sirdar.

"I had forgotten that vile worm of earth until Hahib spoke," said Safar-Hadgi. "You may do with him as you see fit."

"Allah wills the punishment of the transgressor," said the reis, with a stern voice. "Sire, here is the document!"

The emir snatched the accusing paper from the reis's hands, and glanced rapidly over the characters traced upon it, his features gradually contracting as he read, until his countenance was hideous to behold.

"Your desire shall be granted!" said he to Hahib. —"Let them both be impaled."

"Stay, Mozzafar!" cried Safar-Hadgi. "With Mohammed you may do as it pleases you—I little care—it will be but justice; but Hahib is under my shield."

"You have me in your power; go on insulting me. It is most generous so to do!" murmured the emir, with clinched teeth.

"I do not insult you; I protect my slave.—Come forward, Hahib. I pardon you, and take you under my protection. Are you willing to follow me?"

"O seignior! anywhere, and for all time!" said the slave, as he kissed the hem of the hadgi's robe.

"Farewell, Mozzafar! Never shall we meet again. May Allah forgive you!"

"Allah's curse upon you, Safar!" replied the emir.

Safar did not so much as turn his head. With Eminch by his side, and followed by the embassadors and Turcomans, he issued from the palace court-yard and directed his steps toward the city gates.

Mohammed's tortures lasted two whole days—new tortures invented by the emir, who gloated on the sufferings and anguish of his minion.

To the heart-rending cries of the unfortunate wretch, malignantly kept alive by his executioners, Mozzafar would reply:

"Moan and wail; your tortures will never equal the humiliations you have brought upon me!"

The Persian cried aloud for death, and the emir ordered his suffering to be suspended. His body was seared with hot irons, his eyes and tongue taken out, and his feet burned, and in that condition he was lowered into a dungeon, where death did not terminate his agony until three days had elapsed.

On the day on which Mohammed expired, Safar-Hadgi took final leave of the Turcomans, who returned to their desert home on the Black-Sand plains. Unwilling to withhold any secrets from his comrades, the sirdar revealed to them that of his intervention in behalf of Relieff, before bidding them a last farewell.

"I leave you, friends," said he, "for you have been suspicious of me, and confidence has ceased between us. Accustomed to life in great cities, I see things with other eyes than you. Your manner of regarding them may be the right one, but it is in the hands of no one to change his destiny. Adieu!"

"You do wisely," replied the aged president. "You and we no longer understood each other. We dwell in the wilderness, under Allah's watchful eye and the guardian hand of the Prophet. Your subtilties displeased and terrified us. Farewell, Safar! You shall ever be present in the memory of the Turcomans!"

Between Mehemet Ali's unfinished castle and the gorgeous pleasure-grounds of Fuad Pasha, on the Asiatic shores of the Bosporus, stands an elegant mansion, imbedded in a garden which does not yield in beauty to that of Logothetus, situated almost opposite to it on the European side. The mansion is occupied by an opulent Mussulman, not an Osmanli, and whose origin is unknown to any one. He is noted alike for his piety and his benevolence; all the imams in Stamboul associate familiarly with him, and it is said that he rarely allows a week to elapse without paying his respects to the Sheik Oul-Islam.

Now and then a man deprived of both his thumbs, the chief servant of the wealthy foreigner's household, and well known to the inhabitants of all the surrounding villages, is observed at sunset issuing from the gate that looks down upon the straits, and withdrawing from beneath a vaulted shed a *caique*[1] of precious wood with gilded seats and velvet cushions. He is followed by a pair of bony-visaged *caijis*[2] with small, sparkling eyes, attired in costumes dazzling with gold and rich gems, who spring lightly into the craft and seize the oars. Then a lady robed in a silken *feridje*[3]

[1] Pleasure-skiff.   [2] Boatmen.
[3] An overdress worn by Mohammedan females.

descends the granite steps leading to the brink, and takes her seat on the heaped cushions; and the caique skims along the bosom of the waters, within view of the *yalis* and mosques of the Asian coast.

The court-martial had passed sentence on Relieff, who, in spite of the earnest and friendly solicitation of the reporting captain and the judges, maintained an obstinate silence.

"If it is your belief that I am guilty," said he, "condemn me; for I can give no explanation!"

Great indeed was Molotoff's disappointment when he heard that Relieff had been sentenced to be shot.

"You did not take him in the right way, gentlemen," said the governor; "and I am deeply afflicted at the sentence. I'll call and see the colonel myself in his prison, and I hope to bring him to such a confidential avowal of the circumstances as will throw light upon this deplorable incident, and enable me to annul your decision, for it would be painful to me to be obliged to pardon him."

"We all agree with you heartily, general," replied the officer who had presided at the court-martial. "It was with tearful eyes that we pronounced the sentence."

The observance of the formalities of the law was, nevertheless, unavoidable. Court-martial sentences are to be carried out within twenty-four hours after they are given. Accordingly, the president ordered a platoon to be told off and in readiness at noon the following day, at Timour's Round-Point, where the execution was to take place. All this was, of course, regarded as a simple formality, for every one in Samarcand felt confident that the colonel would not be shot.

At ten o'clock the next day Molotoff repaired to the prison, where he was met by the prisoner with perfect composure, almost with a smile. Relieff had slept soundly, and was reading a book when the general entered.

"*Sacrebleu!* my dear fellow," cried Molotoff, "you're carrying your obstinacy a little too far, let me tell you. The court-martial has sentenced you to death, you know."

"Well," replied Relieff, with a ghastly smile, "it cannot be helped! I shall be shot!"

"Why, you're mad! completely mad! raving mad!"

"No! tired of life, that's all! Not that I am unhappy, either; but I have nothing more to hope for, nothing to wish for; and life under such circumstances is void of charm."

"And do you for a moment suppose that I'll allow you to be shot?" interrupted the governor.

"I don't see how you can prevent it," rejoined Relieff, clasping the general's hand.

"You don't see *how?* Well, I should think you'd tell the truth to your friend, your old general; and—"

Relieff interrupted him: "Come, general," he asked, "do you really believe me to be guilty of holding secret communication with the enemy?"

"No, no! A thousand times no! Absurd, stupid nonsense! You in communication with those brutes! —But, after all, why refuse to show your innocence?"

"Do you think a Russian colonel can break his word of honor, although it were to save his life?"

"So your honor is bound?"

"Yes, general. That much I am at liberty to tell you. But pray, question me no further."

"Oh! but I am all-powerful here, and I will not allow you to be shot!"

Relieff drew himself up.

"I trust, general," said he, "you do not contemplate a pardon for me, by virtue of your authority."

"Well, but—my dear fellow—" stammered Molotoff.

"Oh! that I will never accept. Sooner would I take my life with my own hands. The guilty only are pardoned."

The old general was deeply moved.

"Come, come, *mon cher!* Do not excite yourself so. In an extreme case I can use my authority to annul the sentence and call a new trial; and your word of honor to me will then enable me to declare your innocence. The council that sentenced you did so reluctantly, and will readily concur in my decision. But what unheard-of obstinacy on your part not to have told them that you were bound by word of honor! As matters now stand, I am powerless to interfere until the last moment."

"Why so?"

"You are beyond comprehension!—Because I swear to you that, unless you consent to a reëxamination of the sentence, I will pardon you, and then have you placed under close surveillance to prevent you from committing suicide."

Relieff pressed the general's hand convulsively.

"You are really taking too much trouble to save my life," said he. "However, do as you see fit. I will not be dishonored. And, as my innocence is evident to every honest-minded man, death does not frighten me. Hence I say that, if I am once led to the place of execution, it will be just as well to shoot me."

"Well, well, *que diable!* The whole affair will be conducted among ourselves; I will not even send a report to St. Petersburg; the sentence will be revised, and you'll be the hero of the day. You shall even be released on parole, if you choose. The show of taking you to the place of execution is nothing more than a formality in my behalf; for, if I were to merely set aside the sentence, without any further ado, that would be regarded as a very unusual abuse of authority. Yet, if you absolutely insist upon it, as I shall never have a more worthy opportunity for such an abuse—"

"No, no, general!" interrupted Relieff, with emotion. "I submit—I give in! I will not insist! I really don't know how to express my gratitude for all your kindness to me!"

"Ah, bravo! there's a good fellow! The deuce take you for the anxiety you have caused to all of us!" And the warm-hearted old general pressed his former aide-de-camp in his arms.

"No!" soliloquized Molotoff, as he went, "I cannot help admiring that man! So bold and noble-hearted! Could I but save him this show of execution!—If he had only submitted to be pardoned! But he won't, and he's right. Yet, I can't set aside the decision of the court-martial with a stroke of the pen!

What a deplorable example I should set! Besides, I have not even the right to do it, according to the new regulations!—No, no! I can't! That will be the punishment of his obstinacy—the only punishment, it is true; for I'll send an explanation to Tashkend, and request the governor-general to allow the affair to be hushed up. Yes, yes, that's it—a stay of execution, revision of the sentence, and hush the matter!"

As Molotoff ascended the palace-steps, he suddenly recollected a file of papers that had been handed to him after the search made at Relieff's quarters, and which he had not yet looked over, so thoroughly was he persuaded of the colonel's innocence.

"Suppose I should come upon the secret!" reflected he. "All difficulties would be removed. I could proclaim his innocence, and his word of honor would remain unbroken. I must read those papers."

Having thus meditated, the general rather flew than ran to his cabinet, where he had laid the bundle of documents. At the head of the stairs he was met by Martha, who had been waiting for him ever since he had gone out. The pallor of her face was ghastly, and she trembled convulsively in every limb.

"Well?" she inquired.

"I have already promised, Martha," replied he, with marked coldness, "that no hurt should befall Relieff. Allow me, then, to reconcile my duty with justice."

"Well, sir," rejoined the countess, unable to master her emotion, "you are treating the life of a man very lightly."

"Martha! Martha!" cried the general, pushing her aside. "Think what ideas your conduct might prompt to the mind of a man less loyal than myself!" And he rushed into his cabinet.

There he found Bassalsky, who was also awaiting him, and no less pallid than Martha. The anxious expression of his countenance was a silent yet eloquent inquiry.

"In the name of Heaven, do you all think I mean to forfeit my honor?" cried Molotoff. "You have my promise for Relieff's safety. Now, leave me: I desire to be alone."

It was eleven o'clock when the governor sat down at his desk to examine the colonel's papers. Just then the platoon was forming in line at Timour's Round-Point. Relieff had been brought to the palace, and was waiting in a room in the guard-house until the hour appointed for the execution should arrive. When he had carefully perused the letters that had been seized in Relieff's quarters, the general arose and consulted the clock: the hands marked half-past eleven. He called an orderly who was constantly in waiting in the antechamber adjoining his cabinet.

"Tell the aide-de-camp of the day to come here," said he.

The orderly disappeared.

"I see nothing!" soliloquized the general, glancing mechanically over the papers spread out open before him. "The execution must be stayed, and I regret it; I could have wished so much to have a clear and palpable elucidation.—But what is this?"

His eye caught the sheet that had been used to wrap Relieff's other letters. He saw his own name written on it; and, as he gazed at the name, it seemed to be traced in characters of fire and of gigantic dimensions. He snatched up the paper and devoured it with his eyes. It was the unfinished letter which Relieff had left on his desk on the evening of his return to Samarcand.

The governor read as follows:

"My dear Friend: She loves me, and bitterly regrets her conduct toward me! Oh, the cruel situation into which that avowal plunges me!"

Here a knock was heard at the door, and Bassalsky entered.

"Did your excellency send for me?" he asked.

"Yes! yes!" replied Molotoff. "Presently." And he continued reading:

"She has told Lise that she was in despair for having married Molotoff, and that she now sees the extent of her error, for she loves me now. She wishes to see me to-morrow. My whole being thrills when I think of the happiness I shall experience! Yes, dear friend, to-morrow she—"

There was no more. On reaching that point the weary writer had laid down his pen. Molotoff stared for a moment vacantly into space; his visage grew purple, his sight dim, and he sank back in his chair.

The general was of a plethoric, apoplectic habit of body. The terrible blow he had just received sent the blood coursing to his head; his eyes were bloodshot, his brain reeled, and in the fear of sliding to the floor he bent forward and pressed his head tightly between his hands. A spell of complete prostration then ensued.

Meantime Bassalsky, after having tarried some ten minutes, grew impatient, for the fatal hour was fast approaching. He knocked again, and, receiving no reply, he knocked still louder, and at length his anxiety emboldened him to push the door half open.

Molotoff was still in the same position, both elbows resting on the letter, and his head between his hands. He seemed not to have heard the officer entering.

The terror-stricken Bassalsky, persuaded that the general sought to elude his promise, flew to the countess's apartments, and found her in a state of indescribable agitation.

"The general won't answer me, countess. For God's sake, come! Time is flying. It will be twelve o'clock in a few minutes, and the general seems to have forgotten the execution!"

"Can it be possible?" cried Martha. "Oh, the wretch! Come along; I'll soon force him to move!"

Trembling, and with disheveled hair, the countess flew through the intervening apartments, and rushed into her husband's cabinet. At the approach of the woman he had loved, Molotoff sprang erect upon his feet as if electrified, and, placing his finger on Relieff's letter—

"Is what is there written true?" he asked, in a half-stifled and faltering voice.

After a hurried perusal of the paper, the countess riveted her eyes upon her husband's with a dire expression.

"It is!" cried she. "Do you mean to kill him for it?"

Molotoff attempted to speak, but a torrent of blood choked the words in his throat, and a hollow gurgle was the only sound he could utter. Stretching out his hand, as if in search of support, he reeled and fell heavily to the floor.

"The coward!" exclaimed Martha, rushing precipitately upon him and plucking him by his uniform; "he has fainted!" And she shook him with feverish and angry violence.

"The stay of execution, sir!" she went on, frantically. "The time is almost up. Are you going to stop the exection? Your conduct is odious!"

But the general could not reply. He was dead! He had died in an apoplectic fit.

The clock struck twelve.

Abandoning her husband's inanimate body, Martha flew to Bassalsky, and, clutching his arm in an iron grasp—

"And you!" she cried. "So all you men are cowards at heart? Fly, and suspend the execution in the name of the governor. He is dead, and cannot belie us."

The expression of Martha's eyes as she spoke caused an icy shiver to pass through Bassalsky's frame. Nevertheless, he obeyed promptly.

The countess listened to his receding footsteps, and then hearkened with eager attention to catch every sound from without. A few moments of oppressive silence followed; then a sharp report, and Timour's palace trembled to its very foundations.

When Bassalsky returned he found Martha crouched by the side of her husband's corpse. Her haggard eyes were staring fixedly upon the motionless pupils of the dead, and she was tearing her breast convulsively with her hand.

Tears trickled down the officer's blanched cheeks.

"I was too late!" said he. "Let the remembrance of those two men weigh forever upon your conscience, madame, for it was you that killed them!"

For the last two years a woman has been frequently met in one of the small towns of Southern Italy. She is evidently a foreigner, and she has a sad, pale, and sickly countenance. She is still young, and her emaciated face reveals some traces of rare beauty; but her hair is whitened, and her sinister, fiery eyes are surrounded with a sombre circle. She is always robed in black, and never is she seen to smile. The peasants say she has an unlucky eye, and turn their heads aside when they meet her.

Lise and Bassalsky are now married.

THE END.

www.ingramcontent.com/pod-product-compliance
Lightning Source LLC
Chambersburg PA
CBHW022110230426
43672CB00008B/1336